PLOUGH, SWORD AND BOOK

PLOUGH, SWORD AND BOOK

The Structure of Human History

ERNEST GELLNER

The University of Chicago Press

For David, Sarah, Deborah and Ben

The University of Chicago Press, Chicago 60637
Collins Harvill, London

© 1988 by Ernest Gellner
All rights reserved. Originally published 1988
University of Chicago Press edition 1989
Paperback edition 1990
Printed in the United States of America

98 97 96 95 94 93 92   5 4 3

LIBRARY OF CONGRESS CATALOGING-IN-PUBLICATION DATA

Gellner, Ernest.
    Plough, sword, and book : the structure of
human history / Ernest Gellner.
        p.   cm.
    Originally published : London : Collins Harvill,
1988.
    Includes index.
    ISBN 0-226-28701-7 (cloth)
    ISBN 0-226-28702-5 (paper)
    1. History—Philosophy.   I. Title.
D16.8.G413   1989   88-32452
901—dc19   CIP

ACKNOWLEDGEMENTS

I wish to put on record my gratitude to the Economic and Social Research Council and its Chairman Sir Douglas Hague and its Secretary Mrs Suzanne Reeve, who have given support to this purely theoretical inquiry and thus freed me from worry concerning the expenses connected with it.

I would also like to put on record my very great debt to the secretarial and research staff of the Department of Social Anthropology at Cambridge: Mrs Mary McGinley, Mrs Margaret Story, Mrs Anne Farmer and Mrs Janet Hall. Without their sustained help and support the book certainly would not have been written. Valuable additional secretarial help was also received from Miss Hilary Colby.

I am most grateful to people who have read drafts of the book and made useful suggestions: Mark Raymond Bonham-Carter, Graham Fawcett, David Gellner, Julian Jacobs, Declan Quigley, Emma Tristram, Harry Willets, and Anthony Raven. Janet Hall and Julian Jacobs have also been most helpful with the bibliography. Mark Green has been outstandingly helpful and patient as an editor.

The number of people from whom I have borrowed intellectually is too large to be included in full, and no doubt there are many debts of which I am not properly aware. But for years I have run a seminar on historical sociology at the LSE jointly with John Hall and Michael Mann, and my debt to my two colleagues and to all those who have contributed papers or observations in discussion is very considerable. Over the years, I have learnt a very great deal from the writings or conversation of S. Andreski, the late R. Aron, J. Baechler, D. Bell, P. Burke, P. Crone, R. Dore, S. N. Eisenstadt, Y. Elkanna, M. Elvin, C. Geertz, R. Gombrich, J. Goody, J. Hajnal, M. Hinds, K. Hopkins, R. Horton, A. Khazanov, P. Laslett, G. Lloyd, A. Macfarlane, J. Merquior, C.

Renfrew, G. Runciman, T. Shanin, E. Wolf, J. Woodburn, A. E. Wrigley, and many others. The responsibility for what is affirmed in the book is of course mine only.

ERNEST GELLNER
September, 1987

CONTENTS

CONTENTS

Subjection enters the house with the plough

Attributed to the Prophet Mohammed

CHAPTER 1

In the Beginning

The Need for Philosophic History

Men and societies frequently treat the institutions and assumptions by which they live as absolute, self-evident, and given. They may treat them as such without question, or they may endeavour to fortify them by some kind of proof.

In fact, human ideas and social forms are neither static nor given. In our age, this has become very obvious to most of us; and it has been obvious for quite some time. But any attempt at understanding of our collective or individual predicaments must needs be spelt out against the backcloth of a vision of human history. If our choices are neither self-evident nor for keeps, we need to know the range of alternatives from which they are drawn, the choices that others have made or which were imposed on them. We need to know the principles or factors which generate that range of options. The identification of those principles or factors is not beyond our capacities, even if specific prediction continues to elude us.

We inevitably assume a pattern of human history. There is simply no choice concerning *whether* we use such a pattern. We are, all of us, philosophical historians *malgré nous*, whether we wish it or not. The only choice we do have is whether we make our vision as explicit, coherent and compatible with available facts as we can, or whether we employ it more or less unconsciously and incoherently. If we do the latter, we risk using ideas without examination and criticism, passed off tacitly as some kind of "common sense". As Keynes observed about economics, common sense is but dead theory:

    ... the ideas of economists and political philosophers ... are more powerful than is commonly understood. Indeed the world is ruled by little else. Practical men, who believe themselves to be quite exempt from any intellectual influences, are usually the slaves of some defunct economist. Madmen in authority, who hear voices in the air, are distilling their frenzy from some academic scribbler of a few years back.[1]

This is true far beyond the sphere of economic thought. Those who spurn philosophical history are slaves of defunct thinkers and unexamined theories.

The great paradox of our age is that although it is undergoing social and intellectual change of totally unprecedented speed and depth, its thought has become, in the main, unhistorical or anti-historical. "Historicism" has become a term of abuse, designating those who set themselves up as self-appointed prophets, in possession of a secret plan of history and hence of the key to the future, who endeavour to browbeat humanity into the acceptance of their own values and recipes for the future, and who do this in the name of a possibly benign and allegedly inexorable historical necessity.

This is not the only charge made out against historical visions, though it is the one that has been most eloquently expounded. There is also the "genetic fallacy" argument. It consists of the simple point that the *origins* and the *validity* of an idea are independent of each other: hence, it is mistakenly argued, we need not be concerned with our origins and our past, when we assess the merits of our future options. Discovering the roots of our ideas does not tell us whether or not those ideas are sound. So why bother with the roots? Our point here is that we look at those roots in order to understand our options, not so as to prejudge our choices.

The joint result of our inescapable need for possessing some backcloth vision of history, *and* of the low esteem in which elaboration of global historical patterns is at present held, is a most paradoxical situation: the ideas of nineteenth-century philosophers of history such as Hegel, Marx, Comte, or Spencer are treated with scant respect and yet are everywhere in use.

The aim of the present volume is simple. It is to spell out, in the sharpest and perhaps exaggerated outline, a vision of human history which has in any case been assuming shape of late, but which has not yet been properly codified. The attempt to bring it to the surface is not made because the author has any illusions about *knowing* this vision to be true: he does not. Definitive and final truth is not granted to theories in general. In particular, it is unlikely to attach to theories covering an infinite diversity of extremely complex facts, well beyond the reach of any one scholar. The vision is formulated in the hope that its clear and forceful statement will make possible its critical examination.

What method is employed in this undertaking, then? Basically, it is deductive. Conclusions are extracted from clearly stated *assumptions*; various possible conclusions are then checked against available facts. Assumptions are revised if the implications fail to tally with available facts.

The painting of a historical backcloth cannot possibly be a matter of mere description: reality is so rich and diverse that no unselective description could even be begun, let alone completed. Instead, one chooses the crucial and elementary factors operative in human history, selected to the best of one's judgement, and then works out their joint implications. If the resulting picture fits the available record and highlights the relevant questions, well and good. If not, further tinkering with the premises is evidently required. The method is in principle very simple; its implementation is not.

If this be the method, in what way does it differ from theories or models in any other field? There is something here which is distinctively historical: the *sequence* or order in which new important elements are added to the model is a matter of recorded or surmised fact, not just of logical convenience. Food production, political centralization, the division of labour, literacy, science, intellectual liberalization, appear in a certain historic sequence. They do so because some at least of the later developments in human history seem to presuppose the earlier ones, and could not have preceded them. Human history is a play in which the cast tends to increase over time and within which constraints seem to be imposed on the *order* in which the characters appear. The theorist of human society cannot introduce them in any old order at will. Some changes are at least relatively irreversible: agriculture, centralization, literacy, science can of course disappear in areas where they were once established, and occasionally such regressions do occur; but, by and large, there does seem to be a kind of overall cumulativeness.

The claim that certain transformations are only possible on the basis of earlier ones, which constitute their preconditions, may of course be paralleled in evolutionary biology. But historical transformations are transmitted by culture, which is a form of transmission which, unlike genetic transmission, *does* perpetuate acquired characteristics. In fact, culture *consists* of sets of acquired characteristics. A culture is a distinct way of doing things which characterizes a given community, and which is not dictated by the genetic make-up of its members. Humanity is unique in that the communities into which it divides display an astonishing variety of modes of conduct, all of them evidently compatible with our shared genetic inheritance; hence none of them are dictated by it. Some animal species may also display some measure of such variation, but the range of such diversity in other species simply is not comparable with ours. Racialists believe that the differential genetic make-up of human races has significant social consequences. In fact, it seems that any culture on earth can be assimilated and internalized by an infant of any given "racial" group, just as any infant can acquire any language. Cultures are not genetically transmitted, even though cultures can and do use genetic traits as symbols and markers.

Cultures can loosely be defined as systems of concepts or ideas which guide thought and conduct. Much of our argument will be in terms of the kinds of concepts that are possible or likely in various social conditions. Cultures are socially transmitted, but the converse argument – societies are perpetuated by cultures – should not be accepted lightly. It is in fact contentious and deeply problematic. Of course, the concepts deployed in a given culture do make a contribution of some importance to its life. But the precise extent to which concepts help perpetuate a society, and the extent to which on the other hand its perpetuation depends on more earthy factors, such as physical coercion or threats of hunger, is a very difficult question. It is this issue which separates historical idealists and materialists. Why assume that the question has the same answer in all places and at all times? Concepts do constitute a social constraint; but not all social constraints are conceptual.

To say that history does contain steps, such that the earlier ones are preconditions of the later ones, is not to say that the earlier ones necessitate the later ones. It does not mean that the development is predetermined, or predictable. There is no reason to suppose that all possibilities are fulfilled, or that the actual development was uniquely necessary.

Social prediction, outside isolated spheres, is unlikely ever to be feasible. Even if one has correctly identified the factors which enter into a given situation, nevertheless small, unpredictable, even undetectable, changes in their proportions may make enormous differences to the outcome. One can also never confidently predict the presence or absence of new factors. But the impossibility or low feasibility of prediction does not exclude the possibility of *comprehension*.

We understand a social order when we see it as one possible corollary of the basic factors which engender it, but also when we see how other options could have been engendered by that same set of elements. We understand a situation when we see how the same cards, so to speak, could have been dealt out differently. We may or may not be able to see in retrospect why one option has been selected. For better or worse, we are unlikely to be able to foretell future outcomes. So prophecy is neither promised nor threatened. We do, however, complain that our contemporary fashionable anti-prophets have thrown out the baby of understanding with the bathwater of prophecy. Nor is comprehension without prediction useless. It is an advantage to understand the options which face us, even though (or perhaps because) we cannot always determine in advance which will be realized.

The Structure of History

Mankind has passed through three principal stages: (1) hunting/ gathering; (2) agrarian society; (3) industrial society. No law ordains that every society must pass through each of these stages. There is no obligatory developmental pattern. Societies can and do remain stuck in any one stage. What is the case, however, is that the transition to (3) is not conceivable directly from (1), and that regression from (3) to (2), or from (2) to (1), though conceivable, is improbable, and rare. Contrary to the philosophies or sociologies characteristic of the nineteenth century, no ineluctable destiny, no inner necessity, *compels* societies to move either from (1) to (2), or from (2) to (3). On the contrary, the spontaneous, endogenous transition may well be inherently improbable, and due to a near-miraculous concatenation of circumstances (especially so in the case of the second of these two great transitions).

These three kinds of society differ from each other so radically as to constitute fundamentally different species, notwithstanding the very great and important diversity which also prevails within each of these categories. It is as well to give a brief characterization of each of them.

Hunters/gatherers are defined by the fact that they possess little or no means for producing, accumulating and storing wealth. They are dependent on what they find or kill. Their societies are small, and are characterized by a low degree of division of labour.

Agrarian societies produce food, store it, and acquire other forms of storable wealth. The most important forms of such wealth, other than stored nourishment, are the means of *producing* further nourishment and other goods (tools), means of coercion (weapons), goods of "symbolic value", and various objects which assist or culturally enhance the quality of life. These societies are capable of growing to a great size. The need for a labour force and defence personnel inclines them to place high value on procreation, and consequently they display a tendency to push their population to a danger point, in which

16

population presses against the limits of available resources, and is liable to suffer famine if those resources fail.

Agrarian societies tend to develop complex social differentiation, an elaborate division of labour. Two specialisms in particular become of paramount importance: the emergence of a specialized ruling class, and of a specialized clerisy (specialists in cognition, legitimation, salvation, ritual). Differentiated clerisies and ruling classes are not universal in the agrarian world, but common enough to be considered typical.

In the societies which make up what we shall call Agraria, innovation does occur, but not as part of some constant, cumulative and exponential process. Agraria values stability, and generally conceives the world and its own social order as basically stable. Some agrarian social forms at least seem to be deliberately organized so as to avoid the dangers of possibly disruptive innovations. Ancestors, or past institutional forms, perhaps in idealized versions, are held up as the moral norm, the prescriptive ideal.

An industrial society proper is one in which the production of food becomes a minority occupation, and where production is generally based on a powerful and above all continuously *growing* technology, such as is perfectly capable of outstripping population growth if necessary, and often does so. The notion of industrial society (sometimes, for brevity, Industria), is here used in a broad and generic sense, going far beyond nineteenth-century Lancashire and the dark satanic mills. It includes what is sometimes called "post-industrial society", whatever it may turn out to be: I prefer the term "fully developed industrial society". "Industrial society" in the Marx/Dickens sense is best referred to as early industrial society.

Agraria was based on *one* discovery, namely the possibility of food production. Other discoveries or innovations were contingent, and did not come, if indeed they came at all, in any sustained and continuous stream. They came at best as single spies and never as battalions. Industria, by contrast, is not based on any one discovery, but rather on the generic or second-order discovery that successful systematic investigation of Nature, and the application of the findings for the purpose of increased output, are feasible, and, once initiated, not too difficult. The nature of its technology ensures that Industria is characterized by the presence, though not necessarily the exclusive presence, of very large productive organizations. The need to innovate means that Industria is marked not merely by a complex division of labour, but also by a perpetually changing occupational structure.

Some measure of coercion and legitimation is inherent in human societies. It is a simple corollary of the fact that the structure of human societies is not dictated by the human genetic potential: the range of possibilities is so very wide for populations of identical or similar genetic composition. Hence a structure, no longer imposed by nature, must be imposed by some other mechanism. Coercion can be assumed to be one element in it, and legitimacy and conviction another.

The process of legitimation is very often a perfectly humdrum thing. We ought not to think only of great inspired seers and prophets or systematizers, who impose their vision or their code on their fellow men, by some magical charm attaching to their person or their doctrine or both. An equally valid specimen of legitimation is something as humdrum as a cinema usherette, who leads the ticket holder to his appointed place, and without whom audiences would be inconvenienced by chaos. The capacity to assign a place without being challenged is the paradigm of legitimacy. Coercers and legitimators are complementary. Legitimators are underwritten by a given power situation; but equally, the balance of power depends on the nature and size and position of groupings, which in turn are built up by the humble daily activities of the ushers and usherettes of each society, who lead men to their places. Owing to their size and complexity, agrarian societies inevitably possess coercion and legitimation systems of a kind more elaborate than was available to their pre-agrarian predecessors. Industrial society, on the other hand, is characterized, or perhaps indeed is defined, by a very distinctive form of coercion and a division of labour, in some ways simpler, in others more complex than those of the agrarian world.

Trinitarianisms

Trinitarian theories of human history are not uncommon. Some are of considerable interest and merit, and we shall have cause to refer to them. Their beginnings may lie in the medieval thinker Joachim of Fiore, who postulated Ages of the Father, of the Son, and of the Holy Ghost. Hegel thought that the doctrine of the Trinity was the outstanding merit of Christianity, and provided the clue to the understanding of human destiny. Auguste Comte distinguished the religious, metaphysical and positive stages of the human spirit and of human society. Sir James Frazer, an intellectualist like Comte (at least in his main and as it were official theory), distinguished the age of magic, that of religion, and that of science, though he also stressed that each of the ages was defined, not by the exclusive presence, but rather by the mere predominance of one of these three elements of styles of thought. Marxism operates with more stages than three but it can plausibly be reinterpreted as using three basic epochs: one in which men knew neither a surplus nor exploitation; another in which both surplus and exploitation are both pervasive; and a third in which the surplus remains but exploitation vanishes.[2] Karl Polanyi, seeking the defining crucial trait, like Marx, in production rather than in style of thought, argued in terms of the three stages of reciprocity, redistribution, and the market.[3]

The division of history into periods, like any kind of classification, is to be seen primarily as more or less useful, rather than straightforwardly true or false. It seems to me that the three-stage scheme offered here – hunting/gathering, agrarian production, and industrial production – is, in the light of modern knowledge, far more useful, and in that sense valid, than its rivals.

In so far as our own schema deploys a definition of the three stages in terms of their productive base, should it be considered a form of economic determinism? Not so. The contention is that the economic or productive base does indeed determine our problems, but that it does *not* determine our solutions. The evidence seems to show that both hunting/gathering and agrarian societies come in a very wide, indeed bewilderingly wide, diversity of forms. The same seems to hold for the new species of industrial society.

So our position is "materialist" only in the sense that it assumes and claims that each of the three crucial productive bases – hunting/gathering, agriculture, scientific/industrial production – bestows on the societies which use it radically different sets of problems and constraints, and hence, that societies of these three different kinds can usefully be treated as three fundamentally different species. But the argument makes no preliminary assumptions as to which sphere of human activity – production, coercion, cognition – is crucial, either in the maintenance and continuity of societies or in bringing forth new forms.

The only thing that is perhaps obvious is that the two very great transitions – the neolithic and the industrial revolutions – cannot plausibly be attributed to conscious human design and plan. In each case, the new social order, due to be ushered in by history, was so radically discontinuous and different from its predecessor, within which its gestation had taken place, that it simply could not be properly anticipated or planned or willed. Those who sowed knew not what they would reap, nor did those who abandoned the plough and sword for trade, production and innovation. This point in no way applies, of course, to the subsequent *diffusion* of a new social order, once established and successful in one location. On the contrary: once a new and visibly more powerful order is in existence, it can be, and commonly is, consciously and deliberately emulated. Those who emulate may also end up with more than they intended and bargained for, but that is another story.

Production, Coercion, Cognition

The three great stages of human history provide one of the two dimensions for our approach. The other is given by the fundamental classification of human activities: production, coercion, cognition. This leaves us with a simple three-by-three diagram, which constitutes the basic framework for the overall argument:

Our concern will be with the transformation and interrelation of production, coercion and cognition. We shall follow them through the three stages, with all their internal varieties, and across the two great leaps.

The small scale of pre-agrarian society inhibits or in any case limits the division of labour and the full emergence of either political or religious specialisms. These only separate out to a mild degree either from society at large or from each other. By contrast, Agraria encourages, and often perhaps necessitates, the emergence of specialized agencies of coercion and of cognition/ legitimation, sometimes fused with each other, sometimes distinct. By frequently depriving the rest of society of either the privilege, or the burden, of participating in defence or the maintenance of order, it also encourages the development of the division of labour in the sphere where social theory has hitherto stressed it most – the economic. Specialized producers, craftsmen and traders emerge. In most cases, however, agrarian society is dominated either by its warriors or its clerisy, or by both of them jointly.

The hiving-off of cognition and coercion as distinct spheres of activity is at least as important as the emergence of specialization within the field of production. The implications of this *generic* division of labour, between coercion, cognition and production, are different in kind from the consequences of intra-economic or specific division of labour, which occurs within the sphere of productive activity. When the division of labour is made into *the*

21

clue to human history, the differences between these two kinds, the generic and the economic, is crucial.

Exceptions to the rule of military-clerical domination of agrarian society do occur, but they constitute only a minority of cases. Two species of such exceptions are conspicuous. (1) Small communities of producers, often pastoralists or mountain peasants, whose environment makes it possible for them to resist external domination, or to deter it by making it not worth the effort. They can maintain internal order on the balance-of-power principle, with widespread political participation, and without the emergence of any outright internal domination. These self-governing, participatory communities often display great cohesion and military valour, and under favourable circumstances are well placed to turn into the conquerors of more typical, centralized and stratified agrarian societies. For instance, they provided Islamic societies with many of its dynasties and governing groups. (2) City states, within which a relative absence of domination is strengthened in some measure by the fact that trade requires initiative, which is not normally compatible with servile status. These two species of domination-free society can also be combined, as when an association of fairly equal landowners constitutes a city, which at the same time depends for a significant proportion of its wealth on trade. The government of the city may remain largely in the hands of the Landowners' Association, so to speak, even if the wealth of the city depends on traders deprived of full political participation, as could happen in classical Greece.

Notwithstanding this important qualification, the Agrarian Age was basically a period of stagnation, oppression and superstition. Exceptions occur, but we are all inclined, as in the case of classical Greece, to call them "miracles". These are no doubt value-loaded and condemnatory terms, and it might not be difficult to find neutral-sounding, more "scientific" and perhaps lengthy and ponderous circumlocutions. The disadvantages of such a procedure would, however, outweigh its advantages (if any). Our aim is to put things as simply and forcefully as possible; there is little to be gained from denying that from the viewpoint of the currently dominant values of our growth-oriented, liberal society, most agrarian societies seem unacceptably stifling. There is no point in pretending not to have the values and reactions which most of us in fact do have, and which lead us to ask the questions we do ask – provided it does not lead us to distort facts. (Romantics will no doubt protest: but our language aims at simplicity even at the cost of apparent prejudice. It does not beg any question.)

Two further developments are crucial within Agraria: political centralization (state-formation), and literacy, which is followed by the emergence of codified, scriptural belief-and-legitimation systems. Neither of these is actually entailed by agriculture – stateless and illiterate agrarian societies do exist – but each occurs in a very large proportion of agrarian societies, and they also seem to be preconditions of subsequent radical change.

Which Way Will the Stone Age Vote Swing?

Primitive man has lived twice: once in and for himself, and the second time for us, in our reconstruction. Inconclusive evidence may oblige him to live such a double life for ever. Ever since the principles of our own social order have become a matter of sustained debate, there has been a persistent tendency to invoke the First Man to settle our disputes for us. His vote in the next general election is eagerly solicited. It is not entirely clear why Early Men should possess such authority over our choices. Suppose that archaeologists, digging up a very early site, found a well-preserved copy of the original Social Contract: should we feel bound by its terms, and proceed to declare all current statute law which was incompatible with it to be null and void? Would it supplant the United Nations Charter?

Although we might not feel bound to obey the decrees of some Stone Age constituent assembly, the urge to find out just what that assembly – or its informal equivalents – had implicitly decreed, continues to be exceedingly vigorous. The debate takes two extreme forms: on the one hand, some contributors in no way pretend to be practising archaeologists or anthropologists, but on the contrary frankly offer an "as-if" model so as to provide moral guidance. For them, the founding contract is a valuable fiction, even if not a historic fact.

According to some of them, the Constituent Assembly of Mankind has been in a kind of continuous session ever since human societies have existed. Contributions to its debate are made under some version of the convention of a "veil of ignorance" – i.e. one suspends and abstracts from all specific information about current social arrangements and one's particular place within them, and argues *as if* one were just about to set up a social order for the first time.[4] As a conservative philosopher endowed with a strong sense of historic continuity derisively put it, rationalistic thinkers behave – or rather try to think – as if each day were their first.[5] One's moral intuitions, or perhaps rather one's refined and valid intuitions, are assumed by these thinkers to be the same as the conclusions reached by this primeval or permanent assembly, provided its debates were properly conducted. The pretence of starting society as if anew is supposed to lead one to the basic and valid human reaction, which is legitimated by such an intellectual simulation or experiment.

The criticism to which practitioners of this style of reasoning are open is this: do they really suppose that the make-believe suspension of current information is genuine? Do they suppose that this assembly-in-permanent-session would not reach widely divergent conclusions, in accordance with the particular tradition from which its members happened to be drawn? The thinking-away of specific information about one's personal position in no way secures a similar suspension of deep, pervasive, culturally local but contentious assumptions.

Far from sitting in judgment, *independently*, on real societies, the assembly constituted according to this bizarre recipe can only reflect and reinforce the values of the concrete societies from which its members happen to be chosen. Or rather, as this assembly is not actually convened, the conclusions of its imaginary session simply reflect the values of the thinker who is imaginatively reconstructing it.

In many societies, the whole supposition that culturally naked men can *choose* their social order, instead of having it imposed on them by transcendent authority, would be simply unintelligible. Such people, when asked to perform the imaginary conceptual amputation, would in effect be requested to *think themselves away*, to deny their own existence, to ignore their own deepest moral reactions. The "veil of ignorance" method, intended to overcome local prejudice and vested interest, is simply an extreme instance and expression of a special set of ethnocentric blinkers, of the way in which our own rather special, mobile and hence egalitarian society feeds its own values back to itself.

The assumption of a moral identity independent of status and occupation does indeed make good sense in a society such as ours, in which these attributes are supposed to be, and in some measure actually are, redistributed in each generation. We even enhance our sense of community by redistributing *roles*, as some peasant communities enhance theirs by periodically redistributing fields. We identify, not with hereditary roles, but with the cultural zone ("nation") within which roles are redistributable without protest. But what sense does role-detachment make in societies within which such meritocratic principles do not prevail, within which they are not valued and are not normative? What sense does such role-nakedness have in societies in which men find their identity *through* their specific roles, and not in detachment from them?

By contrast, there are other contributors to the debate whose primary, or official, concern is with primitive man as he actually was. They are professional anthropologists or archaeologists, and what they say or write is meant by them to be judged by the normal canons of scientific validity. Any moral, ideological implications or suggestiveness of their ideas is, officially speaking, quite incidental. The most stimulating of these realistic reconstructions are nevertheless heavily loaded with contemporary political suggestiveness. It is difficult not to suspect that it was this element which, at least in part, inspired their authors. The fact that these ideas possess such a political loading does not, of course, render them invalid. Their acceptability can only in the end be determined by the evidence. And if they turn out to be accurate, it may still be doubted whether this makes them binding for *our* political choices. All the same, it is interesting that early man has lost nothing of his political sex appeal.

In between the two extremes – candid fictional reconstructionists and paid-up professional anthropologists – there are others who, while not professional specialists in the area of early man, nevertheless intend their affirmations about him to be realistic, not mere fictions, but who wish them, all the same, to point a moral for the conduct of our own social life.

For instance, one of the profoundest and most influential of prophets of modern economic and other liberalism is F. A. Hayek. Hayek's analysis of the options and perils of modern society do in fact dovetail with a sharply delineated vision of the primitive social order and ethos. On his view, the strong social morality of early man and its survival in contemporary society constitute a positive danger for us:

> There is . . . so far as present society is concerned, no "natural goodness", because with his innate instincts man could never have built up the civilisation on which the numbers of present mankind depend for their lives. To be able to do so, he had to shed many sentiments that were good for the small band, and to submit to the sacrifices which the discipline of freedom demands but which he hates. The abstract society rests on learnt rules and not on pursuing perceived desirable common objects; and wanting to do good to known people will not achieve the most for the community, but only the observation of its abstract and seemingly purposeless rules.[6]

And, should anyone not understand what this implies in practice, let it be spelt out:

> . . . the long submerged innate instincts have again surged to the top. [The] demand for a just distribution in which organised power is to be used to allocate to each what he deserves is thus strictly an *atavism*, based on primordial emotions. And it is these

widely prevalent feelings to which prophets, moral philosophers and constructivists appeal by their plans for the deliberate creation of a new type of society.[7]

The picture is striking and suggestive. Men must have lived in something like "bands", groups too small to be capable of imposing abstract and impersonal rules, for a very long time – during the overwhelming majority of generations since the inception of humanity, however that inception may be dated. So, on this view, throughout most of our history our situation instilled in us an ethic which is directly opposed to all that is innovative, creative, progressive in human civilization. Hence, civilization is based on the overcoming, not so much of our lowest instincts, but on the contrary of all that had usually been held to be moral: the social impulses of mankind, the tendency to cooperate with fellows in the pursuit of shared aims. Respect for abstract and incomprehensible rules must replace love of fellow men and community and a sense of shared purpose, if civilization is to emerge and survive.

In Hayek's vision, an unplanned, unintended culture, which was the fruit neither of conscious reason nor of animal instinct, had somehow arisen, and it alone made possible that automatic mechanism of response to need, that sustained innovative improvement, which is manifested in and fostered by the *market*. Only so can the market, dependent as it is on an unconsciously engendered abstract civilization, on respect for rules rather than on affectionate cooperativeness, come to perpetuate, in a new form, that unconscious natural selection which had, in nature, produced the higher forms from the lower ones, and which can now once again lead to higher social forms. In Hayek's interesting version, neither the perpetuation of natural strife, nor its modification by a peace-keeping state, will on their own trigger off progress. But the two beneficent mechanisms – natural selection and the market – are separated in time by a dark age, in which an excessively social morality had taken over and had, so to speak, *over*-socialized man. For long, too long, we had been under its sway. Anything describable as an abstract, impersonal, rule-bound society only emerged some five millennia ago, and even during that time, most of mankind did not live in it. Seeing how recent and precarious our liberation from over-socialization is, it is surprising that we are not even more thoroughly in thrall to atavistic sociability than Hayek fears. It is a social ethic and cohesiveness, not their absence, which are our greatest threat.

Hayek's way of presenting our general condition differs from what might be called the simplest or classical formulation of *laissez faire* liberalism, in his conscious stress on the *cultural* preconditions of an open or market society. The classical formulation suggests that its only important condition is a *political* one: a just, effective and unrapacious state must be present, a political authority which uses its power to keep the peace and uphold the rules, and does not use it simply to despoil civil society. The presence of a new spirit would then replace natural selection, which eliminates species and individuals, by a market solution, which eliminates inefficient products and bad ideas, but allows their progenitors to live, so as to produce and innovate on another day. Hayek's new way of defining the problem makes him insist that mere political order is not enough, that a certain kind of abstract culture is also required, the emergence of a sense of and respect for abstract rules, and a detachment from communal, cooperative ends. The Hidden Hand can operate only in a suitable cultural milieu, amongst men who are not too sociable, men who respect rules rather than social aims.

A very similar sense of the struggle, not with destructive animal instincts, but on the contrary with an oppressively social morality and the deep feelings which underline it, is also found in the social thought of Karl Popper.[8] This Hayek/Popper vision might well be called the Viennese Theory. One may well wonder whether it was not inspired by the fact that, in the nineteenth century, the individualistic, atomized, cultivated bourgeoisie of the Habsburg capital had to contend with the influx of swarms of kin-bound, collectivistic, rule-ignoring migrants from the eastern marches of the Empire, from the Balkans and Galicia. Cosmopolitan liberals had to contend, in the political sphere, with the emerging breed of *national* socialists. This "Viennese" vision is an inversion, a denial all at once of romanticism – it elevates

28

Gesellschaft (society) over *Gemeinschaft* (community) – and of Marxism. Marx anticipated the restoration, rather than the overcoming, of the alleged social proclivities of early man.

An alternative attempt to enlist primitive man on behalf of current values, an attempt now dated at some points but still profoundly suggestive, is to be found in Thorstein Veblen's classic *The Theory of the Leisure Class*.[9] Unlike Hayek and like Marx, Veblen applauds, and does not deplore, the peaceable sociability which he ascribes to primitive man, who in his view exemplifies the central, essential and defining human quality, the pursuit of fulfilment in *work*. The universality of the work ethic is inferred from the alleged inherent purposiveness of human action. Because we all seek ends, the argument runs, we all love efficiency, and so we value honest, sound work. In this way, Veblen uses a kind of truism – action is purposive – as a premiss, from which he deduces an appallingly contentious generalization: all men are possessed by the spirit of craftsmanship. In truth, even if all men, more or less by definition, do seek the fulfilment of their ends, some men do honour work and find fulfilment in it, and some do not.

> ... man is an agent ... seeking in every act the accomplishment of some concrete, objective impersonal end. By force of his being such an agent he is possessed of a taste for effective work, and a distaste for futile effort. He has a sense of the merit of serviceability or efficiency and of the demerit of futility, waste or incapacity. This aptitude or propensity may be called the instinct of workmanship.[10]

Primitive man clearly was a Yankee, with a taste for efficiency and a distaste for waste. The impersonality of his ends has a certain resemblance to the respect for abstract rules valued by Hayek. But Hayek thought this had to be attained, whereas the *zielbewusst* quality of conduct was, for Veblen, present from the start, a kind of birthright. What kind of community did early man live in? "These communities ... are without a defined leisure class ... They are small groups ... they are commonly peaceable and sedentary; they are poor: and individual ownership is not a dominant feature of their economic system."[11]

The growth and complexity which succeed this happy condition engender a parasitic, leisure- and violence-oriented ruling class, which un-learns the instinct of workmanship, as work becomes a stigma and sign of submission. Significantly, Veblen, so preoccupied with the ruling *class*, is not much concerned with the state, which astonishingly makes virtually no appearance in his book. Presumably this is so because in his America civil society was so very strong, and the state really was, at that stage, little more than its delegated agency.

Marxism in its official and central position claims that the state is but a reflection of a social order which it does not itself engender; but Veblen in *The Theory of the Leisure Class* conveys the strong impression (which Marxism in practice does not) that this is so already, and that one need not worry about the menace of the state. The ruling class and its failings matter, but the state does not.

Hayek would seem to be haunted by the contrast between the creativity of an individualist bourgeoisie and the cultural sterility of kin-hugging gregarious migrants from some Balkan *zadruga*, whose clannish and collectivist feelings threaten liberty and progress. Veblen by contrast appears to express an American distaste for European aristocracies, and the survival, or emulation, of their values amongst the American rich. The wealth zealously acquired on Wall Street had to be conspicuously wasted on Fifth Avenue, much to Veblen's disgust. Hayek's and Veblen's values are not so very far apart, but their perception of their historic incarnations and social roots are very different indeed.

Veblen is probably quite wrong in linking the emergence of a taste for conspicuous leisure and violence to hunting. The fact that the hunter is violent towards his prey does not mean that he is necessarily aggressive to his fellow men. The Italians who spend autumn days roaming the woods and shooting anything that moves then spend the evening in most amiable collective eating and drinking, and one may wonder whether the evening feast is a celebration of the hunt or whether the hunt is merely an excuse for the feast. There is some reason to suspect that early hunters similarly had little cause and perhaps even inclination to fight each other. A hunting or gathering economy with no stored surplus provides little rational incentive for aggression and oppression. In any case, it is not impelled in that direction by the pressing problem of the production and distribution of a stored surplus. Veblen saw that:

> Predation cannot become the habitual, conventional resource of any group or any class until industrial methods have become developed to such a degree of efficiency as to leave a margin worth fighting for, above the subsistence of those engaged in getting a living. The transition from peace to predation therefore depends on the growth of technical knowledge and the use of tools.[12]

So Veblen, or his primitive man, is somewhere in the middle of our political spectrum, between the right-wing Hayek and the left radicals. He values early man for his sociability (which is damned by Hayek), and for his rational work ethic (valued by Hayek, but not credited to early man). Those at the left end of the political spectrum are liable to praise the primitive both for his sociability *and* for his beneficent laziness, uncorrupted as yet by the work ethic, or, as they prefer to put it, by acquisitiveness. Some of them write in an age when a late industrial counter-culture has come to repudiate aristocratic display and bourgeois industriousness alike. Liberals loathe force and socialists detest greed, and some of our rebels claim to hate both, and see an early man untainted by either.

It is worth looking further at this other end of the spectrum, at those who are eager to enlist primitive man on the far left. Marshall Sahlins' *Stone Age Economics*[13] is probably the most influential and important recent work of this kind. Where Hayek damns early man for his gregarious social morality, Sahlins praises him for his freedom from greed and, even more, perhaps, for his freedom from the work ethic. Where nineteenth-century populists idealize the peasant, Sahlins' neolithic populism goes much further back and idealizes the hunter/gatherer. The rot had set in, not with the first bourgeois, but with the first peasant. Indeed the peasant seems to be a kind of proto-bourgeois. We lived far better before the inception of agriculture, with more leisure and greater humanity. Some quotations from his work will convey the flavour of his ideas:

> The hunter, one is tempted to say, is "uneconomic man". At least as concerns nonsubsistence goods, he is the reverse of that standard caricature immortalized in any *General Principles of Economics*, page one. His wants are scarce and his means (in relation) plentiful. Consequently he is "comparatively free of material pressures", has "no sense of possession", shows "an undeveloped sense of property", is "completely indifferent to any material pressures", manifests a "lack of interest" in developing his technological equipment.
>
> Economic Man is a bourgeois construction... It is not that hunters and gatherers have curbed their materialistic "impulses"; they simply never made an institution of them... We are inclined to think of hunters and gatherers as *poor* because they don't have anything; perhaps better to think of them for that reason as *free*.
>
> The most obvious, immediate conclusion is that people [hunters and gatherers] do not work hard. The average length of time per person per day put into the appropriation and preparation of food was four to five hours. Moreover, they do not work continuously. The subsistence quest was highly intermittent.

Want not, lack not.[14]

Sahlins does not deny that there is a certain price to be paid for this early form of affluence, of that hallowed congruence of need and satisfaction, rooted in exiguity of need. Such hunter/ gatherers had to be mobile and to restrict their own numbers. Indeed, the need for mobility is part of the argument which helps explain the freedom of pre-agrarian man from a sense of property. Any possessions he acquires become, quite literally, a *load*, a burden. In a world without porters, no perpetual traveller would acquire or retain a taste for bulky luggage.

If Sahlins is right – and his case cannot easily be dismissed – the initiation of agriculture was a catastrophe, both moral and material, and not a glorious achievement. There is the intriguing possibility, which clearly gives Sahlins some satisfaction, that the hunger/gatherers, far from being unable to progress, wisely reject this option: "Interesting that the Hadza, tutored by life and not by anthropology, reject the neolithic revolution in order to *keep* their leisure."[15] The East African Hadza, admirably investigated and interpreted by James Woodburn, have inspired much of the recent revaluation of the relative merits of agrarian and pre-agrarian economies. The Hadza would appear in many ways to constitute a conscious, deliberate rejection of peasant-bourgeois man. They firmly turn their back not merely on wealth and work, but also on many other values which are the pride of many other "higher" cultures: notably on intense personal relations and on long-term commitments of any kind. Among us, say these neolithic layabouts, there are no debts. Actions performed engender no long-term obligations or relationships. So benevolence, when it does occur among them, is genuinely disinterested, and not a hidden form of investment in the future. There are no trade-offs or hallowed compacts between past and future. Not merely is there little of a social "structure", of a division of labour and of roles at a given moment, but above all there is little corresponding to a structure *over time.*

This has stimulated the anthropologist investigating them, Woodburn, to formulate an intriguing hypothesis, which links the beginnings of agriculture to the kind of minimal social organization which can articulate and enforce long-term obligations.[16] Agriculture involves labour with *delayed return.* A very loose and diffuse social organization, insensitive to the retention of obligations over time, cannot ensure the delivery of the delayed fruits for its members. Anthropologists have long ago abandoned the idea of primitive sexual promiscuity, but a kind of economic/moral equivalent, the transience of productive relations, seems to be alive and well. So agriculture can only be initiated by a community which, for some reason, *already* possesses a sense of long-term obligation and permanent relations. *Some* hunters/gatherers do have social systems of the required kind, and, on this hypothesis, it was they alone who could initiate agriculture, when the need or opportunity for it arose.

It is an attractively bourgeois theory, which turns the Victorian

33

virtues of thrift, continence and patient postponement of satisfaction into the prime movers, not merely of the industrial, but equally of the neolithic revolution. It was the acquisitive primeval proto-bourgeoisie of the late Stone Age which set us off on the slippery path of Progress. Hegel had summed up world history as a progression from a state where *one* was free, to a condition in which *some* were free, and culminating in a consummation in which *all* were free. More soberly, we might now replace this by a schema in which, initially, all had leisure, and then some only had leisure, and finally, under the reign of the work ethic, none have leisure. First there was no delay of satisfaction, then a delayed return, and finally, when work became its own reward, the reign of infinitely delayed return.

It is interesting to see the neo-Marxist Sahlins use Woodburn's material and ideas but resolutely reject the bourgeois values which might seem implicit in them. Sahlins evidently views the neolithic bourgeois revolution with great distaste, as the origin of greed, acquisitiveness, aggression, human enslavement and much else. At the factual level, he is not so very much in disagreement with the neo-liberal Hayek, who disapproves of the sociability, and the immediacy of aims, of early man, and delights to see them replaced by a sense of abstract, impersonal, hence permanent and long-term rules.

Karl Marx himself, be it noted, was the bourgeois to end all bourgeois. He did indeed anticipate the shedding by mankind of the most deplored alleged corollaries of our neolithic work addiction, namely social stratification and coercion. But he wanted to absolutize and universalize the work ethic, by finally separating work from any reward and turning it into an end in itself, the ultimate fulfilment: ". . . in communist society, where nobody has one exclusive sphere of activity but each can become accomplished in any branch he wishes, society regulates the general production and thus makes it possible for me . . . . to hunt in the morning, fish in the afternoon, rear cattle in the evening, criticize after dinner . . . without ever becoming hunter, fisherman, shepherd or critic".[17] The division of labour would disappear (or, strictly speaking, its social enforcement and role ascription would disappear), but *work as fulfilment* would remain and indeed constitute our fulfilment.

The idea of work as its own reward is of course the very essence of the bourgeois spirit. We work because we like it, and despise those who work as a means only, or are constrained to perform work which means nothing to them, or do not work at all. Basically, Marxism is a bourgeois wish-fulfilment fantasy: work is to be its own reward, life really is *about* work and finds its meaning in work, and the secret of history is that, appearances notwithstanding, it is determined, not by the patterns of coercion, but by those of production. That is where the action really is. It is only the faulty organization of work which engenders antagonistic relations between men, and their corollaries, coercion and socially instituted delusion. Work-oriented middle-class producers always wished all this to be true, but only Marx dared say that it actually was true. Production was always primary, even if producers themselves knew it not. The time would come when they would be alone with their freely chosen creative activity, and all constraints, coercive or superstitious, would be gone. Man would be alone with his work and at peace with his fellows. The destiny of the proletariat was to fulfil the bourgeois ideal of peaceful, self-rewarding and unconstrained productivity.

The Suspect Witness

Returning from the political invocations of early man, where does he himself really stand? What are the facts of the case?

As so often when the question is crucial, the facts themselves are ambiguous. Pre-agrarian men, like their descendants, agrarian and industrial men, are not all alike. If we declare one sub-class within any of these categories to be typical, and the others to be mere aberrations, we simply prejudge the issues. In the case of pre-agrarian societies, which leave us no written record, we have the additional problem of deciding whether the few surviving hunting/gathering societies are in any way representative of them all, or whether they are, on the contrary, highly untypical just because they have survived (or perhaps have only emerged) in the agrarian age.

This is indeed one of the great issues in the study of such societies. We have seen Marshall Sahlins proudly invoking the testimony of the Hadza in his own repudiation of the neolithic revolution. But their testimony is suspect. Let us suppose that in the twenty-second century the world is fully industrialized, but that somewhere near Yasnaya Polyana, or in the English shires, a few communities of Tolstoyans or William Morris enthusiasts survive, firmly rejecting the values and practices of the surrounding world, and perpetuating the lives of muzhiks or of English medieval craftsmen, or what they fondly imagine to be such. How justified would a twenty-second-century anthropologist be in studying such communities, and on this basis reconstructing a general model of the agrarian world as it truly was?

Some at least of the contemporaneous hunter/gatherer communities are open to the suspicion that, far from being survivors from a world in which everyone was a hunter or gatherer, they in reality constitute specialized sub-communities within the agrarian world, moral rebels or rejects or both. Complex societies often engender minorities within their own midst, whose function may be not merely to carry out tasks despised by the majority, but also to exemplify values and life-styles *spurned* by the dominant majority. The very degradation of such deviants underscores the virtue of the rulers. The contempt in which they are held, and which they themselves are obliged to internalize, confirms the authority of the dominant values.

Societies like to affirm their own excellence not merely by celebrating their own values, but by seeing them reversed by subgroups weak enough to be publicly despised, and obliged to accept such contempt, and indeed to share it. A proudly sedentary and property-revering agricultural society may covertly delight in seeing and reprobating, in its own midst, nomadic and thieving gypsies. A nominally commerce- and finance-despising medieval society, whose rulers nevertheless desperately needed the fruits of commerce and finance to maintain their own position, could delight in the confirmation of its own faith and merit by both using and despising Jews. Some hunters and gatherers are symbiotic, in different degrees, with their agrarian neighbours; and it is at least conceivable that not merely their specialisms, but also their values and ideology, are formed, not by a past when hunters were living in a world of hunters, but by deliberate contrast, by the image-creation of their non-hunter neighbours. They opt out, or are forced to opt out, by the dominant society of which in fact they are an integral part, and which they serve symbolically as well as economically, by their degradation as well as by their services.

Such an interpretation, strongly suggested by the situation of some at least among contemporary hunting societies, is not equally applicable to all of them, and perhaps wholly inapplicable to some. Some hunters, on the other hand, may also contradict the hypothesis of the tie-up between complexity of organization and delayed economic return. They may combine a very complex ritual and kin organization with a low degree of economic long-term planning or storage. To say that they practise delayed return in the matter of exchange of brides, though not in production, is to concede that long-term obligation, and all it implies, may after all be produced without any ecological stimulus.

In brief, both the roots and the generality of either neolithic embourgeoisement, or current dissident neo-neolithic bohemianism, remain contentious issues. So Stone Age man remains a floating voter in the coming general election. He does not seem either willing or able to settle our destiny and our obligations for us. For the polster eager to predict our future on the basis of our deepest (oldest) nature, early man obdurately remains a "don't know".

The range of options open to, and realized by, pre-agrarian man remains an open question. Archaeological and ethnographic evidence remains incomplete and ambiguous, and may remain so for ever. Whether primitive man may be enlisted on the side of peace or of aggression, on the side of equality of women or of male chauvinism, on the side of the work ethic or of an ecologically beneficent and humanly sensible exiguity of needs, on the side of social sentiments or of individualist ruggedness – all that remains to be explored further. What does, however, remain obvious is that, prior to the agricultural revolution, there simply was no possibility of a growth in scale and in complexity of the division of labour and social differentiation. These alone set the scene, and the problems (in very different forms) for agrarian and industrial man, for *us*.

CHAPTER 2

Community to Society

The Cognitive Evolution of Mankind

One persistent attempt to find a thread in the history of mankind focuses on the notion of Reason. Human history, on this view, is the unfolding of rationality. Human thought, institutions, social organization, become progressively more rational. The idea that Reason is the goal or end-point of the development of mankind can fuse with the view that it also constitutes the principal agency which impels humanity along its path. It seems natural to suppose that changes in human life spring from growth of our ideas, our ways of thought. What is conduct if not implementation of ideas? If we improve, is it not because our ideas have improved? Though somewhat suspect as the fruit of vainglorious self-congratulation by nineteenth-century Europeans, the role of thought and reason still deserves some consideration.

The problems and difficulties facing a reason-centred view of history are considerable. No doubt the idea is far less popular now than it was in the heady days of rationalistic optimism, which stretched, in one form or another, from the late eighteenth to the early twentieth centuries. But, in a sober and not necessarily optimistic form, it remains necessary to attempt some kind of sketch of the cognitive transformation of mankind, from the days of hunting to those of computing. The nature of our cognitive activities has not remained constant: not only have things changed, but the change has also been deep and fundamental. It is not merely a matter of *more* of the same. The changes that have occurred have been changes in *kind*.

A convenient baseline or starting point for the discussion of this problem is provided by the blatant absurdity of some at least of the beliefs of primitive man. Many of us like to think that the standards of what is acceptable in matters of belief have gone up, and that the advance of reason in history is manifest in this raising of standards. We have become fastidious and shrink from the beliefs of our distant ancestors, which strike us as absurd. Perhaps, so as not to prejudge an important issue, one ought to say – it is the *translations* frequently offered of some of the beliefs of some primitive men which now seem so absurd. It may be – and some have indeed argued this – that the absurdity is located not in the original belief itself but in its translation, inspired by a failure to understand the original context. On this view, it is the modern translator, and not the savage, who is guilty of absurdity.

The apparently sustained and systematic absurdity of the beliefs of primitive man helps to set the background for our central question. Are they wrong and are we right? Or are we playing radically different games, legitimately measured by quite independent criteria? And if their problems and their answers are different, are they linked to ours by some developmental series? And if not, what is the nature of the chasm which separates us from them? Is it indeed a chasm?

Let us use the identification of bulls with cucumbers credited, in certain ritual contexts, to the Nilotic tribe of the Nuer, as a code abbreviation for absurd beliefs of primitive societies in general.[1] The frequency with which alleged absurdities of this kind are found – or are credited to – savages or alien peoples accounts for much of the appeal of anthropology. The absurdity shocks and titillates our cognitive voyeurism. It has also inspired a variety of theories about "primitive mentality" and hence of the overall development and nature of human thought.

Two extreme positions are available on this topic. One is that the prevalence of absurd beliefs indicates a special, pre-rational kind of mentality, radically discontinuous with our own.[2] The other position is one already mentioned, namely that the reasoning of primitive man is as good as, and similar to, our own, and not in any way qualitatively different. The apparent pervasiveness of absurdity, of the defiance of fact and logic, in primitive thought, was wished upon it by unperceptive, unsophisticated, and perhaps in some cases malevolent observers.

Take the benevolent or charitable thesis: primitive man is rational. It is supported by the indisputable and conspicuous fact that primitive man is at the very least as good as modern man in observing and coping with his immediate physical environment. One could easily demonstrate this empirically. Take the "bull = cucumber" equation. We could test Nuer rationality empirically. Take ten Nuer selected at random, and also ten randomly selected Fellows of the Royal Anthropological Institute. Place a very small bull and a very large cucumber, or perhaps a prize marrow just to make it a bit harder, in the Nilotic scrub, about 150 yards away from a given vantage point, at dusk, and then ask, one by one, each of the ten Nuer and each of the ten Fellows to identify small bull and big cucumber. Can there be much doubt but that the experienced and clear-sighted Nuer (few of whom have spoilt their eyesight with a lifetime of book-reading) will do better than the Fellows? Where is primitive mentality now?

If this charitable view of primitive thought is accepted, its protagonists face the problem: how did it come about that primitive man was so widely credited with absurd views of the bull = cucumber kind? These protagonists offer various explanations, but one of the commonest runs as follows: these seemingly absurd and really mistranslated assertions are not really statements about the physical environment at all. They generally occur in a ritual context, and they are "really" statements about the social order of which the native is a member. The apparent empirical content is really a re-affirmation of the social order.[3] It just so happens that they employ local terms equivalent to "cucumber" or "bull" which, *in other contexts*, may indeed have just this kind of simple empirical reference. But the semantic complexity, the variability of real meaning with context and purpose, misled the observer, who was, alas, in any case only too eager to find exotic oddities and to indulge his own vainglorious sense of intellectual superiority.

This account is indefensible. If what the member of the alien culture really meant was simply the proclamation of his loyalty to the social order of his community, why on earth is he not

41

translated as saying *precisely that*? Is it really a mere accident that the very same terms are used both in an empirical and a ritual context? Are no absurd beliefs ever pervasively held by a society? Is there really no use for the idea of *false consciousness*, of institutionalized error contributing to the very foundations of a social order? Are there not countless examples of the use of magical connections for purposes of manipulating the environment, treating such connections as if they resembled ordinary causal ones?

Above all – has there really been no overall, long-term change in human mentality? Did primitive man really know how to segregate perfectly sensible empirical observations from culturally specific re-affirmations of adherence to his own social order? Was his basic internal intellectual economy the same as ours? Is there really no tale to tell of the intellectual history of mankind?

Of the two polar positions, one, which credits primitive man with a kind of perpetual logic-shunning inebriation, fails to account for his outstanding and indisputable competence in coping with his physical environment. The other, which re-defines his terms for him so as to endow him with our own logical fastidiousness, and exculpates him from the charge of absurd convictions, fails to account for the radical discontinuity which does exist between primitive and modern mentality. In the name of a tolerant relativism, it pretends, absurdly, that all cognitive systems are equal. Claiming to recognize diversity, it obscures fundamental and deep differences. Faced with the historical battles between rationalism and faith, or indeed between fastidious, codified faith and luxuriant superstition, it has nothing to say. Yet these conflicts were of great historic importance. The charitable view cannot cope with the great tensions which are a central theme of our history, and it can only see them as mere misunderstandings. But they were far, far more than that. Is there an approach which can accommodate both insights, which can recognize the great empirical sensitivity of primitive man and also the discontinuity between him and modern cognition styles?

The error underlying each of these contrasted positions is the failure to appreciate something which is a commonplace in sociology. It is a point which, curiously enough, has not been introduced sufficiently into the discussion of the problem of knowledge. The point in question is the difference between single-strand or single-purpose activities on the one hand, and multi-strand activities on the other. A multi-strand activity (the use of speech, in this case), which serves multiple criteria or ends, *is treated as if it were a single-strand one.* It is assumed that primitive men or man in general must *either* be making observations about the physical world (bulls are or are not cucumbers), *or* recording his loyalty to a given social order, by means of a ritual formula. It is assumed that this distinction is at least tacitly understood. The possibility that these two activities (and others) might be conflated and intertwined in complete and ambiguous and sliding-scale ways is excluded. In other words, the assertions of primitive man are treated as if he were the heir and beneficiary, as we are, of a complex, systematized, conscious and orderly division of labour, within which diverse functions and aims tend to be clearly and distinctly separated. In *our* society, such a separation is systematically inculcated and highly prized, and the muddling-up of aims is reprobated. Primitive man, however, has no need for such distinctions; the functioning of his society may indeed depend on their absence.

It makes sense to ask a modern man whether he is making an empirical observation or affirming his loyalty to the hierarchy and structure of his own society. If endowed with the appropriate educational background, he may understand the question. There is even the possibility that he will answer it accurately. But is there any reason to suppose that this neat separation of functions is so inherent in the very nature of things that – given a bit of trouble about terminology and translation, perhaps – the savage could also grasp it? Is it everyone's birthright, or is it, on the contrary, the special accomplishment of one rather eccentric tradition, the fruit of very unusual circumstances? Is the division of labour, and the separation of functions, inscribed into the very constitution of nature and thought or, on the contrary, does not nature, and society for that matter, prefer to use one tool for a variety of ends, and one end to be served by many tools? We, who have been drilled into acquiring a fine sensitivity for the difference of aims and functions, must beware of projecting it onto all others. It may be an eccentric, perhaps even a pathological accomplishment.

The assumption of the inherent neat separation of diverse linguistic functions is so weird that, once challenged, it should readily be discarded. There is no excuse for projecting our own sensitivity, arduously acquired in the course of a very odd and distinctive historic development, onto humanity at large, let alone onto early man. The division of labour, and the separation of questions which is but one aspect of it, is a late accomplishment, and *not* a birthright of all mankind.

If we refrain from indulging in this misguided assumption, what is the correct way to think of primitive mentality? Multistrandedness, in activities other than cognition, is a familiar and common notion. The idea is simple: in a complex, large, atomized and specialized society, single-shot activities can be "rational". This then means that they are governed by a single aim or criterion, whose satisfaction can be assessed with some precision and objectivity. Their instrumental effectiveness, "rationality", can be ascertained. A man making a purchase is simply interested in buying the best commodity at the least price. Not so in a many-stranded social context: a man buying something from a village neighbour in a tribal community is dealing not only with a seller, but also with a kinsman, collaborator, ally or rival, potential supplier of a bride for his son, fellow juryman, ritual participant, fellow defender of the village, fellow council member.

All these multiple relations will enter into the economic operation, and restrain either party from looking only to the gain and loss involved in that operation, taken in isolation. In such a many-stranded context, there can be no question of "rational" economic conduct, governed by the single-minded pursuit of maximum gain. Such behaviour would disastrously ignore all the other multiple considerations and relationships which are also involved in the deal, and which constrain it. These other considerations are numerous, open-ended, intertwined and often incommensurate, and hence do not lend themselves to any cost–benefit *calculation*.

In such circumstances, a man can live up to a *norm*, but he cannot really serve a clear single *aim*. Norms are complex: aims should be simple and clear. An instrumental and more or less quantified rationality presupposes a single measure of value, in terms of which alternative strategies can be assessed. When there is a multiplicity of incommensurate values, some imponderable, a man can only *feel*, and allow his feelings to be guided by the overall expectations or preconceptions of his culture. He cannot calculate. Single-mindedness and cold assessment of options, by contrast, when it does obtain, requires a rather special social setting, and one that is generally absent from simpler societies. The fewer the members of a community, the more conflated, many-purpose, its agenda. Large societies *can* afford the luxury of neatly separated activities (though even they do not necessarily or universally adopt it).

But the same kind of many-strandedness is clearly also likely to pervade the use of language in simple and smaller societies. A man indulging in a socially recognized and acceptable noise-pattern – in brief, *saying something* – cannot simply be assumed to be doing *one thing only*. He can plausibly be expected to be doing a number of things at once. Our strategy, when approaching our problem, is to invert this baseline assumption. We have tended to assume that men do one thing at a time, and that they neatly separate diverse activities, because that is indeed a central part of our own ethos and education; therefore, if men do a number of things at once, we feel that that needs to be explained. The opposite is true: it is single-strandedness, the neat and logical division of labour, the separation of functions, which needs to be explained, and which is exceptional, and whose emergence is the form in which Reason enters history. The conflation and con-fusion of functions, of aims and criteria, is the normal, original condition of mankind. And it is important to grasp this point fully. A multi-functional expression is not one in which a man combines a number of meanings because he is in a hurry and his

45

language has offered him a package deal: on the contrary, the conflated meanings constitute, for him, a single and indivisible semantic content.

Any given multi-strand use of language may serve two, three, or any number of purposes and criteria. There is no reason whatsoever to assume that any one figure is pre-eminent or privileged, or that the same number is found in all spheres of language. We shall concentrate on a *dual*-purpose model, but only because all the relevant complications arising from many-strandedness, of any degree, are already to be found in the dual-aim model: not because duality is in any way privileged or typical. A mystique of the *binary* is found in some recent theories in anthropology, but it plays no part in the present argument. The relative simplicity of two-term models is only an aid to exposition. Duality is not privileged, but it does constitute the simplest way of approaching the problems of plurality.

Once one recognizes that a given verbal expression serves two purposes, its use in a given society will only be describable by means of an at least two-dimensional diagram. But let us begin with a single-dimensional one:

It is raining   ✓   ?   X

The phrase naively translatable as "it is raining" may, along *one* dimension, be "referential". It is linked, "operationalized", related to an independent reality, namely rain. The phrase receives the high grading (translated as "truth") if it is indeed raining, a low mark (denial) if it is not, and may receive a borderline or ambiguous grading if the weather itself is dubious.

But, at the same time, the native phrase may *also* be part of a ritual, linked to social situations rather than to nature. As such, it may receive high marks if the high priest or village shaman has said the same, a low mark if he has denied it, and a suspended sentence if he has kept silent. Acceptance of the grading by a

member of the society indicates his conformity and his identification with the authority-structure of his own society. In this
context, he is not theorizing about nature; he is endorsing (or of
course repudiating, as the case may be) a social order.

High priest says it is raining	√
High priest silent	?
High priest says it is not raining	X

The gratuitous assumption which we are challenging is that
the speaker must himself be distinguishing the two activities,
reference to nature and loyalty to social order – the supposition
that their separation lies in the very nature of things, or in the
very nature of speech or thought. It does not. On the contrary, an
air of referential objectivity may underwrite his support of the
high priest; and an air of transcendent endorsement may in turn
pervade his recognition of a natural state of affairs. Why separate
them? Why should they not reinforce each other?

Conflation of ends is far more common and in some sense
natural than their neat separation. The conflated multi-purpose
role of the expression, in its particular social setting, *is* its
"meaning". The man in question does not think of himself as
simultaneously indulging in meteorology *and* politics, comment-
ing on the weather *and* emphasizing his alignment. The two are
fused. This endows his politics with a natural vindication, and his
meteorology with a social sanction. This is the life which the
expression leads within its speech community, and it knows no
other. Consider the matrix of the real multiple use of the
expression:

	Raining	Ambiguous	Not raining
Priest says yes	√	√	conflict
Priest silent	√	*CONFIRMATION*	X
Priest says no	conflict	X	X

47

Referentialists, as one may call them, have imposed the referential use of language as somehow primary and basic onto pre-division-of-labour man. They have treated the second rank (when the priest is silent), seen in isolation, as giving us the "real meaning" of the assertion. The rest is a kind of social accretion. Coming across fact-contradicting uses (the two "conflict" squares in the first and third rank), they either had to accuse primitive man of defying logic – if he deferred to priest rather than to nature – or to say that, in these cases, the phonetically identical phrase is used, but in a different sense. The absurdity or fact-denial is then blamed on the translator, who had treated homonyms as a single concept.

By contrast, adherents of what may be called the social theory of meaning have concentrated on column two, in which, *by our act of analysis*, the social aspect (of this simplified situation) is isolated. In this column, extraneous fact plays no part. In our example, it is so because the weather is doubtful; empirical reality has passed no clear verdict. All that is recorded here is the respect which the speaker accords the hierarchical ordering of his own society.

The diagonal descending from left to right may be called the Diagonal of Confirmation. The vision of our high priest, the divine inspiration of our doctrine, is confirmed by the remarkable convergence observable along this line. He saith it raineth, and behold, it raineth. He saith it raineth not, and it raineth not. He keepeth mum, and behold, you can't tell what the devil the weather doeth.

There is another important diagonal, rising from left to right. This may be called the Diagonal of Conflict. Ritual occasions are normally distinguishable not merely by a certain stilted language, but also by the defiance of fact and logic.[4]

A heightened sense of occasion can be brought about not merely by excessively formal or informal conduct and clothing, but also by logical and factual eccentricity. If it really were the case that the savage, or indeed the believer in sophisticated societies, never said anything which defied the normal conventions of logic or meaning, how could such special highlighting be secured? How could the special effect be achieved? Life would be lived permanently in the same semantic key, and it would be dull, without even a quickening of sensitivity.

Without absurdity, no logical fireworks. If the affirmation "This cucumber is a bull" had nothing paradoxical about it; if it were a mere mistranslation of: we carve up this cucumber in a ritual manner so as to reaffirm our adherence to our social order, and whilst so doing, refer to it by the term which just happens on other and ordinary occasions to be used for bulls, would anyone feel any excitement? Attempt a similar re-translation of the affirmation that the wafer is the body of Christ. . . If transubstantiation were merely the use of one word for two, by way of phonetic economy, would it have any deep resonance? The doctrine of the Real Presence is an attempt, in advance of time, to disallow over-charitable anthropological interpretation. Note that Leach's position in his book on the tribes of Highland Burma in effect contradicts the important point he makes in his essay on "Time and False Noses".[5] If indeed the apparent empirical absurdity were generally but a mistranslation of something social and commonsensical, how could the sense of social occasion be generated by defying logic – if in fact no such defiance had occurred?

Our model depicts a so-to-speak two-dimensional sensitivity: a system of expression which responds to *two* sets of constraints, one located in nature, the other in society. In the real life of societies and language, there can often be not two, but many simultaneously operating constraints or controls. We have selected two which are crucial for the argument. Empiricists talk as if concepts were only "operationalized" by being linked to processes in nature. Anthropologists concentrate on expressions which have a conspicuous "social" operationalization, a "function". In fact, expressions are far more often than not linked to social processes. Generally the rules governing the use of a given word "operationalize" it in *both* directions at once. But their multiple life is experienced as *one* single life.

Multiple Sensitivities

A language of a given community may be assumed to possess multi-dimensional sub-systems of this kind; and it may be assumed to be endowed with *a large number of them*. The various multi-stranded sub-systems which make up a language, which constitute the conceptual sensitivity of a given community, will each of them be composed of *different* sets of elements or dimensions. Not only is each such system complex: the elements which enter this complexity vary greatly from one such system to another.

This is supremely important. The "dimensions" which enter into any one sub-system will *not* be the same as those making up other such sub-systems. They may, or may not, overlap in part.

One set of activities, for instance, may fuse courtship, recognition of group boundaries, and the marking out of time; a periodic festival will signal the passage of time *and* the progression of generations, by serving to initiate an age group into a new status. At the same time, participants in the ritual may be allocated parts which indicate permissible marital pairings. Another ritual may fuse the affirmation of status with the organization of the hunt: the timing and location of the hunt may be in the hands of various office-holders, whose decisions will be determined both by objective prospects of a kill and by the political, intra-social consequences of various choices. A third sub-system may be both a "game" in the ordinary sense and the establishment of a rival alternative hierarchy, a counter-weight to the ritual or formal one: a social occasion arises in which a narcotic is consumed, and in which excitement is stimulated in other ways, but within which seating and rank obey rules more flexible than those which prevail on other occasions, so that a rival outlet for ambition and an alternative social court of appeal are created;[6] and so on. The range of possibilities is enormous.

If this hypothesis about the conceptual order of primitive man, and probably of most other men as well, is correct, what is the consequence? The most important corollary is this: if we wish to have a realistic model of "the world" as conceived and as experienced by such men, we must imagine something like a multi-periscope submarine. Something like this:

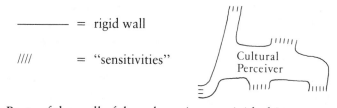

————— = rigid wall

//// = "sensitivities"

Cultural Perceiver

Parts of the wall of the submarine are rigid: this corresponds to those parts of the belief system, normally rather extensive, which during the normal life of society are totally insensitive to the outside world. The background myths and legends, the classification of men, creatures, objects and activities, which also assign them their place and role – all this is fixed and given in the daily life of most societies. Most of what men say, and the content of what they say, has no direct relationship to nature (contrary to the view of naive theorists of language who would treat all acts of discourse as if they were experiential reports). They simply play a part in social interaction. Language is not merely rooted in ritual; it *is* a ritual. Grammar is the set of rules of a ritual performance. Language is the most pervasive ritual activity.

Most uses of speech are closer in principle to the raising of one's hat in greeting than to the mailing of an informative report. The complex variants of greeting may have descriptive content, or allude to it; but the stories which make up the corpus of beliefs are largely fixed. If variable at all, they vary under the impact of something quite other than "evidence". A descriptive picture may be presented, but it is not in any way under the control of any data.

But there is also a variety of apertures, sensitivities, of periscopes as it were, which enable the individual organism, and the language-sharing community of such organisms, to "perceive", and above all to respond to, bits of external reality. A nature independent of society cannot be avoided; but there is no need normally to systematize it into a single, socially independent, unified system, and indeed societies do not normally do anything

51

of the kind. When it does happen, it constitutes a historically rare and difficult achievement. It is in no way any kind of baseline of the human condition, a natural birthright of mankind.

The really important thing is this: few, probably none, of the encounters with extra-social reality are "pure". On the contrary, they are generally many-stranded, and their responsiveness to the outside world (if any) is meshed in with other, intra-social, sensitivities and constraints. Their sensitivity to some external natural feature, to which they are "operationally" linked and on which they are, so to speak, the organism's special spy, is normally blended in with other controls, internal to the system. In this way the external reporting is not "pure", and the pure "empirical" element can mostly be overridden by the other controls or dimensions. If the leader of the hunt is ritually impure, then conditions for hunting are impropitious – never mind the "real" natural circumstances. Moreover, the various periscopes, or sensitivities, are diversely constructed; hence their elements do not, and *cannot*, "add up" with each other. Sensitivity A, which fuses awareness of weather with respect for the high priest, cannot be blended in any straightforward way with sensitivity B, which records both the presence of game *and* the state of ritual purity of the hunter (say). Each lives its own life, governed by its own and distinct set of criteria or controls.

Hence it is wrong to see the traditional use of language as primarily referential (with non-referential elements as a kind of irrelevant impurity); but it would be equally wrong to see it as wholly unrelated to nature. The crucial point is that its links to nature are meshed in with other elements, and that the various diverse links to nature do not and cannot fuse into a single pure, referential account of an independent, extra-social system. Hence the individual sensitivities or nature-links do not have much or any potential for growth, or improvement; the notion of tinkering with terms until a given piece of nature is more efficiently linked to its verbal correlate is missing. This potential for improvement is not merely missing, it goes against the grain; its emergence is normally inhibited.

It simply cannot be repeated too often, or stressed with

sufficient emphasis, that a person who has deeply internalized one of these systems and lives within it, and can conceive no other, does not think of them as being multi-purpose, as a conflation of two different activities. It is no use asking him, When you say tomorrow will be a fine day, are you expressing a probability conviction about the weather, or your deference to the authority of the priest? When you say that game is plentiful, are you speaking from empirical evidence, or merely telling us that your ritual condition is such that you may allow yourself to go hunting? Even supposing one found the words to say all this in his language, he would no doubt look at one blankly. The multiply-controlled concept is, for him, but *one* concept.

Generic Types of Strand

One of the things which make a sound or any signal, emitted or produced by a human being, into a part of a language, and more than merely a sound, is that it is subject to rules of fittingness: it is not equally appropriate under all circumstances. The evaluations and criteria to which acceptable sound or signal patterns are subjected are complex. In sophisticated languages, a properly formed, socially acceptable sentence is often graded on a roughly binary scale: it is deemed *true* or *false*.

Ordinary speech, unlike two-valued formal logic, is not in practice very strictly binary in this way: apart from classifying assertions as true and false, we are rather sensitive to nuance. We do not normally think that a miss is as good as a mile: on the contrary, we think it relevant if an assertion only misses by a narrow margin or by a technicality, or if it is very nearly true and can be set right fairly easily. We distinguish between falsehood and outrageous falsehood, or between lies and whoppers.

Nevertheless, the myth or ideal of a strict two-valued logic tends to pervade our current habitual thinking about thought. This does not matter too much – but it is important to stress that the rules and gradings which govern the various "strands" themselves also come in all kinds of shapes and sizes. Sharp and two-valued evaluations have no monopoly. Multi-valued grada-tions, continuous-spectrum gradations, etc., are all there, ready to be found.

The wide variety of ends and criteria that men may pursue in both their actions and their speech is significant. But despite this great diversity of criteria of grading, which is of the very essence of the situation, this diverse multitude of aims can nevertheless be usefully classified in two great overall general species: the Referential use, and Shared Concept Affirmation. Socially recognized noise patterns receive approbation either because they are "true (1)" (that is, referentially valid, correctly linked to nature), or because they are "true (2)" (that is true/loyal, con-forming to normative conceptual expectations). These are the two important species of "truth". The English language ambi-guously and suggestively uses the word "truth" in both senses. German distinguishes *treu* and *wahr*.

Truth (1), referential accuracy, is perhaps a very remarkable subspecies of truth (2), of loyalty: exclusive loyalty to a uniform and unified nature, and hence indifference to society. In the end, perhaps, you cannot serve two masters efficiently; but most of mankind has in fact done so most of the time. It is important for us to distinguish and oppose the two great species now. There is also an enormous diversity *within* each of these two great species: but it is this overall distinction which matters for our argument.

If we now project this distinction, not made or noticed by most men, onto the past, we erect the machinery which helps us to understand primitive thought. We avoid the absurd and previously insoluble dilemma. So we return to our simplified two-dimensional diagram. It simplifies in so far as it assumes the presence of two "strands" only. We do this because we are primarily interested in the two great genera, in reference and norm-affirmation. Moreover we assume, for the sake of the argument, that each operates with a simple, yes/no, fairly discon-tinuous principle of evaluation. (Nothing in our argument hinges on these simplifications.)

From the viewpoint of the users of the language, each such sub-system constitutes a unitary, seamless sensitivity. It is *we* who have in retrospect sorted it out into two strands, and, above all, into two strands of radically different kinds. One of them is referential: its claims stand or fall in accordance with objective states of affairs. It is properly "operationalized", and linked to its own bit of "nature", which decides its "truth" or "falsehood". The other, despite the great variety of functions it can perform, serves above all the affirmation of commitment to shared concepts by the users of the language. They are, at the same time, members of the same community. Loyalty to concepts makes possible loyalty to the community.

A concept is, of course, far more than a "mere" concept: it encapsulates and communicates and authorizes a shared way of classifying, valuing, a shared range of social and natural expectations and obligations. It makes cooperation and communication possible. It limits behaviour and sensibility, otherwise endowed with a potentially infinite diversity, into circumscribed bounds, and thereby establishes a "culture", and makes communication possible.

One way of looking at a culture is to see it as a set of concepts, and in some sense a *system* of concepts. Each concept groups a set of objects or events or whatever "under" itself. It engenders a set of expectations in anyone who is imbued with it. According to this or that culture, a "man", for instance, is expected to behave in certain ways, and indeed everything in nature that is classified thereby also has some expectations attached to it.

There is hardly any point in separating moral and probabilistic expectations in any sharp and systematic way; the distinction may operate sometimes, but it is not imposed systematically. The "normal" and the "normative" are linked, even if not always identified. Deviation from expectations built into a notion more often constitutes a moral transgression rather than a falsification of a theory. A man who does something that "real" men in his culture "simply don't do" is not falsifying a theory; he is disturbing the moral order.

"Concepts" are simply the summations of such expectations,

and they are generally tied to a word. Concepts are not inherent in the nature of things, but inhere in, make up, and are instilled by cultures; their transmission certainly is not genetic. It may or may not be the case that some concepts are universal and shared by all cultures. They could be, either because nature universally displays certain patterns which are then always echoed by culture, or because the structural prerequisites of any culture, any system of ideas, always throw up the same as it were service notions, ideas which help organize the others. Universally present ideas, if such there be, may reflect fundamental inescapable features of external reality, or they may spring from a shared genetic predisposition of humanity. We do not know the answers to these intriguing questions; happily, our argument can proceed without the answers, though the questions deserve to be raised.

It was Emile Durkheim's central insight to see that concepts are *binding*, and that it was this which really constituted the original unwritten social contract, the distinguishing mark of human sociability.[7] He also saw that this binding power of concepts was not self-explanatory, that it required explanation. The explanation he offered also had great merit, though his main achievement was perhaps the sheer perception of the problem. He did insist, rightly and with great emphasis, that the explanation of the power of concepts offered by empiricist philosophy was inadequate.

Empiricist philosophers tend to suppose that abstract concepts, the ideas which bind a multiplicity of phenomena under them, are attained by a kind of *abstraction* from experience. We see this man, that man, and the other man, and lo and behold, we somehow cotton on to the notion that they share some cluster of features in common, and thus attain the abstract idea of "man". There are many things wrong with such a theory. For one thing, and this was central for Durkheim, it fails to explain the *compulsiveness* of concepts. Even if men can act as they wish, they cannot think as they wish. Concepts precede and do not follow recognition. The "abstraction" model may conceivably hold for a very sophisticated modern investigator, contemplating a domain of inquiry, and tentatively grouping objects together in virtue of shared traits which, he conjectures, may turn out to be relevant for his problem. But that is not how life is normally lived. Concepts hold men in their grip, they guide and constrain their conduct and their expectations.

Men are not free to think as they wish; they are in thrall to their ideas, and their ideas are socially shared. Like Kant, Durkheim supposed that moral and logical compulsion had the same root, though he differed from Kant as to what that single root was. The primary function of ritual, according to Durkheim, was the imprinting of concepts, and hence of the compulsions and obligations built into them, onto our minds and feelings. Collective excitement makes us malleable and fit to receive, not so much indoctrination (that was only to come much later), as *inconceptualization*. Shared concepts and shared compulsions made us into social men: in fact, they alone made us both social and human.

If "association" were the real nature of concept formation, then given that anything can be associated with anything, concepts would be hopelessly volatile. They would trail off in any number of directions, there would be no reason to expect congruence of concepts between speaker and listener, and communication would be impossible. "Free association" is really a pleonasm: *association* is inherently free and undisciplined. Concepts formed in this manner would be subject to a kind of semantic cancer. They would rapidly come to embrace and devour everything within sight, or rather, within association. The interesting and crucial thing about our concepts is that they are themselves highly disciplined, as well as that they discipline us. Associations are born free but are everywhere in chains. Men are better behaved conceptually and linguistically than they are morally. This may be because the temptations to transgress are weaker or because control is stronger, or both. Durkheim's theory of concept formation – through ritual – highlights the problem of the astonishingly disciplined comportment of our concepts, and of the manner in which they discipline *us*. It highlights this problem and offers a solution.

Social and Logical Coherence

To recapitulate: shared concepts, affirmed by the non-referential aspects of each sub-system of language, are not governed by the same aims and criteria within each sub-system. On the contrary, their uses are highly variegated. However, what they do have in common is that they set up clusters of normatively prescriptive expectations. These are shared, fairly closely, by the members of the given conceptual community. Language is a shared system of inhibitions.

Each set-system engenders its own distinctive sensitivity to the external world. The non-referential element or principle contained within each such conceptual sensitivity, however, is *not* identical with the non-referential element in other similar sub-systems. To give examples: one ritual inculcates deference to the high priest, and the recognition of the castes and clans of the given society; another teaches the participant the rhythm of social time, the units of duration in terms of which his obligations are measured. Another ritual still may define spatial bounds, or the beginning and end of a given productive activity. Each of the systems may also contain some "external" sensitivity, a linking of the activities it triggered to outside facts. But these facts are meshed in with separate concerns, and their idiom does not relate them to the factual elements in *other* sub-systems. They may all support each other and form a moral system, and, in general, this is indeed how societies do seem to work: but the various sub-systems are not identical, and do not, so to speak, use a single *referential* currency. Each mints its own.

In other words, the various apertures of our multi-periscope submarine are constructed in quite diverse ways and in accordance with a variety of principles. Hence their findings, the data they feed back to the body of the submarine, simply are not comparable. Each in itself is usable, but they cannot meaningfully be combined and juxtaposed. The verbal accompaniments of diverse rituals are not part of one and the same system.

Does this mean that the world of primitive man, deploying this diversified multiplicity of conceptual organs, is incoherent, fragmented, a thing of threads and patches? Superficially, this would seem to follow; in fact, however, the very reverse is true.

If a conceptual sensitivity is single-purpose, single-strand, and the criterion in question is objective reference, *then*, and then only, the findings become wholly unpredictable and cannot serve reliably (or indeed cannot serve at all) any social purpose. The external world is, by definition, that which we do not control. The external world is what happens to us. It is independent of our will. It constitutes a set of hostages to fortune, or rather, hostages to nature. Data are what *turns up*; no constraints can be put upon them. They will not serve social ends, or only do so by accident. They will not serve social ends because they will not serve any end.

Things are different, however, if the actual *processed* findings fed back by the periscope are only in part data-dependent; and if, as we insist, reference to nature is *at most* one element in a complex of "controls" or "operational links". The system can then be so constructed as to ensure that certain kinds of data are never allowed to come through at all, but are reliably overruled, sifted, screened, by the mechanics of the other, non-referential dimension or dimensions involved. The total system can maintain a stylistic and functional unity, not at the mercy of "factual findings". So the pervasive themes, faiths of a culture, cease to be at the mercy of nature. Nature speaks only through, so to say, delegations sent in by the sub-systems, and within each such delegation, its messages only constitute a minority. If, for instance, the "deferential" element in the rain-language of the tribe always protects the authority and prestige of the high priest, if his say-so overrules the actual facts of precipitation, then "objective" (by our standards) rain-facts will never be allowed to imperil the religious hierarchy of the tribe. Multi-strandedness generally makes it *possible* (though not mandatory) to subordinate the referential to the exigencies of the social, to ensure that no fact will ever brazenly overturn the vision that is socially preferred.

The multiplicity of such socially censored periscopes *need* not, of course, add up to a coherent, harmonious system. There could be some disharmony, or even a lot of it, and, no doubt, there sometimes is. But the neutralization-if-necessary of purely external and hence uncontrollable data also makes it *possible* to form a coherent and hence a habitable system.

Most pre-scientific societies do in fact seem to make use of this feature of their thought-systems, of the absence of any pure and socially unbound referentiality, of any uncontrollable intrusion of the Outside, and build up a tolerably coherent world picture, in which background world-story, social organization, and natural fact are all congruent. The time-ordering sub-system will tend to dovetail in with the personal hierarchy sub-system: the big periodic festival, marking the seasonal rhythm, also under-writes the hieratic rankings. The bigger the festival, the more senior the officiating priest, say . . . The *social* elements in each sub-system form a reasonably coherent whole with the social elements in the other sub-systems of the language; it is the empirical constituents of the diverse sub-systems (when they are present at all) which fail to cross-relate to each other. Unpurified, meshed-in with the social, they cannot cross-relate to other pure "factual" elements, and there is no common idiom in terms of which they could do so. Instead, they generally buttress up the pervasive social vision.

Multi-purpose sub-systems, which do not allow any single criterion to dominate (so that nature is never endowed with a veto), can and generally do help engender a coherent vision of the social and natural world. They produce a *cosmos* in which the natural and the social are not sharply or systematically dis-tinguished. The tendency of societies, especially small and simple societies, to have reasonably coherent visions of the world, to inhabit such a "cosmos", has often been noted, not without envy. The passing away of such a coherent vision in complex and unstable societies, and its replacement by an impersonal, law-abiding, indifferent Nature, is a source of much recent romantic regret, poignantly expressed. The coherence of the world we have lost was thematic or stylistic rather than strictly logical. A fairly coherent picture was sustained by devices which evaded or defied logic.

To anticipate a later theme: it is the complex and cognitively "progressive" societies, within whose internal intellectual economy cognition has become fairly well separated from other activities and criteria, which possess a high level of *logical* coherence. All "facts" can be cross-related and fitted into a single logical space. They all use a common conceptual currency; putative explanation can link or cover any facts, however distant and however enregistered.

At the same time, however, they generally lack *social* coherence: their moral and cognitive orders simply do not constitute any unity. This fills some of the philosophers of such societies with anguish, and some of them eagerly endeavour to set it to rights.

By contrast, simpler societies tend to possess a high level of social coherence. The world one inhabits and acts in is the same world as that in which one thinks, and the moral and cognitive orders reinforce and sustain each other. At the same time, these societies possess a low level of logical coherence. The data of their diverse conceptual sensitivities, their conceptual *senses* as you might say, cannot be added up, and do not constitute a single logical space. It simply makes no sense to postulate general theories, whose claim would be open to testing by any and all of these "sensitivities".

From all this, one may in fact formulate a supremely important if rough law of the intellectual history of mankind: *logical and social coherence are inversely related.* The more you have of one, the less you can hope to have of the other. A scientist in our world working on a problem in one domain, say nuclear biology, is entirely free to invoke findings borrowed from a distant domain, say particle physics, if he is ingenious enough to establish a connection. It is clearly recognized by all that the biologist and the physicist are investigating one and the same world. Mistaken theories of pre-scientific thought generally go wrong at this point: they take for granted the existence of a *single* and morally centred world, and credit it to simpler cultures. In fact, such a world is not given to man as such: it had to be found or invented by one rather idiosyncratic culture.

The failure to bring findings from diverse fields together into one unified picture is in our society a sign of insufficient advance in one field or the other or both, but not of some inherent insulation of diverse phenomena. On the other hand, the concepts deployed by either scientist will normally have no authority, or even resonance, when he comes to choose his spouse or his political party. His moral and his scientific life are generally distinct, and when links are established – when nature red in tooth and claw is claimed as a support for a market economy, or boiling kettles are alleged to illustrate the "dialectical" nature of social processes – the connections are suspect and generally spurious. By contrast, the ritual system which helps primitive man choose a propitious time for productive activity will be linked to the manner in which he chooses his social alignments; but it will *not* lead him to try and connect diverse natural phenomena with each other.

The Terminus

It might seem logical at this stage to proceed from the preferred model of primitive thought directly to whatever the next stage can be surmised to be. Instead, the next step in the argument is the provision of a sketch of *our own* cognitive world, of the distant terminus – so far – of the human intellectual pilgrimage. The path between the starting point and the terminal will be explored a little later.

The reason is that our procedure is, inevitably, both simplified and speculative. We have some firm points: we know, in rough outline, what our own intellectual world is like. I also believe that the baseline, the starting point, *must* have been of the kind outlined in the preceding passages. This conclusion was reached by means of a strong, but of course not definitively conclusive, argument-from-elimination: no other model can explain *both* the presence, in primitive societies, of an indisputable and fine empirical sensitivity to the physical environment, *and* at the same time of a pervasive tendency to absurd and idiosyncratic, but socially unifying, belief. The model fits in with the salient data (primitive man is both an accurate observer of nature *and* the upholder of absurd and socially supportive beliefs). It also fits in with a highly persuasive assumption: the division of labour, the separation of functions and aims, is not humanity's birthright or baseline, but a rare and near-miraculous achievement. We have no reason to expect such a division of labour, and its cognitive by-product, to be a permanent constituent of the human condition. We need to explain its rare emergence, and treat the old conflation of activities and criteria as "natural" and pervasive, as our baseline starting point. It is the imposition of this division of labour, the specification of precise and distinct aims and criteria, which alone made possible a cognitively united, and at the same time socially disconnected, world.

The baseline and the terminus are relatively clear and well established – especially, perhaps, the terminus, which is the world we now recognize. But even if they were not, they help us set up the problem. How can one arrive at the point at which we find ourselves?

The basic features of *our* world were codified by the theory of knowledge of the eighteenth century, and recodified in the twentieth. In outline, it is very simple: simplicity is of its essence. It teaches that all facts are separate and equal, and all form part of one single interconnected logical space. Any one fact can be conjoined with any other, and the conjunction will make sense. (Contrast this with the multi-periscope submarine, where the conjunction of items drawn from diverse periscopes makes no sense at all.) Theories, generalizations, may and do cover any range of facts drawn from within this single world, this single sensibility. In fact, theories are meant to cover as wide a range as possible: the wider their range, provided they retain plausibility, the greater their merit.

Though forming part of a single logical space, all facts are independent of each other: any one of them may hold or fail to hold, without any other being affected. They are not allowed to present themselves to us as parts of indivisible package deals. This was the old practice, but is so no longer. The republic of facts is Jacobin and centralist and tolerates no permanent or

63

institutionalized factions within itself. This atomization in principle is not merely so to speak lateral – disconnecting each fact from its spatial neighbours – but also, and to an equal degree, qualitative: each trait conjoined in a fact can in thought be disconnected from its fellows, and their conjunction depends on factual confirmation alone. Nothing is *necessarily* connected with anything else. We must separate all separables in thought, and then consult the fact to see whether the separated elements are, contingently, joined together. That is one of the fundamental principles of the rational investigation of nature.

This picture has been challenged of late, and indeed the Jacobin proscription of factions, of clustering for mutual protection, may not be fully implemented even in science. A certain amount of package dealing, of clannish cohesion amongst ideas and facts, does perhaps survive. But this is a furtive, surreptitious practice surviving only in a shamefaced and camouflaged form. When contrasting the rules and realities of our current intellectual world with that of pre-scientific humanity, what is striking is the degree to which the atomistic ideal of individual responsibility *is* implemented. If a factual claim is false and persists in being falsified, its favoured place in a kinship network of ideas will not in the end save it, even if it does secure for it a reprieve and stay of execution. It is not true that ideas face the bar of reality as corporate bodies:[8] rather, in the past, they *evaded* reality as corporate bodies. They are no longer allowed to do so, or at any rate not for very long. Occasionally, they succeed in doing so for a while. In the traditional world, the factional gregariousness of ideas was allowed to become a stable structure, sacralized, and to inhibit cognitive growth. Even if a bit of informal temporary corporatism is still tolerated, it is no longer allowed to become overt, sacred, rigid, meshed in with the social role structure, and to thwart expansion.

This is a single world, and the language which describes it also serves but a single purpose – accurate description, explanation and prediction. It is also notoriously a cold, morally indifferent world. Its icy indifference to values, its failure to console and reassure, its total inability either to validate norms and values or to offer any guarantee of their eventual success, is in no way a consequence of any specific findings within it. It isn't that facts just happen to have turned out to be so deplorably unsupportive socially. It is a consequence of the overall basic and entrenched constitution of our thought, not of our accidental findings within it.

This world has certain additional significant features. It is a unified orderly world, in which general explanations are in principle available, even if they have not yet been found. In other words, not only are data recorded in a single conceptual currency, but there is also the anticipation that the same laws hold for all data, and that the laws form a single system which tends towards one apex. Notoriously, it is impossible to prove that this anticipation is justified; but the anticipation does prevail, and makes it possible to judge exploratory ideas by one criterion, namely, the extent to which they contribute to the advancement of this ideal.

A very important corollary of all this is that this world has, so to speak, a *turnover ontology*. The "objects" i.e. the terms in which we classify the continuum of experience into "things", are not there for keeps. In trying to handle, explain, manipulate the continuum of experience, it is held to be legitimate and proper to experiment with diverse conceptualizations, diverse ways of clustering the flux into "objects". This is an essential trait of our world; without it, cognitive expansion is not possible and cannot be understood. It was all very different under the cognitive *ancien régime*: the multi-purpose disconnected apertures onto the world each worked with their own terms, their own ontology, and each such ontology was permanent, rather than ever-replaceable. The world was endowed with stable if untidy furniture.

There are various ways of demonstrating the moral and social inertness or taciturnity of the new world. The atomization of facts, laterally and qualitatively, entails it. This was the main way in which David Hume established the fact/value separation: it simply follows from the separability of everything from everything else. The value-component is separated from the cluster of traits to which it happens to be attached, and we are reminded that the evaluative assessment could just as easily have been attached to something else: nothing in the very nature of things glues it to its position. The contingency of all clusterings applies to evaluation as much as it does to everything else. Values are distinct from facts just as all facts are distinct from each other.

The conclusion can also be approached from the outside, so to speak, by insisting on the single-purpose construction of this world: if reference to reality, the collation and ordering and predicting of facts, is its sole and ruling principle, then evidence is king. We cannot prejudge or guarantee what the verdict of this severely and genuinely independent and unpredictable court of last appeal will be: hence if our values were firmly linked to fact, they would be unacceptably precarious. They would be hostages to an intolerably capricious fortune. Hence they must be detached.

Within the new world, there also is and can be no room either for magic or for the sacred. Magic presupposes the existence of operations, of connections, which are specifically linked to the operator or a guild of operators, to their inner personality, ritual condition, or special qualification or private personal essence. But in our world, not only are all facts equal, but so are all observers and operators. The validity of connections is and must be a matter of public testing, and the verdicts are inherently blind to the status or sacramental condition of the propounder. The equality of facts precludes the possibility of sacred, privileged, normative facts or sources of revelation. This is, as its critics insist, a manipulative world. But manipulation and testimony are inherently linked. Un-manipulative knowledge may sound nobler and disinterested, but in fact it is simply self-indulgent. It serves the predilections of its propounder or the interests of his society, but is subject to no extraneous checks and engenders no cognitive growth.

This, in very rough and general outline, is the world we inhabit, as codified by our philosophies, or some of them. Serious, authoritative cognition in our world is bound by its rules, and its findings reflect the principles of its construction. Of course, this is just a purified ideal type, and in day-to-day practice its rigours are often softened and evaded. Some philosophers do a brisk trade in supplying some gentle comforts and modifications for this austere world – interior decorations which hide, modify and diminish its severe austerity. Neither individuals nor societies are consistent. Nonetheless, for all the minor compromises and evasions of daily living, some of them endowed with highbrow theoretical support, this is now the dominant mode of our cognition and world-construction.

The Overall Plot

This may be an appropriate point at which to summarize our problem and our plot, and to indicate the direction which the argument will take.

The transition to humanity proper may be assumed to have occurred at the point when the genetic equipment of man became so permissive as to allow the wide range of social comportment which in fact we find in history and ethnography. It can reasonably be assumed that the observed range is only a small part of the possible, genetically permissible, range.

When this occurred, culture and language, in some appropriate and strong sense, became indispensable. Though the social diversity of mankind is enormous, the diversity within any one community or society is very limited. Communities whose members behaved in an utterly volatile way could hardly survive. So a set of markers indicating limits (i.e. a language) became indispensable. A set of such markers and their involvement in social practices constitutes a culture. Cultural transmission complemented, and to an important extent replaced, genetic transmission, as an agency of stability. But sustained cultural change, unaccompanied by genetic changes, thereby became possible.

Whether mankind has remained genetically stable and homogeneous since this occurred we do not know, but the argument is pursued independently of this question and without prejudice to it. It is obvious that a great deal of what has happened is open to explanation in non-genetic terms.

Since the emergence of mankind in this sense, two very profound revolutions have transformed the human condition so thoroughly that it is tempting to speak of radically different species, at least of societies if not of men. The institution of food production and storage has led to vastly increased size and complexity, permitting and encouraging the hiving off of rulers, coercion specialists, and of human markers, or guardians of symbolic markers, in other words of a clerisy. The activities of production, coercion and cognition have become separated, especially since the initiation of conceptual storage by writing.

By and large, the agrarian world was stable or stability-seeking, and its internal logic has been such as to militate against the sheer possibility of the second fundamental transformation, the emergence of the scientific-industrial world. What are the basic features of this world?

The most important feature is this: the environment within which man now lives is unified into a single continuous Nature, assumed to be law-bound and homogeneous, devoid of privileged ("sacred") elements, open to sustained and never closed exploration, tending towards ever more general and conceptually centralized explanation.

Modern man (including some professional anthropologists) tends to take such a unified world so much for granted that he has some considerable difficulty in realizing that earlier men did not live within a version of it. The sensitivity of earlier men to an outside world was not unified into a single system; such considerable unity as they did possess, those earlier "worlds" owed to their linkage to social needs, and not to external data.

Living within such a unified yet socially detached world has certain supremely important implications. For one thing, such an open, ever expanding and corrigible world is not really available for the underpinning of social organization. Social values, the allocation of social roles and obligations, must now find some other base. For another, the technology associated with such a world has terminated the age of ever-present scarcity, and has simultaneously made coercion easier and less mandatory.

It is appropriate to define modern man, man as he now is, as

68

the inhabitant of such a world. The basic problem to which this book addresses itself is simple: how is man in this sense possible at all? How could he emerge?

The subsequent chapters approach this problem as follows. Chapter 3 attempts the sketch of a general theory of ideology and generally the role of concepts, of cultural markers, in script-endowed agrarian society. Chapter 4 discusses the subsequent tension between communally oriented, fragmented cultural-ideological systems and more centralized ones, on the assumption that this tension was to become one of the central factors helping to bring about the next big change. It also discusses the interrelation between political and ideological centralization and the implications of their distinctness. Chapter 5 discusses the nature of the self-conscious codification of the modern vision when it makes its appearance. Chapters 6 and 7 discuss the interrelations of the three spheres of human activity, the break-out of the economic from the constraints of the coercive, and the problems faced by the new, intra-worldly legitimation of the new order. Chapters 8 and 9 attempt a more detailed discussion of some of the salient features of the world which has emerged, and the final chapter considers future possibilities, and attempts a final summary of the overall argument.

CHAPTER 3

The Coming of the Other

Paths of Cognitive Transformation

We must speculate about the route followed in this very prolonged and profound transformation. Our speculation can be aided or checked by a fair amount of historical and ethnographic knowledge. What path can lead from the cosy social cocoon of early man to the expanding, cognitively powerful, and socially disconnected world of modern man?

Within the multi-periscope submarine, the diversity of many-stranded sub-systems is accompanied by a low degree of division of labour. Concepts do many things at once, but men do much the same things as their fellows. This lack of specialization is made mandatory by small numbers and paucity of resources. Here too there is an inverse relation: men are alike, but what each of them does is multiple. Each man takes part in many activities, and each activity is complex.

The first step out of the primitive stage is taken when food production, and storage of resources, lead to a demographic explosion. A surplus, jointly with large population size, make possible the hiving-off of a ruling class, and a class of ritual specialists, and in due course of doctrinal specialists. In cases in which an agrarian society itself remains fragmented in distinct and independent units, the ritual specialists may, many of them, remain separately tied each to his own distinct locality and serve its various ends in isolation from each other. If on the other hand a large and populous society becomes reasonably centralized, the chances are that centralization will eventually also affect the clerisy itself.

A centralized or well-defined clerisy will generally compete with freelance competitors, notably local practitioners of ritual and therapeutic functions. Often, it will endeavour to assert and defend its own monopoly. Sometimes, on the other hand, it may be contemptuously indifferent to defiant forms of folk religion and magic. It is unlikely that these deviant forms will disappear: the ancient centralized state, notwithstanding its much-proclaimed absolutist pretensions, is seldom powerful enough to control effectively the daily life of the populations under its sway. Characteristically it governs, not a mass of atomized individuals, but a collection of at least partly autonomous local communities. These in turn will normally engender their own ritual specialists, who may or may not be linked and obedient to the central clerical organization.

So the scene is set for a permanent dualism between a high culture and a folk variant, a tension which in different forms, and with different degrees of acuteness, is endemic in agrarian society. But the truly crucial step in the cognitive development of mankind is the introduction of literacy,[1] and its deployment in religion (i.e. scripturalism). Earliest deployments of writing may occur in administration, tax-gathering and similar spheres: but the mysterious power of writing in recording, transmitting and freezing affirmations and commands soon endows it with an awe-inspiring prestige, and causes it to be fused with the authority of ritual specialists. The priest takes over writing from the accountant. Just as literacy facilitates bureaucratic, administrative centralization, it also makes possible the codification and logical centralization of doctrine.

The Disembodied Word

The most significant thing about writing is that it makes possible the detachment of affirmation from the speaker. Without writing, all speech is context-bound: in such conditions, the only way in which an affirmation can be endowed with special solemnity is by ritual emphasis, by an unusual and deliberately solemnized context, by a prescribed rigidity of manner.[2] But once writing is available, an affirmation can be detached from context. The fact that it is so detached in turn constitutes a very special context of a radically new kind.

In a sense, the transcendent is born at that point, for meaning now lives without speaker or listener. It also makes possible solemnity without emphasis, and respect for content rather than for context. Thereby it facilitates iconoclasm: an insistence on taking *all* affirmations seriously and with equal seriousness, revering all affirmation as such, and the avoidance of that special solemnity which implicitly devalues less solemn occasions. The sacred markers of special solemnity can now be shunned. The written word can dispense with trumpets; reverence for the written word as such may allow all trumpets to be spurned. Cognitive and moral egalitarianism is made feasible. This is of the utmost importance for the later history of mankind. Semantic content acquires a life of its own. It can dispense with artificial animation by ritual solemnity.

In the case of the multi-strand sub-systems of primitive thought, it is difficult to say whether the (to us) weird entities or beings, which they often seem to invoke and to which they seem to refer, should also be seen as "transcendent". For one thing, they often seem cosily familiar, intimate, not at all *distant*. They are close and homely. All we can say is that to *us*, who have learnt to separate that which is empirical from that which is not, they seem to belong to another realm. They seem such to us largely for the very simple reason that we consider them to be obviously fictitious and gratuitously invented. If we believed in them at all, *we* would consider them to be beyond the reach of perception. Those among us who cling to such beliefs, justify them, and logically clean them up, so to speak, by endowing them with such a transcendent status.

All we can say of the primitive is that he refers to them in language which we naturally translate as referential. For us, if such language were allowed to be referential at all, it could only be such transcendentally – for it fails to refer to anything genuinely observable. But these things or beings are in practice spoken of as existing and active and interacting with other beings, whose empirical reality is obvious to us. They do indeed operate in the world otherwise populated by natural beings. Yet, at the same time, the language in which these beings are spoken of does not seem to be fully (by our standards) under the control of empirical reality. Instead it seems related to the social order of the society in question.

We like to explain their invulnerability to factual counter-evidence by invoking their social or psychic usefulness. At any rate this is what anthropologists now prefer to believe: professionally averse to denigrating the primitive, and with a vested interest in finding "functions" for whatever he does, they link magical beliefs to the social order rather than to nature. Thus they make them appear sensible. To call such ideas "transcendent" would, in most or all cases, seem to force onto earlier men the idea of a clear and sharp distinction between this world and the Other. This projects a sharp cleavage that is absent from the local stock of ideas, or which, if it exists at all, is drawn quite differently. In Hinduism and Buddhism, *this* world includes a multitude of spirits; the mundane and animistic worlds are *jointly* distinct from the truly *Other*.

It is only after the coming of literacy, and in special circumstances, that this situation is at least liable to change. The Other may then acquire a genuine independence.

Writing makes possible the codification and systematization of assertion, and hence the birth of *doctrine*. A clerisy, a set of specialists who provide ritual, legitimation, consolation, therapy, will in due course, like any other sub-section of society, have a tendency to define its boundaries so as to restrict entry, and to attain monopoly. Adam Smith's famous remark about businessmen is liable to apply equally to shamans: when they get together, they will automatically try to impose a closed shop and establish a monopoly. The solemnity of ritual was the only way, really, in which they could do this in pre-literate days. But who can enforce similarity and the limits of ritual over a dispersed area? With writing, the situation changes. Standardization and conceptual quality control become possible. A written message is a kind of genuine universal. It can be identically present in many,

73

many places. . . Doctrine can be defined and delineated, and heresy also becomes possible at that point.

The impulsion to delimit its prerogatives impels a clerisy to record its affirmations as written doctrine. The tendency to centralize and systematize may cause it to codify the doctrine as a reasonably tidy system. The consequence is that, for the first time, something emerges which at least approximates, in some not very great measure perhaps, to a single-purpose "cognitive" system, an interlocking body of concepts and propositions. Multi-strandedness, though by no means wholly eliminated, is reduced: a unity is approached in the pursuit of monopoly, and a kind of orderliness, or an approximation thereof, is attained.

But note – and this is by far the most important twist in the argument – what is attained at this point is *not* the single-strand, single-aim *referential* system, resembling the one with which we are familiar from the modern theory of knowledge, and which we credit to ourselves. Quite the reverse. The emerging single purpose is not the pursuit of pure empirical reference, sloughing off all social concerns and value saturation. The first occurrence of something resembling a single-strand system is based not on eliminating Concept Affirmation, and replacing it by Reference; on the contrary, it is Concept Affirmation which is made dominant and unified, though perhaps not fully exclusive.

Concepts are unified in a system which requires propositions for its articulation. Such a system normatively defines the vision and ethos of a society, or rather of its high culture. The centre of gravity shifts from norm-loaded, ritually inculcated concepts to explicit affirmations and injunctions, welded into a mutually supporting structure. They may possess some empirical content, but that is negligible compared with the non-verbalized, unre-corded practical skill in the possession of members of the society directly in contact with physical reality, such as craftsmen. A marked and very characteristic trait of this kind of society is that the empirical knowledge built into the fragmented and unofficial practical skills of its members, who are *not* official cognitive specialists, is considerably greater than that which is formally codified in its official doctrine. "Theory" is at best a pale and inferior echo and distortion of practice, and lives a life of its own.

Such unified scriptural systems can usefully be called, generically, "Platonic". Much of the actual thought of the historic Plato provides a neat specimen of most, though not all, aspects of such an intellectual structure. What this kind of system does is to take shared concept affirmation with the utmost seriousness: in effect, it tries to eliminate the rival aims from the matrix. Knowledge is equated with the reverent apprehension of morally binding norms. Empirical referentiality is spurned in pure Platonism. The Ideas stand in moral judgement over facts; facts do not, as with us, stand in cognitive judgement over Ideas.

The erstwhile two-dimensional or multi-dimensional matrix is modified, and comes eventually at least to approximate to a single-dimension one, by systematizing and underwriting the authority of shared concepts, and making them "universalistic", i.e. valid for all comers, and context-free. The system is designed to serve primarily *one* purpose, the provision of a unified charter of a social order and of its vision. This trumps any secondary services it may perform on the side. Concepts had once been danced out in ritual, and thus tied to a community: mankind may have been defined by the possession of thought, but men did not all think in the same terms. All men thought, and thought compulsively, but they did not all share the same compulsions. Now, concepts came to be written out in doctrine, available equally to all readers and binding for all, and a single set of them claimed authority over all men, independently of community. It could in fact console those who were losing any well-defined, supportive community, and this is no doubt one part of the explanation of the spread of universalistic, scriptural salvation religions.

By generic Platonism I mean the kind of ideology that makes its appearance with the religious use of writing, and which is sustained by an organized clerisy. It stands sharply contrasted with the community-oriented traditional religions which preceded it. They used ritual, not script, and were primarily concerned to underwrite and fortify communal organization and the rhythm of communal life, and seldom if ever made universalistic claims. Generic Platonism clearly delineates the Transcendent, and makes it morally and doctrinally authoritative without bounds, i.e. universalistic in its claims. By sharply defining its claims, moral and doctrinal, and detaching them from communal limits, it sets up a tension between the transcendent and man. This tension may well have been decisive for the subsequent development of human cognition and ethos.

"Platonism"

The central intuition of generic Platonism is the independent existence of concepts, "Ideas". These entities simultaneously constitute logical and moral models for reality. The transcendent receives formal recognition. Reality does not constitute a check on Ideas: on the contrary, *they* are the norms by which reality is to be judged and guided.

In brief, there now exists an explicit theory which *says* what previously man had only practised. Men had formed communities by ritually instilling in each other shared notions, endowed with a pervasive, insistent and authoritative moral loading. These notions governed – in large measure – men's conduct. Thereby they made both social coexistence and communication possible.

Overt Platonism now does all this with a new and significant twist: it turns it into an explicit doctrine. For the first time, so to speak, man not merely speaks prose, but *knows* that he is doing so. He knows that he is thinking in terms of concepts. And secondly, the authority of these norms–concepts is universalized. When it had been merely a practice, unhallowed by theory or self-consciousness, the authority of the concepts remained socially bounded. It could not transcend the limits of the region within which the rituals which instilled the concepts were practised. Now, the allegedly authoritative conceptual compulsion becomes, or in any case claims to be, universal, trans-ethnic, trans-social, trans-communal: *it becomes Reason.*

Cultures had always consisted of systems of concepts, which contained their own suggestiveness, anticipations, imperatives.

Societies instilled those in their members by ritual and otherwise, thereby engendering cohesion and making communication possible. Concepts had always been confirmed by *stories* within which they figured. Now they were also confirmed by well-articulated doctrine, their moral suggestiveness codified in formal works, their premisses supposedly *proven* and made logically binding. The actual Platonism of Greek history, through its doctrine of the divine status and moral authority of the concept, unwittingly lays bare the mechanisms of traditional cultures. The Transcendent is formalized and endowed with a metaphysical charter, and made to underwrite culture and its obligations. But by making all this into a doctrine, it creates a new situation altogether.

The Indirect Route

The overall problem of the cognitive path of mankind can perhaps best be conveyed by a diagram.

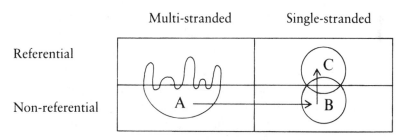

A   Primitive conceptual systems. Unified socially, their referential tentacles are disconnected from each other, though linked to each other indirectly by a shared social context. Its fragmented referential terms are stable (i.e. have fixed ontologies).

B   Unified doctrinal system of some agrarian clerisies. Unification attained; referential content is small. Ontology stable, social corollaries pervasive and powerful.

C   Ideal version of genuine knowledge. Unified, referential, socially detached, with provisional, expendable, turnover, experimental ontologies. Social suggestiveness small if present at all.

The two-by-two schema opposes referential and non-referential intellectual structures, and single-stranded to multi-stranded ones.

The world *we* inhabit, and treat seriously, is single-stranded *and* referential (C). The world inhabited by primitive man was many-stranded and largely, though by no means wholly, non-referential (A). Its concepts organized behaviour and expectations, but were not deployed – nor deployable – in a continuous and sustained exploration of nature. This vision extended various tentacles into the referential world, none of them exclusively dedicated to seeking pure information. These tentacles were, all of them, connected to the "world" as lived in by the primitive. But they were *not* logically connected to each other. The periscopes are, each of them, logically independent of each other. But at the same time they all feed into the total, socially, but not cognitively, integrated picture.

It is hard or impossible to imagine any social mechanism which could ever lead directly from the primitive to the modern vision. What on earth, literally, could ever induce or enable the various tentacles to cut themselves off from the non-referential main body? What could lead them to purify themselves, by cutting off their non-referential, socially servile "controls", then fuse into one unified sensitivity? Theories of knowledge, which naively retroject onto the past of humanity our own single-strand commitment to a single, unified, socially detached nature, do in effect presuppose precisely that something of this kind had indeed occurred. But it is very difficult to imagine the mechanism which would have brought this about.

Sir James Frazer, and in our time philosophers such as Popper and Quine, believe, or rather, uncritically assume, that the transition could have been inspired and guided by a purely cognitive impulse into perpetually improving its referential control over nature. This most misguidedly projects the division of labour, and notably the separation of cognition from other concerns, onto a historic situation in which it was not, and could not conceivably be, present.

On the other hand, it *is* perfectly possible to imagine, and moreover it is also in some measure possible to illustrate historically, a circuitous, *indirect* route. This is the path by which the plural, multi-strand world could be transformed into a homogeneous, conceptually centralized nature, governed ideally by a few main principles. This route leads by way of a more unified but, ironically, *less* referential world. This world is serviced and unified and codified by a clerisy endowed with writing and, for some important but mysterious reason, inspired by a persistent drive towards unification, order, homogeneity. A world comes into being which has something like a single master, a central purpose, a single criterion of validation and legitimacy. But this near-monopolistic single principle initially is not and cannot be reference to nature. It is, on the contrary, an extreme form of norm-affirmation. It produces a world of the authoritative concept, of a generic "Platonism", of a unified, centralized, apex-endowed authoritative system of ideas.

Once a system of this kind is available, and is widely internalized, diffused, familiar, then, and only then, another possibility arises: one day, or rather one age, the system may flip over, and replace one single master by another. The initial unification under one master was perhaps the hardest step. The replacement of a non-referential master by a naturalistic one, by Nature, though difficult, was perhaps less hard, though it did only occur once. The transition from unified concept affirmation to unified reference is not obvious or easy or inevitable: but it is far less of a leap than the first transition, from plural multi-purpose worlds to a homogeneous "Platonic" one. This second transition is easily imaginable. Moreover, it seems to be historically observable. It took place during the Scientific Revolution.

The First Unification

What on earth can initially impel the clerisy towards unification of world-picture, and thereby to disengagement from other aims and social involvement? What can lead to the transition from Stage A to Stage B?

Part of the background, in certain historic traditions, may be the success of what might be called Transcendent Cognition. Some of the early successes of human cognitive effort seem to have taken place in astronomy and geometry: the charting of the movements of heavenly bodies, and the acquisition of knowledge (in due course, demonstrative knowledge) concerning the properties of abstract spatial objects. As Burtt's *Metaphysical Foundation of Modern Science* shows, the Pythagorean mathematization of nature must be seen in terms of a mathematics centred on geometry. Heavenly and abstract entities have this in common, that they seem to be distinct from and contrasted with ordinary, earthly objects. Movements of heavenly bodies are tidy, stable, orderly, permanent or knowable. They may be held to illustrate the same opposition as obtains between abstract concepts (simple, elegant and normative) and earthly things (complex, messy, and generally imperfect and defective). Thus a contrast which may, in anachronistic retrospect, look like an encouragement of pure referential science was, in fact, in the context of time, read as incitement to normative, prescriptive, "Platonic" inquiry: true knowledge is concerned with ideals and not with things.

Another impulse towards the provision by the clerisy, or by some of its members, of a socially disembodied system may stem partly from the demand rather than the supply side. The earliest large-scale polities were either communities grown large or assemblages of communities. Their ritual/religious life can be assumed to have continued to exemplify the features of communal religion. It was tied in with the social organization and with the pattern of its life in time and space. But at some point in their development, urbanization, complexity, social upheaval, produced a new spiritual clientele, seeking salvation that was individual and universal, not communal. Communities providing context and support for individuals were now lacking. Salvation was sought by persons coming in isolation, not in groups, and requiring a generic salvation, an escape from an overall intolerable condition, rather than merely the rectification of a specific ailment or complaint. A day comes when pilgrims arrive not as clans praying for propitious rainfall, but as individuals yearning to be made whole.

The "Axial Age" is Karl Jaspers' term for the period when a unified and demanding Transcendent appears in human history, and partly replaces the communally oriented cults. Sages begin to appear who endeavour to satisfy the new need: sophists, prophets, are men who offer not a socially prescribed place at a ritual, but an omnibus, to-whom-it-may-concern guidance towards generic recovery. They promise salvation, or a specification of self-guaranteeing good life, no longer at the mercy of capricious fortune.

The idea of salvation has a number of crucial features. It is not merely some kind of total bliss, but also generic fulfilment, and it is not the overcoming of some single ill. It is made available in retail to individuals, and not merely supplied wholesale to entire communities. The Good Life is total in content, but it can be supplied, or is even preferentially supplied, to isolated individuals. Those who offer such salvation often like to deal directly with the consuming public, bypassing the wholesale channels of traditional political rulers and command organization.

In the traditional community, rituals are habitually made to measure for the participants, and are adjusted to their social position. Stalls, gallery, boxes are available, in accordance with the social status system of the audience. Non-members of the community have no places reserved for them, and are unwelcome or formally excluded. Their exclusion is a major mechanism of social control in the Ancient City, as Fustel de Coulanges insisted. But how is one to deal with a new and growing kind of uprooted public, endowed with no proper place, or only places they find unattractive or unacceptable? Even the troubles they want healed may be unspecific or multiform. There is an Arab story of a man who prayed to God to remedy so many personal disasters that his prayer-neighbour caustically remonstrated – it is far easier for God to make a new one, than to mend one like you! It is for men plagued with so many ills that a generic salvation, a new Condition, a new Order, has special appeal. Universalism and generic salvation or wisdom doctrines were born, presumably, from the need to cater to a diversified and uprooted and frequently urban clientele.

In some cases, as indicated, the availability of patently trans-social, trans-ethnic truths, such as those of astronomy and geometry, may have provided a model for what such omnibus wisdom could look like. But there were other factors which could lead in this direction. Monotheism was one; a centralized and orderly legal system such as the Roman one could be another. A single Reason, a single God, a single Law...

A single, exclusive, jealous and iconoclastic deity, averse to magic and graven images, was perhaps one of the most decisive, formative influences in the education of the human race. One can only speculate about the origins of this notion. There is an old theory that such a deity arose in emulation of the monarchs of the great centralized states of the ancient Near East – a theory castigated as bad sociology by the late Sir Edward Evans-Pritchard, to whom it obviously caused some irritation. Muslims sometimes say that the Sultan is God's shadow on earth, and it is unclear whether the Caliph was initially the representative of God or merely of the Prophet.[3] The contrary supposition, that the exclusive deity is the shadow of the Great King, is not calculated to please believers. David Hume supposed that this idea emerged by the same mechanism as that to which great concentrations of power can be attributed: the competitive sycophancy of worshippers, who vie with each other in trying to secure the favours of the High God, by crediting him with ever more unique powers and denigrating all his rivals.

But the origin of this notion, intriguing though it is, concerns us rather less than its implications and consequences. A unique and jealous god, once he becomes the central and dominant notion of an intellectual structure erected and carried by a given clerisy, constitutes an overwhelmingly powerful impulse towards the establishment of a single-strand system. It was jealous Jehovah who taught mankind respect for the Principle of Excluded Middle. It was he who insisted on the avoidance of easy cohabitation, within a single mental world, of multiple diverse ways of speaking and thinking, untroubled by their failure to cohere in a single logical system. A deity that tolerates no rivals teaches its adherents that they may not be spiritually opportunistic. Eventually, this may also teach them not to be opportunistic logically.

The well documented emergence of a jealous God is of course somewhat paradoxical. He emerges in a community which fears and resists great Near Eastern monarchies, but is far too small and weak to have much hope of constituting one itself. At the time of the emergence of the jealous God, the people in question was still communally organized, and its religious life was centred on acts of sacrifice performed by an ascriptively chosen ritual elite. These features would not normally lead one to expect a unique and universal God. Initially, though requiring unique attention from those bound to him by covenant, the deity was only potentially universal, retaining very special links with one community and location. The fact that the community in question had a pastoral background, and was locked in struggle with an agrarian population, whose ritual life was so often more luxuriant than that of pastoralists, may help in finding an explanation. Exclusive monotheism was a boundary marker.

A jealous God, eventually detached from a circumscribed ethnic base and its self-identifying rituals, and also in due course endowed by a well-centralized clerical hierarchy, proved to be a powerful agent of the modification of the human spirit. This became specially evident when the hierarchy set about the codification of faith and morals, and brought to the task the logical fastidiousness of the Platonic tradition, and a Roman sense of orderly law.

The intellectual elite could then flex its logical muscles, and on occasion experience highly educative inner anguish, when coping with the internal problems of its own unified doctrinal system. These problems arose partly from the content of the doctrine itself, and partly from the customary striving of the clerisy for a monopolistic position. The logic of the promise of salvation as a *reward*, for instance, required free will. But the sheer possibility of unaided salvation by personal merit or exertion would also undermine the monopoly of the source of salvation. Believers had to be spurred on to try hard, but believers were not to be encouraged to think that they could ever manage on their own, without aid from the spiritual monopoly. The tortuous attempts to combine these conflicting requirements, by St Augustine and his successors, greatly helped concentrate the Western mind. It could lead to a kind of intellectually and socially fertile anxiety.

The problem of the rival claims of appeals to "reason" (i.e. logical compulsion supposedly independent of any specific culture) and of the monopolistically controlled sources of moral and doctrinal legitimacy, also became manifest. The tension occurred no longer merely between transcendently rooted doctrine and social reality, but within the doctrine itself: it had preached exclusiveness. The fastidiousness which this inspired concerning the limits of faith led to internal strains.

The Authority of Concepts

In the Axial Age, human faith detached itself from the ritualistic celebration of community and its internal structure, and attached itself to the Other.[4] A purified form of a selfconscious transcendent had emerged. It gloried in its Otherness and derived authority from it. It was serviced by something much more like a clerisy proper and less like a guild of shamans, and it lived in much greater and more sustained tension with the lower world. The main tool of the transcendent was writing, which disembodied the Word, and made it possible to revere it irrespective of context. The expansion of the faith was also connected with political centralization. A literate clerisy was a good supplier of candidates for the new royal bureaucracies.

Thus one well-known and significant path to the new kind of generic transcendent leads from the jealous and exclusive deity. Another path, equally familiar to participants in the European tradition, leads through Greek thought and in particular Platonism. The profound paradox of Platonism proper is that it preached a return to, or a fortification of, the closed communally organized society: but it did so by means which themselves illustrated, highlighted, and sprang from that liberation from traditional ritualism and communalism. Plato represented dogmatism pursued by liberal means, an authoritarianism with a rational face.

The rationalism, openness, or liberalism of the mode of argument was in the end perhaps as significant as the illiberalism of the intended conclusions. The dialogues convey a clear and obvious fascination with logical, as opposed to social, compulsion. The participants, unlike most of their successors in the Mediterranean world, do not feel it incompatible with their rank and dignity to submit to logic, irrespective of the standing of the speaker. They are able to honour content of assertion more than the status of the speaker. Logic, "the wind of argument", is no respecter of status. It is very hard to imagine later Mediterranean machismo ever submitting to such an indignity.

The most influential modern liberal critic of Plato is Karl Popper.[5] His diagnosis of Plato is in effect a depth-psychological one: Plato, it is claimed, feared and resented the open society which was emerging in Periclean Athens, and yearned for a return to a closed tribal society, with its freedom from doubt or status uncertainty. Popper's virtually Freudian diagnosis credits Plato with a social equivalent of a back-to-the-womb longing. Plato's attempt to stabilize society and hierarchy is seen as an expression of this longing.

Plato's alleged recollection of and yearning for a bygone *Gemeinschaft* and a possibly hypothetical stage of Greek history is an unnecessary speculation. What Plato in effect did in *The Republic* can be characterized without invoking any desire, on his part, to return to a much earlier social order. Plato codified and tried to absolutize an arrangement which is in fact the commonest, most pervasive way of running an agro-literate society. It is a blueprint of a society endowed with agriculture, arts and crafts, with a surplus which needs to be guarded, with writing, and with a fairly stable, or in any case not visibly expanding, technological base.

Society of this kind needs political and ideological order, and the majority of its population is destined to submission and the full-time commitment to production. The relatively small surplus can only sustain a fairly small minority of rulers, warriors and clerics. This threefold stratification of agrarian society – producers, warriors, clerics – is historically very well diffused, and prevails in all but exceptional circumstances. It seems inherent in the logic of the situation. It is not, as some have claimed, characteristic of some particular tradition or branch of the human race.

Plato in effect schematized, legitimized and absolutized this arrangement. He also tilted it in favour of the clerics, by claiming that all this was inscribed into the very nature of things by transcendent decree, accessible to their own wisdom. The wisdom was attainable only by means of prolonged special training, which in turn was under their own exclusive control. Justice and excellence were to be defined in terms of the maintenance of the system.

The anti-empirical bias of Plato was, of course, modified by his successor Aristotle. But this injection of a bit of respect for the observable world was not so very important. Aristotle's world was still a socially functional cosmos rather than an impersonal, socially detached Nature. What did matter was the ideal of a unified orderly world, exemplifying mathematical and geometrical order, and symmetrically, universally accessible to a generic human faculty, "reason". The confluence of this tradition with a unique, exclusive, jealous and hidden deity may well have been decisive for the eventual emergence of the modern notion of Nature.[6]

Plato's Sociological Mistakes

Mankind had lived in what one might call the age of Durkheim when it unselfconsciously imposed the authority of concepts on itself through ritual. In that age ritual, fortified only by legends, was the favoured or sole path to legitimation. Mankind entered the age of Plato when the authority of concepts became a *theory*, when the Transcendent became manifest as such, and when the paradigmatic incarnation of the concept was no longer, or not exclusively, found in ritual, but rather in writing. Ritual had once underwritten the Word, but the Word itself now became a ritual.

The concrete social blueprint which Plato extracted by his particular dialectic was amazingly perspicacious in some ways, and curiously defective in others. In many ways – in proposing the rigid and stagnant rule of clerics and warriors over producers – it was not merely a norm, but a pretty accurate account of the prevalent social condition in the agro-literate age. In recommending that his Guardians be deprived of kin and private wealth, he anticipated some of the most effective bureaucracies of the agrarian world, notably the Church and the monasteries and the Mamlukes. In other ways it was rather inaccurate, and constitutes a bad and altogether misleading guide to the real social and ideological organization of the great pre-industrial, script-using agrarian civilizations.

There is the obvious fact that Plato failed to anticipate Alexander and the demise of the independent Greek city, and thought of the city state as the natural social unit. In fact, of course, city states were to become rarer, and empires – political or religious – more common, more typical frameworks for the social life of men. But far more than mere scale is at stake.

No great theological civilizations of what could be called the Age of Plato – dogmatic, clerisy-ridden, thug-dominated, scripturalist systems – in fact employed Platonic rationalism and concept-worship as their overt ideology. Instead, they personified an authority from which the concept emanated. Nonetheless, their scripturalism and transcendentalism did implement his programme. The main explanation is probably simple: concept-worship, however poetically expressed, is pretty anaemic stuff for the common run of mankind. (Plato had no objection to the perpetuation of existing Hellenic ritual practices – far from it – but made no attempt to link it to his ideas or his Ideas.) But the

87

notion that men are to obey and observe the duties of their station, because abstract *concepts* say so, is simply not strong enough meat to strike terror in the heart and enforce obedience amongst the general. Something a little more awe-inspiring is required; and something a little more intimidating was indeed found. The Word had to become flesh.

Plato also in a way deified *all* concepts, even if some were holier than others. In a sense this is sociologically correct (all concepts are indeed norms, rather than mere summations of data, though some are more normative than others). In another way, it leaves too much latitude, and creates a kind of devaluing inflation. If we revere them all, we do not sufficiently revere any. One has to be a little more selective in one's emphasis. (In the previous age of Durkheim, when concepts acquired their authority through ritual, and not through any theory or metaphysic, ritual was indeed rather selective in the choice of the concepts which it chose for special and solemn emphasis. Big rituals, big concepts.) In the interest of inspiring awe and terror, some concepts, some norms, some models must be very specially revered.

Secondly, concepts have fuzzy or contentious edges: if you deify concepts (the *hero*, the *saint*, the *gentleman*), they become, in Bryce Gallie's celebrated phrase, "essentially contested".[7] People can read different things into them, they pick and choose, and what happens to social order then? The emphasis on *Commandments* or rules is a far better model for a script-carried social ideology than the mere apotheosis of concepts. It is in the form of worship of sacred *rules*, rather than the literally Platonic *forms*, that a scriptural ethic really forged the monotheistic super-ego.

Propositions and imperatives are of course not free of ambiguity and of contested interpretation either. But their flexibility and pliability is considerably smaller than that of concepts. Orders are orders, but no sergeant or petty official has been heard to yell that concepts are concepts. What might have been good enough, perhaps, for an Athenian intellectual, was not good enough for the commonalty of men, who need to be constrained by less ethereal markers. They need *rules*, though they had better be fortified by highly personal exemplars, and sanctioned by personal threats. Abstract models will not do: Platonism, in the particular form which Plato actually gave it, is not nearly enough. When the centre of gravity of the instilling and enforcement of cultural norms shifted from ritual to writing, there also had to be a shift from concepts to rules, to *prescriptions*.

The deification of concepts, as such, is also anaemic in quite another way. Plato makes their authority inhere in the concepts themselves, as such, or at most to derive from the high concept, the ultimate concept of the Good. Men may dread a high god, but they will not quake before a high concept. Concepts are not sufficiently vindictive. And so it turned out to be. The crucial agro-literate civilizations, which in effect and in broad outline implemented and exemplified the Platonic programme, did so, not by deifying concepts, but by revering propositions, prescriptions, commandments, and forming them as the words of the deity (or deities). The Word of God, not the divine Word, was made authoritative. To keep men in order, a personal authority is required: abstractions will not inspire awe. Yet the abstractness, the transcendence, the externality turned out in the end to be crucial. A single and hidden deity could inspire fear, yet also provide that unification and the otherness which would transform the intellectual life of mankind.

Plato also did not consider the implications and possible merit (either for him or for us liberals) of a separation of the clerisy from the rulers. In *The Republic*, the wise are only separated from the warrior/administrators by age and by some extra meritocratic examinations, not by caste or estate. This particular fusion was seldom practised, though examples of it can be found in military religious Orders or in Mamluke-type trained-slave bureaucracies.

So the scriptural civilizations usually made the authority of their codified rules emanate from a *personalized* transcendent, and not from self-authenticating abstractions. The transcendent rules were revered but linked to an Author. So Plato's aspiration of imposing order, discipline and stability on agrarian man, apart from misjudging the size of the operative units, also grossly overestimated the amenability of men to reason – even a reason fortified by retaining a few myths and perpetuating the given Hellenic customs and rituals. In one way, India exemplified Plato's recipe more than the West ever did; and China, with a powerful ethic not locked into theology, was a variant exemplification of the scheme, and perhaps came closest, in Confucianism, to revering an un-personalized morality. But the ideal of an abstractly formulated, ordered cosmos, crowned by a unique divine apex, was eventually to bear a kind of fruit which Plato himself could hardly have anticipated.

CHAPTER 4

The Tension

A Divine Order

The problem of evil is liable to exercise the clerisy of the centralized doctrine. Max Weber sometimes gives the impression that theodicy, the answer to the problem of evil, is central to all religion. Man needs to persuade himself that the world is legitimate and acceptable after all. This had not been the case with communally oriented traditional religions: given their specific attention to concrete ills, they rather took the overall meaningfulness of the world for granted, even though they had done so much to maintain it. They did not feel obliged to supply guarantees of the overall goodness of the world. Meaning was conferred on the world absent-mindedly, without a codified revelation. Centralized faiths, on the other hand, offering as they do generic all-purpose salvation, do seem to be called to account on this score. If a salvation-guaranteeing force governs the world, why do we suffer so? Why is the world so arbitrary, and so unjust?

The transition from communal to salvation religions is one of the big divides in human history, and it occurs within the agrarian age. Fustel de Coulanges' *Ancient City*[1] traces this transition in the classical Mediterranean world. In the East, the switch was not fully accomplished: in China, an ethical vision at the top co-existed with communal rites lower down, and in India, a generalized communal system, though containing generic salvation themes, prevailed over abstract salvation faiths.

Once established, these salvation-oriented, as it were socially disembodied faiths are liable to live in tension with the more blatantly incarnated, more patently social religious practices.

The high religions emerged because an important part of the population to which they appealed had become socially disinherited and uprooted; but by the same token, they are hampered by the fact that not the whole of that population is uprooted, or is not uprooted permanently. Urbanization uproots some of the people all the time, and all of the people some of the time, but it does not uproot all people all the time. So, to a considerable extent, the social base and need for some communal religion remains effective: hence a form of ritual which underwrites and reinforces social organization, rather than one which replaces it and consoles for its absence, also continues to be in demand.

But there is more to it than that: the very success of a universalistic salvation religion helps, at least in some measure, to restore those very conditions whose absence had initially helped bring about its own emergence. The messengers of a universal and impersonal, trans-social redemption gradually turn into the maintenance and servicing personnel of a new and symbolically codified social structure. So the surviving old shamans and the emerging new priests, jointly or in rivalry, come to be in competition with the severe guardians of the "pure" version of the faith. This conflict was destined to have profound consequences for mankind.

The central device for presenting doctrine as trans-social, trans-ethnic, as endowed with extraneous legitimation, is to have it located in writing, *and* to have it endowed with a meta-theory, a theology, which circumscribes, defines and limits the sources of authority. Without some such addition, sheer scripturalism avails little. After all, it would always be possible to add a little, or a lot for that matter, to the written and sacred corpus. The corpus must be bounded, and meta-principles established, defining the limits. This inevitably sets off a regress. The famous and absolutely fundamental political regress is – who guards the guardians? Its ideological equivalent is: who checks on the authority of the interpreters? Who interprets the interpreters?

Who indeed? In practice, diverse ways exist for terminating (or rather, claiming to terminate) this regress. The source and fount of revelation can be narrowed down to a single entry point. It can then be tied to a self-perpetuating institution within this world, whose continuous links to the sacred entry point legitimate its particular interpretations of the recorded doctrine. The doctrine in turn then legitimates the institution.

Alternatively, a lineage of sacred beings, linked genealogically to the entry point, may be available. The incorruptibility of these beings is asserted to be so complete as to ensure their interpretations of the written doctrine against all possible doubt. Or again, a doctrine can deify the written record alone, thereby in effect conferring great power on the scribes who have privileged access to it.

Logically, the regress is interminable. A question can always be raised about the authority of an interpretation. Socially and emotionally, however, the codified theologies and cosmologies of the agrarian age succeed in terminating the regress. The ultimate and key revelation or its source are surrounded with such awe and reverence that the questioner is, in general, silenced. Political sanctions may silence him if doctrinal ones fail to do so. Nonetheless, by offering proofs at all, at any point of their logical edifice, these systems implicitly inculcate the generic notion of a Reason, of a unique faculty whose capacity is to secure truth, or to subject it to a quality test. Scholastic theology is not merely the compliment of faith to reason: it also constitutes an important method by which the notion of a generic Reason is instilled.

Church and State and their Separability

The independence of truth from the merely political order can be assisted by various concrete circumstances. The institutional underpinning of the revelation, the authority structure of the clerisy, can become distinct from and independent of a more immediately political order. On a petty scale, this possibility was present even in small and pre-literate, communal societies: the priest or prophet may be in conflict with the chief. But when the conflict arises on behalf of a written, abstract doctrine, a new situation arises.

In principle, the opposition of church and state can arise even within a single polity. But in such a situation, the likelihood remains that one of the two protagonists will prevail and absorb the other: the priest will become king, or the king will become priest. The situation is different if the geographical domain of the secular power and that of the clerisy are not co-extensive, if the clerisy serves a wide area, which makes it independent of any single ruler, or if it possesses bases or ritual centres outside the territory controlled by the secular ruler. The Christian Church survived the Roman Empire, the Muslim clerisy survived the Caliphate. The Indian case is perhaps the strangest: a communal type of religion became generalized throughout most of the sub-continent, and scripturally codified, with a salvation-oriented element, even though it was carried by communities, kin groups, which were not linked to any one polity, and which survived the endemic fragility of political units in the sub-continent.

A number of systems can be envisaged within which the sword-wielders and script-users are distinct, and within which the latter, notwithstanding their lack of countervailing physical force, can share effective power. In any one single encounter, there is of course no question of any equality of strength: he who has, and knows how to use, the sword, need brook no nonsense from the penpusher, and is indeed most unlikely to tolerate any opposition from him. To understand the manner in which pen-pushers nonetheless can and do effectively oppose and overcome swordsmen, we need not invoke or overestimate some mysterious power of superstition in the hearts of the swordsmen which would compel them to bend their knees to the upholders of legitimation and truth. We need only look at what happens when both thugs and scribes are enmeshed in a complex overall social order.

Consider a society in which a stratum of land-tilling peasants is governed by a much smaller stratum of professional warriors, more or less monopolizing the means of coercion. Each member of the warrior class controls his own stronghold and band of armed followers. Within each small fiefdom, the warrior or head-of-gang is magistrate and administrator as well as defence specialist. The maintenance of order is, in practice, or even in theory, delegated to such local power-holders, who bequeath their position to their sons. These local lords are, however, loosely organized in a kind of pyramid or series of pyramids. Lords higher up on the scale are entitled and able to mobilize the lower lordlings in a joint defence of the local "realm", if it is threatened by a force too large to be resisted by each little lordling on his own.

So the maintenance of order *and* justice is in the hands of this loosely organized hierarchy of lords. But general doctrine, ritual, legitimation and the keeping of records is in the hands of a territorially disembodied, discontinuous organization, somewhat more effectively centralized, but in the main devoid of direct access to physical force. The more effective centralization of this organization is due in part to its peculiar principle of recruitment and perpetuation: its members are vowed to celibacy. Consequently they cannot acknowledge whatever offspring they may have, and so cannot easily retain for their offspring whatever power position they happen to occupy within the structure of the organization. Hence they are assigned to their position on a bureaucratic principle, by nomination from the centre rather than by inheritance on the spot. This in itself greatly strengthens the central secretariat of the organization.

The lordlings, by contrast, even if allocated a post and location in return for service by a central overlord, who in principle retains control over the fief, nevertheless in practice build up a local power base, and transmit the position to their sons. So the political organization is far more fissiparous than the spiritual one.

The main point about the loose and fluid congeries of lords of diverse rank is that they are indeed loose and unstable. There are diverse reasons for this. For one thing, they are prone to conflict and warfare simply in virtue of their pervasive ethos: violence is their honour, their specific skill, and they are in effect required to demonstrate, almost perpetually, their competence at inflicting and resisting it.

There are also other reasons. The balance of power which keeps the peace between thugs and coalitions of thugs is unstable and unpredictable. The power of a lord high up on the scale, of a king in effect, depends on how many lower-level thugs he can mobilize. The availability, the "loyalty", of a lower-level thug will in practice depend on his private assessment of the strength of the king, and so, indirectly, on the lower-level thug's assessment of the loyalty of *other* low-level thugs. They are all tacitly watching each other.

But at the public, overt level, all positions in the secular hierarchy are occupied in virtue of birth – *legitimate* birth. And here's the rub: legitimacy of births is a matter that in the end falls entirely into the domain of the organization. Its ascription of legitimacy or otherwise may well determine, in a "dynastic" or "baronial" conflict, the commitment of crucial support by the minor swordsmen. This does not, once again, imply that individual thugs are so overawed in their hearts by the organization's claim to exclusive moral authority, and by its right to confer legitimacy on the birth of others. It merely requires that all of them publicly go through the appropriate motions of respect, and hence that each single one knows that the others will respect the doctrine, so that, in following it, he will join the larger battalions. Hence the crystallizations of loyalty and of political legitimacy will conform, very frequently, to the verdicts of the representatives of the organization.

In a famous passage, Keynes described how investors act, not on the basis of the performance of a company, but on their estimate of the assessment of its performance by *other* investors, and so on in a regress. Similarly, in civil strife, potential supporters of rival claimants to legitimacy are swayed not so much by their own assessment of the real merits of the case, but by their private, unavowed prediction of the loyalties of others. If the organization has the authority to ascribe legitimacy, and is endowed with the machinery for disseminating and publicizing its verdict, this confers great indirect power on it. It can crystallize the consensus which then brings together the larger units.

Consider another, quite distinct, social system. Assume that the clerisy is not at all centralized, and lacks both a permanent central secretariat and a head, and even any bureaucratic system of ranks and a command structure. Instead, it is severely scrip- turalist, revering a strictly delimited corpus of sacred writing, and it admits into its own ranks anyone whose scholarship gives him access to it. This corps of scholars is concentrated largely in trading towns, precariously protected by a number of central states. These, however, fail to dominate the countryside effec- tively. Large stretches of it are occupied by self-help, self- administering units known as "tribes". Within these groups, there is none of the separation of peasant-producers and warriors so typical of the other system: all male adults tend to be both producers and warriors. The need for perpetual collective self- protection endows these groups with considerable cohesion, and turns them into the most formidable fighting units in the land. What stops them from pillaging the towns? In the main, it is the fact that these groups, and indeed their sub-groups, are habitu- ally locked in conflict, in "feud", with each other, and also that one set of them is linked to the state, and so to the protection (and exploitation) of towns. In return for such benefits, it helps guard the city against potential pillagers. The tribes only become truly formidable when they fuse into a larger unit, which, however, happens but seldom. Their entire ethos, their mutual jealousies, at most times prevent them from melding into a larger body. At the same time, this perpetual indulgence in violent petty conflicts endows them with their organization and keeps them fighting fit.

But they and the trading, scholarly towns, and their rulers, are all of them committed to a shared faith, even if the manner in which they practise it varies from milieu to milieu. Once again, the men who are repositories of the legitimating truth can on occasion attain great influence, and indeed power: the faith is a highly moralistic and censorious one. It regulates all aspects of social life. This time, the scholars determine, not so much the legitimacy of births, as that of moral-political conduct, including the limits of legitimate taxation. By damning a central authority, and blessing a rival, and the tribal coalition which he heads, they can help to crystallize one of those temporary fusions of

97

otherwise feud-enmeshed groups. It alone can lead to a turnover of personnel in the political system. Though devoid of force, the scribes, and perhaps they alone, can forge that unity among as yet unprivileged swordsmen, which alone will make them formidable and capable of overcoming the previously established swordsmen in the central citadel.

Another model still is conceivable. An important faith exists which combines, hybrid fashion, traits drawn from both "communal" and "salvation" religions. On the one hand, it consists, as communal religions do, of ritually enforced role-ascription, of a kind of religious orchestration of a social organization. On the other, it deploys writing and contains a high theology and a doctrine of ultimate, generic salvation. In such a social order, the clerisy is hereditary, simply because virtually all social positions are such. Its power lies in its indispensability: it is required for all those rituals which alone render all else legitimate. If the previous society was rule-pervaded, this one is suffused with ritual. This society, despite its partial use of script and reason, still lives by ritual, far more than it does by proof. This no doubt is true of all societies, but is quite particularly conspicuous in this one. Rituals, not doctrinal commitments, assuage the inner terrors of its members.

But the governability of its non-clerical population depends on its enlistment in ranked, professionally specialized social units. Their preoccupation with their place in this ritual hierarchy dissipates their energy, just as the lateral feuds of equal units dissipated the energy of the tribal units in the previous model. In Muslim polities, it is collective violence between equals, carried out in the idiom of honour, which is the opium of the people; in Hindu polities, it is instead the collective snobbery between unequal groups, carried on in the idiom of purity. But the ritually mediated and enforced grouping can only be established, maintained and serviced by the senior ritual monopolists, who thereby, once again, notwithstanding their lack of physical force, have a firm hold over the society. They are not wholly helpless in the face of the specialists in coercion; temple-linked wealth may even protect some of the surplus from central rapacity.

The types of order that have been sketched are of course not exhaustive. No doubt many other variants can be found. But generically, this much can be said of agrarian society: its dependence on storable and seizable surplus and on land, the principle of escalation of conflict and of the rationality of pre-emptive action, jointly ensure that they tend to be governed in an authoritarian way by a group or stratum which monopolizes the means of coercion. Nonetheless, the frequently inescapable fragmentation, territorial and other, of this stratum, and the difficulties of extensive organization in pre-scientific conditions, mean that central control is loose, and conflict ever latent if not endemic.

The alignments in these conflicts, given the ambiguities of loyalties and the unpredictability of outcomes, tends to depend in large measure on the *legitimacy* of contestants – which helps floating voters, or rather floating fighters, to decide whom to support. The manifest legitimacy of a claimant will also attract the support of *other* floating voters/fighters, and thus make him attractive to those who wish to be on the winning side, i.e. to most people. This in turn gives considerable indirect power to those who, through a mixture of literacy and ritual competence, possess the near-monopoly of legitimacy-ascription. They may be bureaucratic office-holders of the unique organization linked to revelation, or members of an open class of scholars who alone can decide upon rectitude of social and political comportment by comparing it with codified divine rules, or they may be hereditary members of a caste without whose ritual services all social conduct and status loses its legitimacy. The pen is not mightier than the sword; but the pen sustained by ritual does impose great constraints on the sword. It alone can help the swordsmen decide how to gang up to the greatest advantage.

It is in this way, generically speaking, that social elements other than military ones interact with brute force on something like equal terms. On the whole, however, this countervailing non-violent power does not enable a society to break out of agrarian stagnation. That has happened once only. To understand this unique occasion, we need to look at a specific situation, rather than at that which all agro-literate societies share.

Protestantism, Generic and Specific

The role of Protestantism in helping engender the industrial-scientific world is one of the most complex and disputed topics in sociology and history.[2] Modern capitalism, and the institutional and cultural forms associated with it, emerged largely in those parts of northern and northwestern Europe which are also predominantly Protestant. Over and above this argument from association, and perhaps of greater weight, there is a kind of inner elective affinity between the modern or capitalist spirit on the one hand, and the Protestant vision of the world on the other. The precise nature and relevance of that affinity continues to be the subject of vigorous debate. Yet the deep affinity seems to be more important than the questions concerning causal priority.

The overall picture is roughly this: Europeans had lived in a world in which salvation, and mediation with the divine and the sacred, were ascribed to a special organization. The divinity with which the organization maintained contact was appeasable, especially so if the pleas addressed to it were mediated by the organization and endorsed by it. The deity was held not to be averse to intervening in the world which it had initially created. It followed that any laws, natural or moral, which it had prescribed for its world and creation could be, and on occasions were, suspended. They were provisional and negotiable rather than absolute. The deity allowed itself, as the theologian S. A. Kierkegaard put it, a "teleological suspension of the ethical", and indeed of the causal.

Great stress was placed by the divine organization on miracles. The importance which miracles played both in the vindication of the faith, and in the ritual pattern of social life over which the organization presided, forcibly and vigorously reminded men of the possibility of divine intervention. No doubt a sense of its pervasive possibility was profoundly internalized. The organization acted as a kind of monopolistic divine agency and patronage network on earth. Rewards could be expected by those who supported its representatives and agents. All this encouraged men to think of the moral order in patronage, opportunistic terms. Appeasing the patron mattered more than heeding and comprehending his rules, especially as his own comportment did not always seem to be rule-bound. Loyalty was prized more than fastidious rule-abidingness. The heavenly court rather resembled earthly ones, and the Other world seemed to be as patronage-ridden as this one.

The deity was also willing to reveal important truth to mankind, and make the world intelligible by such a discriminating procedure. It was not averse to a certain measure of rationalism: to some extent, a generic reason could at least confirm, and even attain a significant part, though not the whole, of revelation. This revealed intelligibility and partial rational accessibility would encourage the seeker after illumination to make straight for the central truths. A short-cut seeking reason was in a way closer to revelation than to research.

By contrast, an inscrutable, inaccessible, unappeasable, anti-rational yet orderly deity might in effect strongly encourage scientific method. It would do so by turning the orderly facts of its creation into the only evidence of its own design. Such a rigid and austere deity had no cognitive favourites, and would not disclose its secrets capriciously to some. Patient investigation of its rules, as revealed in its creation, would be the only path towards enlightenment.

It would of course be wrong to see the old vision as wholly capricious: the organization had put a good deal of order into this conceptual world, it was jealous of its monopoly of magic and the sacred, and it discouraged or suppressed freelance manifestations of the exceptional and the sacred. It monopolized and bureaucratized magic, it certified authentic examples and imposed quality control on sanctity. In the main, it did indeed embrace and incorporate, but thereby also control and restrict, the spontaneous manifestations of magic: if you can't beat them, oblige them to join you. If the notion of a single and exclusive deity resembles that of an early Near Eastern monarch, then the Church resembled that of a *fairly* effectively centralized patronage network, with a single apex, and one intolerant of rival networks, especially if they refused to be incorporated.

Throughout much of the Middle Ages, notwithstanding occasional schisms and setbacks, the spiritual patronage network was markedly more successful in its efforts to centralize than was its political counterpart and rival. If the role of the "state" is to provide the model of the good life, the fount of legitimacy, and the moral identity for those who live under it, then in a very important sense the medieval Church *was* the medieval state. In the conditions which then prevailed, it delegated, whether in virtue of its own doctrine, or simply making a virtue of necessity, the task for direct enforcement of order to a class of professional violence-virtuosos. But their internal organizational cohesion was markedly inferior to its own. Amongst the thugs, fissiparous and centrifugal tendencies were usually far stronger than centralizing ones.

In such a world, the incentives making for either economic or cognitive accumulation are necessarily limited. The fact that, barring exceptions, the sword is more powerful than either the plough or the counting house, means that producers and traders are ever liable to spoliation. One consequence of this situation, which is endemic in the agrarian world, is that specialists in production or trade, if at all successful, would be tempted or impelled, partly or wholly, to switch their resources to coercion. Norsemen could trade in the Dark Ages because they could defend themselves. This also meant that, when it was feasible, they did not need to bother with trade at all, and would switch to pillage or permanent conquest. Karl Marx formulated a theory according to which an economically defenceless proletariat sees its remuneration reduced to the minimum needed for its reproduction: a similar law can at least as plausibly be formulated for the bourgeois class of the agrarian age. Its rulers allow it to retain only as much as is required for its own reproduction, and no more. This mechanism is highlighted by the preference shown by medieval rulers for traders drawn from populations deprived by their religion of the moral protection offered by the Church.

But fear of spoliation by the virtuosos of coercion also works in another and indirect way. The best way to escape violent confiscation was to link one's wealth to religion, seeking the protection of the sacred. Pious foundations of one kind and another could benefit the original owner and donor, or could at least help him retain the residue. So wealth flowed to the temple, the monastery, the upkeep of a mosque school. It is almost meaningless to ask whether the faithful benefactors were buying the favours of heaven, or merely escaping the rapacity of the political/military thugs. They were doing both, fleeing robbery, and securing merit both in this world and the next. The manner in which they subjectively presented it to themselves hardly matters. When men perform acts which are part of their cultural repertoire, the ascribed motives come as part of a package deal, and need not be taken too seriously in any one individual case. What does matter are the situational constraints which operate overall.

In a society of this kind, the surplus accumulated by producers, if not forcefully seized by the monopolists of violence, is naturally channelled either into purchasing entry to the ranks of the swordsmen or into enhancing the ritual equipment of the society. So, one way or the other, the clerical-military elite benefits, whether or not its own ranks are replenished with new entrants, and whether or not there is a circulation of elites. Neither way, however, is the surplus used to augment the productive equipment of society, or to enhance its cognitive potential. The entire organization of society, in both its coercive and ideological institutions, works against this being so. Almost everything in the ethos, and in the balance of power of the society, generally militates against the possibility of an explosive growth in either production or cognition.

Consider, by way of contrast, the model of a Protestant society. Let us define Protestantism generically as a creed which denies the existence of a sacramentally distinct priesthood, of personnel specially qualified to mediate with the sacred, and hence its right to form itself into a distinct body representing the divine on earth. The deity is thereby deprived of a holding company on earth, one which can simultaneously receive donations and protect them and the donors from political spoliation. That way of disposing of the surplus is henceforth blocked: conspicuous religious display, enhancing the status of the donor in this world and his prospects in the next, ceases to be feasible. The Protestant ethos is characteristically averse to display, whether cis-mundane or trans-mundane in spirit or purpose. This on its own would not, of course, prevent the swordsmen from benefiting from the withering away of the clerics, and pocketing the lot. Some top specialists in coercion, such as Henry VIII and his clients, did of course benefit precisely in this manner. But what if violent spoliation as a permanent way of life *also* becomes difficult at the same time, in virtue of other factors? *Then* the new rules of the game are indeed liable to have very profound consequences.

This postulated generic Protestant ethos has other features of great relevance. It is not merely the great leveller of all believers: it also levels out the universe itself. A mysterious, distant, ineffable deity no longer stoops to interfere in the daily events which make up the life of Its creation. Miracles cease to be the centre of religion, and order reigns supreme. The days of divine conjuring performances are over. Sacredness is evenly spread out over creation, and no longer singles out some objects, places or events. The orderly and severe deity also becomes unappeasable; Its favours can no longer be bought or influenced. Twice over, It ceases to be eligible to act as the apex of a patronage network. It spurns the use of middlemen, spiritual brokers, and It is not receptive to pressure or other inducements. It cannot be fixed, and will not act as fixer. Notoriously, in the most severe version of Protestant doctrine, It has firmly and irrevocably assigned men to salvation and perdition. Any attempts to influence the outcome by pleasing Its agents, even if such agents were still available, is now pointless, if not blasphemous.

The most famous and influential of the theories linking Protestantism to capitalism and economic accumulation and growth lays great stress on this point: Calvinist believers, deprived of any means of influencing their own posthumous fate, but believing that success in their vocation is a sign (though not a cause) of their Election, will unconsciously cheat. They will endeavour to prove their own salvation, to themselves and others, by prospering in their vocation. A category of producers eager to prosper primarily for this peculiar reason, and no longer anxious or obliged to turn their profits into either pleasure or power or salvation or into the means of entry into the coercive stratum, will form the ideal class – perhaps the *only* class – capable of continuous and disinterested accumulation. Such a class alone seems capable of taking humanity spontaneously around the painful hump of economic growth, and helping it reach the point where a wholly new economic order is born. Once its enormous potential for wealth and hence power becomes manifest, it can of course thereafter be emulated from more mundane and ordinary motives.

To what extent this rather tortuous but ingenious psychic mechanism, postulated by Max Weber, really operated, remains contentious. It is important to note that it does not constitute, by any means, the only possible link between the Protestant ethos and economic growth. Consequently, even if the historical objections which have been raised against the Calvinist paternity of the modern world is sustained, the complicated nexus between generic Protestantism and modernity remains important.

In a Protestant world, a symmetrical population of believers, no segment of which is endowed with a privileged access to the sacred, faces a similarly symmetrical and orderly world, subject to firm laws. No parts of it are selected and eligible for special reverence, or treated as refractions or emanations of the sacred. The equality of concepts makes genuine theoretical exploration possible: visions cease to be conceptually anchored and ritually immobilized. The inscrutable and hidden nature of the deity obliges men to investigate nature impartially, if they wish to discern its laws and the divine will: the hope of direct access to truth, by a clever conceptual *combinazione*, or by deity revealing the nature of things to those whom it favours, bypassing tedious observation, has been dashed by its severe and uncompromising inaccessibility.

The absence or attenuation of ritual specialists places a special onus on internal moral sanctions, by diminishing the relevance or availability of external ones, or at any rate diffusing them among the total community. If Max Weber is right, the fear of an inscrutably imposed damnation greatly increases the power of the internal sanction, by giving it a very great deal to be anxious about. From Augustine to Kierkegaard, a self-tormenting theological streak weaned some men at least from a facile reliance on external reassurance.

So, a Protestant world is one in which the sacred is absent (hidden) or, if you prefer, in which it is evenly diffused. Hence there are fewer bounds and prescriptions surrounding economic activities. Existing practices, and the combination of elements which they embody, cease to be hallowed. So the way is free to innovation and growth by means of new devices, by new combinations of elements. Instrumental rationality becomes more common and acceptable. The diffusion of moral authority, the stress on the internalized voice within each believer, rather than on the special authority of some, means that Protestant respect for codes of conduct is less dependent on public enforcement, on the anticipation of reciprocation. Hence it becomes more genuinely trustworthy, and thus more conducive to the flourishing of economic activity.

Trust becomes far more widespread, and less dependent on external sanctions. Those governed by inner sanctions will behave in a trustworthy manner without first waiting to make sure that others do so as well. This breaks the vicious circle of distrust, and sets off a kind of moral multiplier effect. If a man's motive for economic activity is the desire to demonstrate his saved status and to fulfil his calling, he is less likely to cheat than if he is activated by the desire for gain. His rectitude is not at the mercy of his anticipation of the rectitude of others. Thus Protestantism has a double (and somewhat contradictory) role: it makes men instrumentally rational in handling things, and non-instrumentally honest in their dealings with each other.

The dominant morality is one of rule-observance rather than of loyalty, whether to kin or patron, and whether political or spiritual. The spiritual egalitarianism leads to the participatory self-administration of the sect. This sets a political precedent, and provides training for participatory and accountable politics. The stress on scripturalism is conducive to a high level of literacy; scripturalism and an individualist theology lead naturally to an individualist theory of knowledge. This suggests the sovereignty of the individual consciousness; the right, and duty, of the individual to judge for himself, and to refrain from passing on responsibility to some external authority. Claims to truth are to submit to the bar of individual and symmetrical judgement: neither claims nor judges can claim special, unequal privilege.

The stress on scripturalism and hence on literacy eventually engenders a community in which, for the first time in human history, the high culture becomes the genuinely pervasive, majority culture. A high culture is one which is dependent on normative texts and is transmitted by formal education. It is contrasted with a low or folk culture, transmitted orally and in conduct, and linked to norms embodied in ritual rather than in writing. Under the conditions prevailing in the agrarian age, a high culture, if it exists at all, is at best a privileged minority accomplishment. A tension between it and the low culture is endemic.

A modern society is inherently one in which a high culture becomes *the* culture of the entire community: dependence on literacy and formal education, the standardization of procedures and measures (in a broad as well as a literal sense), all require it. A style of production which is simultaneously innovative *and* involves the cooperation of countless, anonymous agents cannot function without shared, standardized measures and norms. Protestantism points humanity in the direction of such a social order, well in advance of the actual arrival of modernity.

In the Weberian account of the contribution of Protestantism to the emergence of modern rationality, the notion of "vocation" is prominent. The overall argument is paradoxical: the modern world, in which occupational mobility is great and vocations are rapidly rotated, especially between generations, is brought about by men who treat "vocation" with the utmost seriousness and revere it as god-given. Some agrarian communities regularly rotate village land, thus enhancing communal cohesion. A modern society rotates vocations, with much the same effect. The paradox is there, but there is logic in it. A rigidity in the attitude to vocation broke the logic of the agrarian age, which decreed that power trumped wealth, and that consequently wealth should be transmuted into power and status at the first opportunity. A non-economic inducement to economic single-mindedness engendered a world in which wealth could, on the whole, be pursued without the intrusion of other considerations. A "vocation" may be an authoritative "call", but it is not imposed by precedent and parentage. It heralds, at the very least, inter-generational occupational mobility.

Here there is a certain parallel with another modern notion, that of "romantic love", the authority and importance of unpredictable, aura-endowed passionate attachments. Some have seen its origin in the work-situation of the apprentice knight, unable to consummate the passion engendered by the proximity of the "mistress" (in the original sense) whom he serves.[3] The real explanation of this phenomenon seems to me to lie in conditions of a genuinely open and individualist marriage market. It makes men choose partners, without heeding any rules of preferential, let alone prescriptive marriage. They are no longer bound to consider the interests of their kin.[4] In such circumstances, an excuse is required if a man is not to choose the most obvious bride, suggested by social or geographic proximity. The cult of the *coup de foudre*, outside a man's control yet binding and so to speak sanctifying, provides just such an excuse.

Similarly, the *coup de foudre* of personal vocation, which might seem to endow professions with rigidity, in fact legitimizes and facilitates free occupational choice, unconstrained by social ascription. It also heralds and confirms the dignity of all productive occupations. It frees them of the stigma attaching to them in the agrarian age, when, on the whole, only sacerdotal and military/political roles were granted true dignity.

Once productive employment is allowed to constitute a vocation, this destroys the presumption that it is a *pis-aller*, an inferior alternative to the only real human fulfilment as priest or warrior or ruler. These dominant occupations cease to be the exemplary models for men. Productive activity can at long last acquire full *droit de cité*. So, at the same time as circumstances no longer oblige a man to turn his profits into pious symbols of salvation, or status, or political or military strength, the conceptual impulsion to do so also lapses. The ethics of production and commerce cease to be stigmatized second-class codes. Morality is internalized rather than externalized. The claims of productive or commercial morality, of the work ethic, also become stabilized and permanent. They lose their interim status as something to be abandoned at the first opportunity. Men imbued with this ethos not merely plough back their profits, they remain within their profession even when successful. Success confirms them in the pursuit of their vocation instead of enabling them to escape its political precariousness and moral stigma.

In the Weberian version of the argument, there is stress on the fact that here, for once, we find asceticism combined with this-worldliness. The argument is that the more customary *other*-worldly asceticism led to a disposal of the surplus on religious symbols, whereas the intra-mundane version leads to economic accumulation and growth. It seems to me that the this-worldliness is a corollary of effective spiritual egalitarianism: if *everyone* in a community is ascetic, the asceticism *must* be this-worldly: otherwise all would starve. Genuinely other-worldly, economically sterile asceticism can only be practised by a minority. It simply is not open to a *whole* society. If all men become beggar-monks, they will all suffer. When ascetic monks come to form a high proportion of a society, they also turn to productive activities, and constitute a kind of clerical crypto-bourgeoisie. Marxists looking for an emergent bourgeoisie in the allegedly feudal conditions of lamaistic Buddhist societies had to seek this elusive burgher class in the lamaseries.[5]

Few things symbolize the low- and even-keyed and ecstasy-avoiding ethos so much as the avoidance, characteristically found in some Protestant sects, of formal oaths. All commitments are equally binding: the special solemnizing of some acts, with its implicit devaluation of ordinary acts unaccompanied by ritual fuss and posturing, is repudiated. The whole diffusion and predominance of Protestant-type attitudes indicates what might be called the transition from Durkheimian to Weberian rationality.

Durkheim stressed the separation of the sacred and the profane. This underscores the use of the sacred for the purpose of highlighting the special occasion, and thereby instilling the *special* idea, and endowing it with awe-ful authority. On his view, it was this subjection to concepts which made us human, and made society possible. Reason stamps its foot in ritual: mankind is cowed into obedience, and social cohesion and intellectual communication become possible. An inherently unequal humanity faces inherently unequal concepts, and only the sacred ones truly bind and command us. But though the mechanism as such is universal, it bestows its aura in diverse ways. The sacred varies from one ritual system to another. Each ritual zone has its own, unconvertible moral currency.

By contrast, once endowed with writing, initiated into and habituated to the notion of a conceptually unified single universe, and persuaded by an egalitarian theology which levels out both men and things, mankind becomes able to observe an altogether different kind of rationality. All like cases can be treated similarly, in production *and* in cognition. Men can respect all concepts equally, and can listen to a reason which communicates in writing without needing to raise its voice in histrionic reinforcement. Protestantism levels out concepts as well as men. Concepts as well as men become rational, in the sense of observing the same orderly rules and claiming no exceptions for themselves. Ritual loses its importance: indeed its absence, a constant and even sobriety, acquires a special aura and authority. Orderly conduct throughout, the like treatment of like cases, and the recognition of symmetrical obligations contained in rules, replace differential awe restricted to ritually heightened situations, and an ethic of uneven loyalty. The sanctions are now within, freed of dependence on loud and insistent reinforcement of audio-visual aids; and the ethic they sanction is also different in kind. No special external markers indicate obligation: it is ubiquitous, symmetrical and emanates from within.

This makes possible an anonymous society of individualists, proud of their occupational specialism, internalizing its rules without need of constant reinforcement or surveillance or threat. The pursuit of the aims of that specialism can be freed of respect for tradition: efficiency can rule unimpeded. Men become respectful of rules rather than loyal to patrons, willing to innovate in the pursuit of their aims, rather than being cravenly respectful of the habitual procedures deployed at their old tasks. A world and a humanity of this kind seem well suited to produce our kind of society, and are compatible with it.

The two great sociologists of rationality were really concerned with radically different species of it. Durkheim's problem was – why are *all* men rational? All men recognize and respect concepts – but some concepts much more than others.

Sacredness is stratified, and stratifies the world. Weber's problem on the other hand was – why are *some* men more rational than others? Why do *some* men treat *all* concepts in an orderly way? Durkheim meant by rationality the fact that men are bound, in thought and conduct, by the concepts shared by a culture. He found the solution to his problem in ritual. Weber's problem was the emergence of a distinctive style of rationality, rule-abiding, capable of instrumental efficiency in disregard of tradition – yet ignoring personal advantage in obeying the rules of each calling, and finding fulfilment in productive activity for its own sake.

The customary formulation of the question concerning the role of the Reformation in the history of Europe and the Western world has been changed somewhat in the present argument. The stress is different. The habitual question is – what was the role of *the* Reformation? By contrast, we treat Reformation as a generic concept. Throughout the later, post-axial period of agrarian society, there tends to be an endemic tension between universalistic, script-carried, egalitarian, generic-salvation doctrines, and ritual-centred, inegalitarian, community-reinforcing religious traditions. There is an enormous difference between cults which underwrite and reinforce a stable and differentiated social order, and a universal message offering an identical all-purpose salvation To Whom It May Concern. The latter inspiration often appears, brought by some sage-saviour, but in the long run the message does not prevail. The social factors inhibiting its permanent and full implementation are far too strong to allow it to prevail. The factors favouring it may be strong enough to bring it forth, but not strong enough to allow it to prevail, to save it from "corruption". But on one occasion and in one area, the message did prevail, thanks to very special circumstances: and the world was transformed for good. So the new question is: how did one, amongst so many reformations, succeed in being permanent?

CHAPTER 5

Codification

Reformation to Enlightenment

The Enlightenment codified the vision of the world as a unified, self-sufficient Nature, governed by orderly laws, and including man within itself as a part of Nature and nothing else. It is the codification, in outline, of the world we now inhabit. The supposition that the Enlightenment is but a kind of continuation and completion of the Reformation is sometimes attacked as naive and over-intellectualist. Yet the logical connection is obviously there: the notion that it is legitimate to scrutinize the claims of a self-proclaimed sacred institution, by checking it against the independent testimony of scripture, would seem to lead naturally to the idea that everything, including scripture itself, can be scrutinized in the light of the independent testimony of "Reason" or fact.

At the same time, obviously, a Reformation does not automatically lead to an Enlightenment. On its own, were it really or even partially successful, it might be expected to lead to a rigid and perhaps anti-rational theocracy. This is precisely what in fact happened in at least one other tradition, namely Islam. More probably, in the conditions normally prevailing in agrarian societies, the reformation would be followed by a swing back of the pendulum, and by a revival of the provision of sacred services, mediation, hierarchy and so forth by "unreformed" brokers of the sacred.

But the one uniquely successful Reformation did not continue to flourish in the stable old social order. It was uniquely successful when compared with reformations which occurred elsewhere in other scriptural religions. It initiated, or confirmed and accompanied, radical and irreversible changes. The social order was transformed for good. The Reformation was not fully successful in the sense of conferring victory on its extreme wing. On the contrary, the defeat of the extremists converted them to toleration. If they could not impose the Kingdom of God on society by force, they settled for withdrawal into the world of their sects, and preached pacificism and toleration. The fact that their defeat was not complete, reinforced by a precarious international balance of power, enabled them to secure the required toleration.

David Hume was one of the first to reflect on the social and political implications of both traditional priesthood and zealous egalitarian scripturalism. He concluded, quite correctly as far as pre-modern conditions are concerned, that a specialized traditional clerisy is far less inimical to civil liberty than scripturalist enthusiasm. He recorded this conviction in his *Natural History of Religion* (Chapter IX): "The tolerating spirit of idolaters, both in ancient and in modern times, is very obvious to anyone. . . . The intolerance of most religions, which have maintained the unity of God, is as remarkable. . ." But in his essay *Of Superstition and Enthusiasm*, he reaches quite a different conclusion, and one compatible with more recent historical experience: ". . . superstition is an enemy to civil liberty, and enthusiasm a friend to it".[1] By "enthusiasm" he meant puritanical unitarian scripturalism, such as that of the nonconformists, and by "superstition" an indulgent pluralistic pantheon.

How is the contradiction to be resolved? First, he says that unitarians are enemies of liberty, and then he says that their zeal is a friend of it. A cogent argument makes unitarian scripturalism anti-liberal in general, but a friend of liberty *on one occasion*. Hume notices this, but his attempt to deal with it is feeble. The real answer would seem to be that it is important for the zealous enthusiasts to be defeated but not crushed. Their defeat converts them to toleration (in any case consonant with the view that truth can only come from an inner light and not from external enforcement). The fact that their defeat is not total helps them secure toleration. A spiritual as well as political balance of power helps maintain a situation in which central coercion is not exercised to the full. The societies in which this has occurred in due course demonstrated, by their own wealth and power, the astonishing economic and military advantages which can follow this compromise. The very societies which had eschewed the old obsession with exemplary display became the models and exemplars of the world. The less centralized British monarchy repeatedly defeated the more absolutist French one. But it was itself twice, in the course of two successive centuries, defeated by its own civil society – once in the home country, and once across the Atlantic. A strong civil society, conjoined with a relatively weak or at least non-dominant central state, constituted a unit *more* powerful than more thoroughly centralized polities. The Enlightenment pondered the lesson.

So the societies in which a reformed compromise prevailed, or some of them, proceeded to flourish so much that, by the eighteenth century, they displayed enormous economic, military and imperial vigour. They eventually came to be a model, a source of envy and puzzlement and emulation, for the societies which had followed a different and more customary path. The Enlightenment was not merely a secular prolongation and more thorough replay of the Reformation. In the end it also became an inquest by the unreformed on their own condition, in the light of the successes of the reformed. The *philosophes* were the analysts of the under-development of France.

So perhaps one should distinguish between the Enlightenment of the reformed themselves, which was a ratification and analysis of changes which *had* occurred, and the Enlightenment of the unreformed, which consisted of an often angry insistence that changes *should* occur. In Edinburgh and Glasgow, thinkers tried to explain the changes which had already happened; in Paris, to call for changes that ought to happen. One may also add a third category, that of the backward-reformed, the Third World of the time, on the other side of the Rhine, in Berlin or Koenigsberg. There the aftertaste of the ravages of the wars of religion plus political authoritarianism gave the Enlightenment a quality distinct from either that of Scotland or that of Paris.

The differences between the two styles were due to persist right up to our time. Those who codified the "enlightened" intuitions did so either against the background of a pliable, elastic, self-modifying and plural religious tradition, or in opposition to an organizationally and doctrinally full-blooded church. Such a church, though it may have incorporated many of the reformed attitudes and ideas, nonetheless retained, or even greatly strengthened, its absolutist and truth-monopolistic pretensions. By contrast, the dominant ideological institution of the plural and developing society, interestingly, opposed enthusiasm rather more vigorously than it rejected disbelief. Hence it did not itself cling to doctrine with any excessive zeal. That would set a bad example, one emulating its own principal rivals, the nonconformists. It practised monotheism with a human face. By the nineteenth century, this lack of zeal impelled some of its own spiritually more eager members to return to the more uncompromising and total clerical organization.

The consequences of this general situation are obvious and well known. The "British" style of Enlightenment stresses empiricism and scepticism. Though it codified a severely this-worldly criterion of social policy ("utilitarianism"), and the empiricist principles of cognition, it did not really attempt to formulate a complete counter-doctrine, a new secular or naturalistic credo. By contrast, the "French" or Romance style, whether in the form of the doctrine of the Encyclopaedists, in Comtian positivism, or in its prolonged later addiction to Marxism, is drawn precisely to some such counter-doctrine and counter-church. It is drawn to systems built of mundane, naturalistic or historicist elements, but one, in its general architecture and spirit, mirroring all too faithfully that which it would repudiate and replace.

The Sovereignty of Knowledge

The Enlightenment contains a number of themes. One of the most important, perhaps ultimately the most important, is the autonomy and sovereignty of knowledge. This philosophy was to ratify the single-purpose vision of a unitary Nature, orderly, and only knowable in an orderly manner. This is perhaps the most important corollary of the division of labour, and of instrumental rationality which is linked to it: knowledge is to serve its own purposes only, and be constrained by no other considerations. In world-construction, the principles of cognition become sovereign. These principles insist that explanation be symmetrical and quite free of any discrimination between the sacred and the profane. The elements of which the world is made up are, all of them, equal, and so are all investigators.

The idea of autonomous cognition was articulated initially, in the most forcible manner, by the seventeenth-century philosopher René Descartes. With Descartes, this knowledge-centredness appears only in the formulation of his *problem*, and not at all in his solution. His solution returns to the vision of an absolute and authoritative world, whose basic structure is indubitable and linked to the ultimate authority presiding over it. Reality then dictates the legitimate forms of knowledge, rather than vice versa. As a problem *and* a solution, the great inversion only appears in the eighteenth century, above all in those two great culminating points of the Enlightenment, David Hume and Immanuel Kant.

Modern society is the only society ever to live by, through, and for, sustained, continuous, cognitive and economic growth. Its conception of the universe and of history, its moral and political and economic theory and practice, are all profoundly and inevitably coloured by this. It is entirely fitting and natural that such a society should begin by placing knowledge at the very centre of its philosophy, and making it sovereign. What may be called the Cartesian tradition consists of doing precisely this.

Initially it was knowledge as such that was stressed, and growth was a bit incidental. It was admittedly assumed that sound knowledge would also grow perpetually. It was only later that growth as such, no longer primarily or exclusively cognitive growth, became the central idea. First it was the theory of knowledge which dominated; the philosophy of Progress came later.

All this constitutes one of the great and profound revolutions in the intellectual history of mankind. One could initially divide all philosophies into two great species: Platonic and Cartesian (although a third species also makes its appearance in the nineteenth century). The difference between them is fundamental. Platonism is the supreme expression of agro-literate man, of a society endowed with a large and steady food supply, capable of sustaining a minority elite endowed with a high culture, and also endowed with writing and hence the capacity to codify, formalize, and preserve its ethos and cognitive capital. It is stable, and aspires to stability; and it is liable to consider radical change pathological. It recognizes and endorses the joint roles of the transcendent and of coercion in securing stability for society. The community is divided into the wise, the aggressive and the hardworking. Cartesianism, by contrast, appears at the point of transition from such a social order to modernity, when the wise cease to constitute a caste. Whether it will also continue to characterize and dominate us is another question.

One enormous difference, perhaps the most fundamental, between the two styles of philosophizing is this: Platonism sees knowledge as an event in the world. The world, its permanent and sacred structure and its inherent values, validate knowledge. Although Platonism tries to establish the ultimate social authority of Knowers, the authority of their special cognitive virtuosity *follows from* the ultimate nature of the world, assumed to be stable and definitively, finally, revealed to man. Cartesianism by contrast sees the world as an event within knowledge. Knowledge validates the world, and is independent of it. In a society which in the last analysis is built on and wholly dependent on the growth of knowledge, knowledge is not treated as sacred, and also confers no social authority. The difference could hardly be more profound, and its implications are boundless.

Platonism assumes that a definite, stable, norm-giving reality is there, hidden perhaps from some or from many, but nonetheless there, and sovereign. So knowledge, and morality as well, can be vindicated from within this fundamental constitution of reality.

Definitive legitimations are the hallmark of the Platonic style. The basic reality is attainable in a so-to-speak penetrative and global and final way, not by piecemeal and provisional sorties. Such access, however, is a privilege, linked to the status system of the society. Knowledge is sound if it leads us towards the absolute reality, and delusory if it does not. Men convey their moral worth by what they can claim to know. So, in the end, it is knowledge which is on trial, not reality.

All this of course enables Platonism to operate its fusion of fact and value, its joint buttressing of social, moral and cognitive hierarchies. This capacity it shares with the simpler communal, ritual-based religions, though it employs more sophisticated and abstract devices in the attainment of its end. By a procedure which seems brazenly circular to us Cartesians, sound knowledge is that which is possessed by morally sound men, and it is from the nature of ultimate reality that we read off the criteria of moral health, which then enable us to identify the trustworthy witnesses. They in turn reconfirm the message concerning the true nature of reality. The circle is complete, and with variations of detail it is repeated by most or all the codified belief systems of the agro-literate age.

Cartesianism inverts all this. The world is to be located within knowledge. The criteria of sound knowledge are independent of the structure of the world, and *precede* it. The same criteria would apply in *any* world, and they are in no way beholden to this one. We ignore and suspend this world whilst we formulate those criteria, much as any honourable juror would refrain from socializing with litigants while judging their case. Know first, live after. Do not allow yourself to be beholden to the world you investigate. No corruption, if you please. So the division of labour finds its culmination in the severe autonomy of knowledge. The cognitive judiciary at long last becomes fastidiously independent.

This strategy of cognition owes everything to the division of labour: all separable questions to be separated. The old world which had been beyond the reach of doubt, by contrast, secured its stability by linking all its facets in mutual support. The new atomization of evidence, the individualization of men, the separation of questions, the externalization (to society and to culture), so to speak, of the cognitive judge, are all of them mutually related.

Descartes' actual method was in its way curiously Platonic. It consisted of a strange kind of residual but selective concept-worship: concepts, *provided they were clear and distinct*, were trustworthy. The concepts selected for special respect were not those which induce ecstasy and awe (that was the old way), but those which manifest the sober and solid bourgeois virtues of clarity and distinctness. They were to serve but one purpose at a time. Their clarity and distinctness was itself a supreme expression and exemplification of the division of labour, of single-strandedness. This plainly was an exceedingly bourgeois Platonism. *Ordnung muss sein.* No package deals, no untidy, messy agenda. Such clear and distinct concepts then helped him to establish the existence of a cognitively benevolent deity, which then in turn guaranteed the intellectual operations undertaken with the help of the said concepts. In the course of this it also reconfirmed its own existence. The privileged concepts helped to establish its existence, and it in return guaranteed their reliability. Orderliness and the exclusive deity went into a symbiotic partnership. The deity had the role of underwriter to cognitive inquiry, but *only* if it was careful, tidy and sober. Descartes' philosophy mirrored in its logic a process that was also taking place within the actual life of West European culture.

In his substantive views, Descartes thus rapidly relapsed into the kind of circularity characteristic of the belief systems of a pre-Cartesian and Platonic age. An absolute and absolutely trustworthy reality vindicated the way of knowledge. So he refrained from being circular and reality-invoking only in his initial moves, which squarely and unambiguously placed all reality-claims before the bar of knowledge, where knowledge itself was to govern by laws of its own. Those laws were *not* in any way to be derived from the alleged deeper layers of the reality to be judged. It was those initial, opening moves which really counted.

There is another great difference between the Platonic and the Cartesian visions, over and above the contrast between reality-centredness and knowledge-centredness. Cartesianism is individualistic, and hence implicitly egalitarian. The principles of cognition, which sit in judgment on reality, are located in individuals, not in collectivities. Implicitly and explicitly, Platonism makes man, cognitively and otherwise, into a social animal, who cannot operate on his own. The key unit is not the individual, who is essentially incomplete. Society, not the individual, is the effective cognizing unit. The basic world-explorative strategy works in terms of the contrast between good and bad men: it is the goodness of good men which alone allows them to know truly, and they are required, as guides for the others. The complementarity and interdependence of men is specially deep and pervasive in Platonic visions.

In Plato's own works, the social and cognitive stratification, and its normative authority, are of course very firmly worked out. Of the great literate civilizations, Hinduism is the one closest to the Platonic blueprint (and I have always suspected that there is a historic link between the two, though evidence is lacking). Cartesianism, by contrast, stands for a kind of Robinson Crusoe stance in the field of cognition. A Hindu Crusoe would be a contradiction. He would be destined for perpetual pollution: if a priest, then his isolation and forced self-sufficiency would oblige him to perform demeaning and polluting acts. If not a priest, he would be doomed through his inability to perform the obligatory rituals. The crucial fact is that a society emerged in which single individuals could apparently carry the entire culture within themselves, unaided, and if need be reproduce it single-handedly on their island. This is intimately linked to the emergence of a society in which knowledge was autonomous, a judge but not the judged.

The predicament of the hapless Robinson Chatterjee only symbolizes the permanent cognitive condition of agro-literate humanity. The division of labour in this social order is such that not everyone can be a specialist in cognition, in full possession of the cognitive equipment of the society. Only a minority can aspire to this, and it and the rest of society are in a complementary and mutually dependent relationship.[2] This feature complements the other traits of this kind of system: its stability (pejoratively: stagnation), its authoritarianism (absolute reality trumps criteria of cognition, cognition is not allowed to be autonomous), and its cosiness: fact and value dovetail, reality confirms and sustains social and moral hierarchy, life is "meaningful".

The new cognitive style implies a double declaration of independence, both of the self and of Nature. An autonomous self favours an orderly and independent nature, and vice versa. Human self-sufficiency and a mechanical nature go together.[3] The separation of powers (itself an aspect of the division of labour) let natural inquiry and morals go their separate ways. Specialization, atomization, instrumental rationality, independence of fact and value, growth and provisionality of knowledge are all linked with each other.

The Dethronement of the Concept

Descartes proposed and pioneered the emancipation of cognition from the social order: knowledge was to be governed by its own law, unbeholden to any culture, any political authority. Such a view is indeed presupposed by the possibility of cognitive growth, of endless, untrammelled, interminable exploration of reality. Where the old linkage with the social order is maintained, it inevitably puts brakes on cognitive advance.

There are some paradoxical features in this emancipation: in one sense, cognition had been hived off from the rest of social life ever since a distinct clerisy had come into being. But in the days of such a clerisy, cognition, though claiming to tower over society and issue commandments to it, in fact still covertly served social ends. It aided the maintenance and perpetuation of order, social if no longer narrowly communal, far more than it served what we now consider the proper ends of knowledge. But when cognition really became emancipated from its social bondage, it also ceased to be linked to a distinct social category.

The clerisy had been formally, and often sacramentally, separated from other men. In this sphere as in the economic, when the division of labour really reaches its apogee, as it does with us, it ceases to define segregated species of men. Fully distinct activities become open to all men. It was an *in*complete division of labour which divided mankind. Its culmination leads to a homogeneous humanity.

So enhancement of the division of labour in one sense means its diminution in another. When knowledge is the slave of social considerations, it defines a special class; when it serves its own ends only, it no longer does so. There is of course a profound logic in this paradox: genuine knowledge is egalitarian in that it allows no privileged sources, testers, messengers of Truth. It tolerates no privileged and circumscribed data. The autonomy of knowledge is a leveller.

This paradox will appear again in other spheres: the one society based on cognitive and economic growth, and hence on an accentuated division of labour, is at the same time more egalitarian, and less haunted by the social echoes of the division of labour, than were its agro-literate predecessors. The division of labour no longer casts its shadow over humanity in the form of deeply differentiated kinds of human being. In the newly emerging world, men do different things, but they are all done by the same kind of man, and in much the same spirit. More accurately, one should say: a mobile, unstable differentiation of activity, carried out on the basis of a shared literate high culture, leads to a greatly diminished differentiation among men.

Descartes had formulated the view of the individual sovereignty of consciousness in terms of the alleged luminously clear inner *concepts*. This aspect of his doctrine was rapidly subjected to criticism by the philosophical tradition known as British empiricism, which insisted that the individual obtained his data from the senses, rather than from some inner reservoir of *ideas*. The culminating doctrine of this school was that concepts were but the echoes, the aftertaste of sensations. This view has tremendous consequences. The doctrine that we learn from experience may seem a trite truism. The idea that we learn *in no other way* totally transforms the world. The sovereignty of experience dethrones other putative authorities. The world constructed without their instructions is radically different from the world erected under their auspices.

Consider the fate of the *concept*. Of course, mankind continues to be guided by concepts. Men can only live by recognizing objects as specimens of wider species and genera, and by allowing their comportment, in the face of individual specimens, to be guided by their expectations concerning the whole class to which the specimen belongs. The conduct of an individual is also guided by the implications of the concepts which he believes *himself* to exemplify, or which he aspires to exemplify. All these expectations are only in some very small measure formed by individuals. In the main they are drawn from the pool of notions carried by an entire culture and language.

Men are guided in their moral responses and intuitions by the inherited, accepted suggestiveness of the concepts by which they live. A poet once observed that a single writer can contribute the occasional line, but the tradition writes the poem. Like such writers, we may on occasion vary our lines, and on even rarer occasions contribute an altogether original one: but in the main we draw on the available cultural stock for what we think, feel and do. As far as this goes, the life of mankind has not changed very much – though it is true that we have abandoned the explicit Platonistic worship of the concept, or rather of its historically more persuasive, scripturalist variants.

But at the level of argument where concrete moral disputes arise, a very great change has come about. Empiricism, the mature form of the Cartesian sovereignty of knowledge, is not just a philosopher's theory. It constitutes or codifies a profound social revolution. It transforms the rules concerning the manner in which rights and duties can be justified.

Consider what now happens to the theory of the concept. This is profoundly symptomatic. Hume and Kant had much the same view on this matter. What is contained in a concept is put there by *us*, by our optional definitions, which we can vary as we do our apparel. Concepts maketh man. Man, and not the nature of things, nor the deity, ordained them. They are human artefacts or conveniences, not supra-terrestrial imperatives. They do not descend upon us from on high. We replace them at will and in the light of their effectiveness; they are our tools, not our masters. They are subject to cost-effectiveness assessment. We can no longer be humbly guided by them, let alone deify them, or be commanded or overawed by them.

Man is no longer socialized by rituals highlighting some concepts and endowing them with a special aura. He is trained by sustained orderly education, instilling moderate respect for all concepts, provided they work tolerably. He is taught to distrust disorderly concepts, which fail to be linked to conditions of employment in a tidy or reliable manner. We can reformulate concepts to suit our convenience. We revise them just as we revise techniques. Neither concepts nor techniques are prescribed by our caste or station; and our caste and station are not prescribed either. An overtly pragmatic system of concepts mirrors an avowedly pragmatic and variable system of roles.

This condition is reflected in the philosophical theory of the exhaustive distinction between "analytic" and "synthetic" judgments. The terminology is Kant's, but the idea is also present in Hume. When we say something, we may simply extract the content *we* already put into the subject of the sentence (by definition, possibly tacit). In such a case what we say has no authority greater than the good sense (or otherwise) of our initial and alterable conventions, which happened to cluster together a set of traits in the definition of a given term. Alternatively, however, what we say about the subject of our sentence is not already contained in it, and the attribution is "synthetic". In that case, what we assert can *only* be justified by the empirical, external facts of the case. To give a hackneyed example: when I say that bachelors are unmarried, I am merely explicating the conventional content of the term "bachelor", bestowed upon it by the tacit consensus of the users of the English language. If, however, I say that bachelors are unhappy, I affirm something that can only be substantiated by a suitable investigation into the emotional state of mind of unmarried men.

All this may look like a bit of technical philosophic scholasticism. But it is more than that. What hinges on all this is something of shattering importance for the life of mankind. It determines the manner in which disputes about how we are to live, how we are to think, how we are to run and organize our society, can be settled.

What it all amounts to is this: cognitive claims can be settled in two ways, and two ways only. They can be settled by *our* decisions and convenience; and they can be settled by empirical fact, independent both of our will and of our social order. *Tertium non datur.* The secularization of the world can hardly go any further. All this is contained in a seemingly dry, pedantic, scholastic theory of judgment. Thus only two kinds of basic legitimation of knowledge are possible; and one of them inheres in *us*, and the other, in *nature*. Our convenience, or blind nature, are the only two authorities which can validate our cognitive claims.

This theory reflects a culture which no longer accepts its own concepts as ordained from on high, but which chooses its own, and endows them with only a conditional authority. Neither ritual inculcation nor Platonic meta-theory sanctifies concepts any longer. Our convenience, and not any transcendent imperative, is our master. The fount of honour and of validity now lies within us, and us only. In fact, concepts, like men, come to be valued for their efficiency rather than their honour. External nature and the social order are now mutually independent, and neither can impose itself on the other. The independence and externality of natural truth is the complement of the human foundation of all authority.

It is true that Kant (and on this point he differed from Hume) recognized some further forms of necessity or conceptual compulsion. These, on his view, underwrote our mathematics, some of our physics, and all of our morals. But the mechanisms or guarantee of this necessity, once again, did not stem from the nature of *things*; it stemmed from the structure of *our* minds and/or the preconditions of our systematization, the unification of our perceptions into *one* coherent picture. That we must so unify nature he took for granted; that early man had failed to do so eluded his somewhat ethnocentric attention. Authority was within us, or it was merely factual and contingent: the nature of things had become morally mute.

By way of example, consider Hume's best-known doctrine, his view of causation. In simplest term, Hume contended that there was no inner necessity in things, manifesting itself as causal regularity: anything could cause anything, and only experience could tell us what connections were in fact to be found in nature. This is, in effect, a denial of the doctrine of an essential natural order. It constitutes a charter, not merely for free cognitive enterprise, but also for free economic enterprise, for the untrammelled combination of factors of production. The rules of such a style of production were being explored at the very same time by Hume's good friend Adam Smith. The notion that anything can cause anything (as opposed to the existence of connections mirroring a natural *and* moral order of things), corresponds to the idea that, in production, any combination of factors is right and proper, if, but only if, found to be effective. This is in marked contrast to the old way of going about things, which allowed productive activities to be governed by hallowed traditional procedures, embedded in a *settled* division of labour.

The most important difference between the world we have left behind and the world we now inhabit, the world explored by Durkheim and the world analysed by Weber, is the status of concepts in either. In the first of these worlds, concepts were sacralized, and some were sacralized much more than others. They were markers of thought and conduct, and the markers were hallowed by ritual. In the new world, concepts, like men, were levelled out; none were hallowed, all were treated instrumentally, all were expendable and replaceable. This does not mean, however, that the new world was less orderly than the old: quite the contrary. What was hallowed and sacralized in the new world was the formal order of thought, the requirement that all like cases be treated alike, all issues separated, all referential claims subjected to exterior arbitration, all explanations fitted into an orderly whole as far as possible. If social and intellectual order was maintained in the old world by deeply entrenched concepts-sentinels, in the new world it is maintained by devotion to second-order, symmetrical procedures. Durkheim had laid bare the basic mechanics of the first procedure, and Weber had analysed the way in which the new world differed from the old, and put forward a hypothesis about how the miraculous change had come about. Durkheim explained why all men were rational, and Weber, why some were more rational than others.

Concept-Implementing and Instrumental Cultures

The revaluation of the concept, its transformation from a norm, first hallowed by ritual and later fortified by doctrine, into a mere public convenience, accompanies, expresses and ratifies that switch from concept-implementing cultures to instrumental-rational ones. In a variety of ways, rational instrumentality, the cold, calculating, single-minded choice of means for a given end, is impracticable and barely conceivable in the agrarian order. Many-strandedness, poly-functionality and interdependence of institutions and activities prevent the emergence of single, sharply delineated aims. Without such aims, instrumental rationality makes little sense. You cannot be efficient unless the criterion of success is reasonably clear. General rationality can indeed be seen as a pervasive application of instrumental efficiency.[4]

But this explanation itself does not yet go to the root of things. The dominance of many-strandedness was not wilful and accidental, but essential and inherent in the old situation. Agrarian societies can contain some markets and some science, but these inevitably remain mere islands, awkward ghettoes, within their cultures. The market cannot absorb and dominate a society's production, and science cannot absorb and dominate its ideas. The ghetto of rationality resembles the rationality of the ghetto. Those who are morally disenfranchised in that world are also debarred from forming multiple, "fully human" links with those whom they serve economically. In the stigma-induced insulation of a single functional relationship, they can be expected to do one thing only. Their usefulness and survival depends on doing it well. They are not allowed to offer anything else. In this way, as Werner Sombart claimed, the ghetto may be the source of instrumental rationality.[5]

A society with a small surplus cannot possibly become a generalized market society. By contrast, in the developed modern world, endowed with an enormous surplus, the individual hands over his labour and buys virtually all he needs with his wages. In the physical sense, there generally isn't any *thing* to hand over: the individual simply takes part in a very complex activity. With his remuneration, he draws from the market what he needs for survival, when he needs it. An analogous procedure in agrarian society would be absurd and disastrous. If the agricultural producer handed over his entire output and then relied on purchasing what he needs, the first fluctuation in prices, occasioned, let us say, by shortages in a neighbouring area, would leave him starving. In consequence, a very large part of production is stored for safety. Agrarian society is, in effect, a collection of protected storage units.

With a small surplus, production retains much of that absolute, yes–no, non-negotiable quality which we now associate with coercion and total conflict. There is not much leeway for seeking small advantage, and seeking a refined, sophisticated equilibrium of satisfactions or interests. Either one has enough, or one perishes. In such a context, there is no autonomous economy – only a binding set of simultaneously economic and political-coercive institutions. The crucial division of labour, the insulation of spheres of activity, which eventually engenders affluence, cannot emerge unless there is already some measure of plenty available. Here as elsewhere, there is a chicken-and-egg impasse.

What is stored needs to be protected if the storage is to be effective. Agrarian society's storage systems vary: the crucial unit can be the individual farmhouse-fort, coexisting on terms of equality with others; or the baronial keep; or the collective storehouse of the tribal segment, which still functioned within living memory in the *irgherm* or *agadir* of the peasant cousin republics of the Atlas mountains. The *nuraghi* of Sardinia, surviving from the first millennium BC thanks to their sturdy stone construction, must presumably have had the same function. The storage and protection system can be based on a set of individual houses, surrounded by a city wall, and protected by and exploited from a citadel; or again, it may be based on a centrally controlled silo.

Whatever the particular form it takes, one thing is always true: the preservation of this political-social infrastructure, from either external aggression or internal disruption, is at least as important as any augmentation of output. Generally speaking, it is *much* more important. In other words, there is no question of productive strategy being dominated by a single and primarily economic criterion. Rationality and experimentation based on insulated aims are excluded. The preservation of the system and its internal order is the first consideration. This calls, not for the pursuit of isolated and economic goals, but for the satisfaction of a complex and intertwined set of social requirements. This diffuse need is dominated by the socio-political considerations concerning the maintenance of the social order, and the protection and security it affords. So multi-strandedness, the impossibility of insulating and pursuing a pure and economic end, is built into the system. It is its essential precondition, not an accidental imperfection or retardation. A complex and precarious order is to be preserved, and this is hardly compatible with ruthlessly innovative pursuit of sharply isolated ends within it. Chayanov's celebrated studies of the attitudes of Russian peasants to production is a good example.[6]

What defines the market is not that people exchange things (they can do this on very unmarketlike, ritual occasions), but that they do so in the spirit of maximizing economic advantage, and, above all, that they do it with an almost total disregard of other considerations. A man selling stocks or shares generally has no idea of the identity of the purchaser. What defines a market society is of course not the presence, but the predominance, of such relations. One, but only one, precondition of the emergence of such instrumental rationality is indeed the availability of a large and expanding surplus, which creates a situation in which there is no longer the need for storing and protecting the major part of what is produced. The expanding surplus does, of course, depend on sustained innovation. This, if it is indeed to be persistent and continuous, depends not on any one discovery or even set of discoveries, but rather on a sense of the intelligibility and manipulability of nature. In other words, it calls for a secular, unified, single-conceptual-currency vision of nature.

So, the instrumental spirit in the economy (which, jointly with politically independent producers, helps set up the market), is paralleled by the unified and instrumental attitude to nature. The fusion of data and explanation into a single ideal currency, subordinated to the single aims of explanation and prediction, is essential. The two are parallel, and mutually constitute each other's condition. Commercialization of a city, or of a linked system of cities, or, on one occasion, of a favourably placed island, was possible even with a *relatively* low level of cognitive expansion; but the general expansion of the market, culminating in its domination of entire societies, and the international system of societies, required perpetual and tremendous cognitive and technological expansion.[7]

The orientation towards the market of a society possessed of but a small surplus would lead to an intolerably precarious situation. Such a society would be even more perilously poised at the edge of famine than most agrarian societies in fact were. Cognitive growth alone made it truly possible to follow through with the pervasive domination of a society by the market. This constitutes the element of partial truth in the Marxist doctrine that the growth of the "forces of production" engendered the radical social transformation. What is true is that without the expansion of knowledge and technology, the augmentation of productivity could not have occurred. But Marxism is in error, and strangely teleological in its explanation, when it goes further, and claims that this increased effectiveness-potential of tools somehow dragged a new social organization into being, as a new "task" imposed (by whom or what?) on humanity:

> No social order ever perishes before all the productive forces for which there is room in it have developed. . . Therefore mankind always sets itself only such tasks as it can solve; since. . . it will always be found that the task itself arises only when the material conditions for its solution already exist or are at least in the process of formation.[8]

What did happen was that a miraculous political and ideological balance of power in the non-economic parts of society made the expansion possible, at a time when the technological potential was also available. Just as miraculously, the impulse to make use of the uniquely favourable concatenation of cognitive, ideological and political circumstances was also present in some at least of the producers.

If the instrumental spirit and growth orientation in the economy presupposes the instrumental and autonomous spirit in the sphere of cognition, the converse is also true. It is hard to imagine perpetual and radical cognitive transformations occurring in a society in which the old alliance of coercive and clerical elements continues to prevail. They would suppress and smother it. They might do so from a valid if semi-conscious perception of their own interests, or from a sincere devotion to whatever orthodoxy their society happened to uphold. The most advanced society of the Middle Ages, the Chinese empire, behaved somewhat in this manner.[9] Only an individualist and instrumentalist society, committed to toleration as part of its internal compromise, can provide the required milieu. It is then able to carry on with its favoured productive activity. It can then constitute the matrix within which perpetual cognitive growth becomes firmly established and institutionalized.

The single-purpose, instrumental attitude towards a unified and as it were levelled-out nature, paradoxical though this may seem, has an elective affinity with the Protestant autonomy of the self. Superficially, one might be tempted by the contrary argument: the modern attitude to nature and natural inquiry places the sovereignty in matters cognitive squarely, unambiguously *outside*: the facts, the data, and they alone, can decide an issue. Man would seem to be devalued by this diminished control over natural fact. But the theory of knowledge which accompanies and codifies cognitive growth seems individualist, and hence strangely subjectivist: it is the individual's *private* data which are ultimately sovereign. Truth would seem to be private. But the cutting edge of this argument is that it deprives the inherited, habitual-custom-born cultural vision of its erstwhile authority. It liberates nature, or rather it liberates inquiry into nature. Individual cognitive sovereignty goes with the autonomy of nature. The end of holistic and social knowledge frees both the individual *and* nature.

The basic contrast is between a concept-implementing society – whose concepts (inevitably endowed with contested and ambiguous edges) are systematically implemented, form a system within which *both* men and nature have their prescribed places, and are sanctified by ritual and doctrine – and a society in which concepts are at least tacitly de-sacralized, where their application is in some measure based on single, isolated criteria, and within which isolated men face an orderly, "mechanical" nature.

The Enlightened Solution and its Problems

It would be an exaggeration to credit the Enlightenment, which codified the new vision, with a single and wholly coherent, consistent and fully worked out doctrine. Intellectual history does not possess that degree of neatness. Nevertheless, the Enlightenment is endowed with a considerable measure of coherence. Its themes – liberalism, rationalism, naturalism, empiricism, materialism – are conspicuous and fairly pervasive, even if its various themes are not always consistent.

Perhaps one should distinguish between vulgar Enlightenment, and the higher Enlightenment. Vulgar Enlightenment was articulated and disseminated by men who were far from vulgar socially or culturally: by the *philosophes* of the elegant salons of pre-revolutionary Paris. They wrote with brilliance and wit, sometimes with depth, and their widely accessible literary productions are plausibly credited with the transformation of the moral and intellectual climate, and with having made possible the proclamation of a new social order in the French Revolution, thereby turning a *fronde* into a profound transformation, a revolt into a revolution. They enthroned Reason and Nature. This pair of deities are highly complementary and indeed mutually interdependent, though also in conflict. For some reason, only one of them was actually symbolized by a naked actress at a revolutionary ritual.

Reason is a kind of generic faculty of cognitive discovery or validation, held to be at least potentially present in all men. But at least as a potentiality, it is present equally in all of us. Nature is the system of orderly reality, revealed unto us by Reason. Nature, in turn, is meant to repay the compliment by assigning to Reason, within its own system, the monopoly of legitimate cognition. Reason reveals Nature: Nature enthrones Reason.

A work in which this vision was systematized, more so than in any other, was Baron d'Holbach's *System of Nature* (1770). Given its brazenly subversive content, it first appeared anonymously, and was indeed condemned to be burnt by the public hangman. The Baron was rich as well as learned, and for a long time played the host, at regular Thursday dinners, to the French *encyclopédistes*. The book in question was a kind of compendium of the new enlightened wisdom, and can be assumed to be, in content, a cooperative work. The extent to which the new vision was both the inversion in content and the perpetuation in style of the old, can be gauged by the remarkable Hymn to Nature with which it culminates:

> O Nature, sovereign of all beings! and ye, her adorable daughters, Virtue, Reason, and Truth! remain for ever our only Divinities: it is to you that belong the praises of the human race: to you appertains the homage of the earth. Show us, then, O Nature! that which man ought to do, in order to obtain the happiness which thou makest him desire. Virtue! Animate him

with thy beneficent fire. Reason! Conduct his uncertain steps through the paths of life. Truth! Let thy torch illumine his intellect, dissipate the darkness of his road.[10]

So much for vulgar Enlightenment. The higher Enlightenment is constituted by those supreme thinkers of the eighteenth century who did more than merely codify the new vision. They also laid bare, and faced, its deep problems and its internal strains. The greatest among these were Hume and Kant.

There is a number of such profound strains, but it is as well to name the most significant ones. They are: the *conflict* between Reason and Nature; the strong tendency of Reason to cut its own throat, and the conflict between universalism and relativism. The problems are related to each other.

The twin goddesses of the Enlightenment are not in harmony. It was only the more popular, less rigorous propagandists of the new vision who thought otherwise. Nature is a unique, orderly, all-embracing system, permitting (indeed encouraging) human control of events by the recognition and use of regularities. It does not on the other hand allow wilful manipulation through magic or incantation, indeed it allows neither exceptions ("miracles") nor propitiation. Reason is the generic human capacity to investigate nature, which, by the eighteenth century, was largely understood to consist of use of evidence and experiment, to test ideas none of which were any longer allowed to claim any authority by right of birth. No idea can claim recognition in virtue of its origins. Rational inquiry excludes invocation of authority, or claims to cognitive privilege. Ideas, like men, must earn respect by achievement, not by ascription. Each of these ideals – an orderly nature, an egalitarian, evidence-respecting form of inquiry – is admirable. But: are they compatible with each other? In other words, if we heed data and data alone, have we any justification for believing in nature?

Hume made it plain that we did not. The data we possess are fragmentary and incomplete. Above all, they have no hold whatsoever on the future. They cannot guarantee that the future will repeat past regularities; so, if data alone justify our convictions, we have no right whatsoever to believe in the perpetuation of an *orderly* nature. Thus there is no warrant for our rational procedures. Reason may have destroyed nature's rivals and precursors, the coherent theological or magico-ritual visions; but it cannot vindicate its own. The reality of nature cannot be established. By reason's own criteria, we cannot claim to know nature either, any more than we can establish a "cosmos", an interlocking system of social roles and natural concepts. We have no right to suppose that events or things form an orderly system, eligible for successful cognitive exploration.

There is another conflict between the two ladies. If nature is indeed both orderly and all-embracing, she also embraces our own cognitive and moral performances in her orderly system. But if, like the rest of nature, these activities are bound by laws linking them to their antecedents, can these activities really be credited with autonomy, responsibility? Are they *our* activities at all? Being governed by impersonal causal laws, can they be expected to be cognitively valid? They are determined by their causal antecedents, and these are indifferent to rational principle. Our cognitive mechanisms are part of nature and serve its ends, and not those of a unique and universal truth.

The division of labour has endowed cognition with autonomy; autonomous cognition has engendered a nature within which no activity can be autonomous. That is the problem. So our cognitive activities can at best stumble upon truth by accident. The old Western anxiety about being able to attain salvation seemed to be replaced by a similar worry about the possibility of attaining truth. Predetermination replaces predestination.

The problem of the self-devouring nature of reason is a generalized version of the first problem. If reason be defined as the generic faculty for eliciting truths without extraneous aid, can she really conjure up, from her own resources, all those principles – moral and political as well as cognitive – by which we are henceforth to conduct our cognitive and social lives? Hume's central contention was that she could not; Kant accepted the force, and in some measure the conclusions, of Hume's arguments.

The vulgar Enlightenment had hoped and supposed that the

new Outer System would possess the same unquestionable, luminous authority which had surrounded the old hierarchical, revealed Cosmos. They hoped that a new vision would be available, endowed with all the authority which had once characterized the old. It would of course differ in content, and it would be orderly and egalitarian. Nonetheless it would perform the same role for newly liberated humanity that the old vision had performed for mankind enslaved to kings and priests. It would be recognized and explored and validated by its new and distinctive revelation, reason. This would differ from the old authority in not being capricious. It would neither claim nor give rise to privilege.

But all this was not to be. The new revelation turned out to be deeply flawed *by its own criteria and standards*. It could not deliver, or at least it could not guarantee, the goods. The new nature left no room within itself for the new revelation; the new revelation would not vindicate and underwrite nature. The greatest thinkers of the Enlightenment were those who laid bare this internal crisis.

There is also the related problem of universalism and relativism. The new vision claimed universal validity (as indeed had its scriptural religious predecessors and social ancestors). Without such a claim, it could hardly justify its own vigorous and enthusiastic eagerness to proselytise. The encyclopaedic propagandists of Paris knew full well, and with a touch of bitterness and fear, that what seemed self-evident to them had little plausibility, or even intelligibility, for the vulgar, for the masses. They wished to convert all men, but when they contemplated the task of persuading their humbler and less educated fellows, they found the task daunting and awesome. But they had cause to fear not only the credulity of the vulgar, but also the self-corroding critical spirit of their peers.

Yet, at the same time as they attributed universal validity to the new conception of nature, that conception itself included, as an integral part of itself, a view of all knowledge as functional. Knowledge itself is a natural part of the functioning of each biological or social organism. But organisms, of either kind, differ a great deal from each other. Each species can be expected to have its own adaptive cognitive practices and criteria. So, inside nature, one may logically expect cognitive diversity, a general relativism. Each organism or culture could be expected to have its own vision, functional and binding for it and it alone. Yet the vision of nature itself, which inescapably implied this relativist corollary, also supposed itself to be *uniquely* valid. . .

Hume and Kant did not properly face the problem of this kind of relativism. They did, however, possess a solution to the first two problems, which loomed large in their thought. The solutions they offered were rather similar, notwithstanding the fact that histories of philosophy generally present them as doctrinal rivals rather than as allies. Their differences, however, are more in stress and idiom than in real substance. The similarities are far deeper and more important.

The solution is simple. Let us grant that nature, i.e. an orderly and intelligible system, accessible to human comprehension, is in no way self-guaranteeing. Neither nature itself nor some other, higher authority has underwritten or can underwrite the availability of such a system. To require or expect such a guarantee is to suppose that there is some finally and definitively knowable basic reality, which can prescribe in advance of the event what may be discovered by cognitive exploration. To say this is to deny the autonomy of knowledge, and make it subject to a kind of precognitive fundamental or entrenched constitution of the nature of things. Inquiry cannot be both free and guaranteed, reliably underwritten, though many philosophers seem to wish it to be both.

In a world ruled by the sovereignty of knowledge, we no longer look to such higher authority – for how could we *know* of its existence and its legitimate authority? No matter, Hume and Kant argued: we ourselves, *our own minds*, function in such a way as to ensure that *our* knowledge at any rate is of this kind. The warranty is to be found within ourselves, in the constitution of our own minds.

When they spoke of *our* minds, Hume and Kant meant humanity at large. There is, admittedly, a considerable difference in tone between the two thinkers. Hume speaks as if it just so happens that our mind habitually picks out regularities and expects them to persist. It is this psychological regularity of ours which has as its consequence that we see all nature as composed of regularities. A contingent regularity in one small part of nature – our own mental habits – is in a way echoed, multiplied a thousandfold, in nature as a whole. Hume can offer no guarantee that our minds must continue to operate in that fashion. He simply finds that, happily and providentially, they do so. Kant by contrast uses an idiom which, if taken literally, inspires much more confidence: our minds not only have, but are bound to have, a certain kind of structure. This then inevitably guarantees that what we know will have the orderly form which we call *nature*.

The difference between them is less important than their shared attribution, *to our minds*, of that which other, less perceptive thinkers continued to attribute to the external nature of things. Hume and Kant shared the same error: the supposition that all minds were indeed alike. They did not see the mind they described as the culmination of a unique historical development. They perceptively described their own minds, the new emergent intellectual style, and attributed it to all of mankind. Hence they did not, at any rate directly and in the main strand of their work, confront the problem of relativism. They could not do so, because the main solution of their central problem denied the fact of relativism (even if they noticed it in other contexts).

It was left to the nineteenth century to try to cope with this problem. Hume and Kant had codified the general procedures, not of the human mind, as they supposed, but of one kind of human mind: a mind which sees all data as articulated in one single currency, all facts as equal in kind, eligible for symmetrical explanation, with the explanations ideally constituting or at least aspiring to a single system with a unique apex. In this book, we have tried to put forward a schematic account of its historic emergence. It is an important corollary of the vision of such a mind that the facts are not merely equal, but also morally colourless: values, moral rules, whatever source they may have, cannot be underwritten by the unique orderly external system of objects. It was natural for Hume and Kant to solve this problem in a style similar to their vindication of nature: the rules of morality also had their basis in the very constitution of the human mind.

But, in fact, the human mind in general does not resemble the Enlightened mind, which is a distinctive and most unusual historic product. The generic model of primitive mentality we have put forward earlier proposes a multiplicity of sub-systems, each of them morally saturated, and each linked to its social context by its own rules.

Once the Hume/Kant error concerning the alleged universality of the Enlightened mind is recognized as such – and it did not take long for it to become conspicuous – the question arose: given that the new vision is *a* vision and not *the* vision, why should it be preferred? And indeed, *should* it be preferred at all? What, if anything, makes it binding?

The Age of Progress, or Operation Bootstrap

Human diversity could be, and was, invoked as a *solution* as well as a problem. This solution became the most prominent and characteristic philosophy of the nineteenth century – the faith in Progress.

A society had now emerged which, for the very first time in history, was based on sustained, perpetual cognitive and economic growth. Looking backwards, this society thought it could discern a similar continued trend of improvement, culminating in itself. A trend which in the past had sometimes been too small to be perceptible, and was sometimes interrupted by regressions, was now visible and conspicuous, and came to be seen plainly and unmistakably. Looking forward, some thinkers felt justified in expecting that this sustained improvement would continue. The perpetual amelioration was not confined, in the estimation of some, to the spheres of cognition and production. Morals and politics, and all aspects of life, would share in this upward sweep. This conferred a new meaning on life. It constituted a new theodicy, a justification of all tribulations that mankind endured. Bliss in an earthly future, not in the Beyond, compensated for the injustices and tribulations of life. A new theodicy was born.

This vision of Progress solved the problem of relativism, which the simpler form of the Enlightenment could not handle. The idea of Progress does not contest the fact of radical diversity of outlook and spirit amongst different cultures and periods. On the contrary, it requires such diversity and glories in it. It treats it as a starting point. There is indeed diversity: but it is not random or chaotic diversity. The diversity in belief, values, organization or whatever, is arranged along a grand series. The later members of the series constitute a completion, superior continuation, consummation, of the earlier ones. Moreover, by and large, this serial arrangement by merit also corresponds to the temporal series, revealed by recorded history.

Western thought was now ready for a deification of history. History was supposed to reveal, not a random succession of diversity, but a series of continuous and endogenous improvements. History, or even the universe itself, was assumed to resemble a bourgeois life. This was, after all, a bourgeois age. The middle class believes in perpetual education and self-improvement, and history was declared to be the Education of the Human Race (a phrase dating back to the eighteenth century). A bourgeois life is, above all else, a *career*. It is justified primarily or exclusively by the progression in achievement, rank, reputation and wealth. It now transpired that the universe did the same: the world itself was upwardly mobile.

This new kind of philosophy was distinct from both the Platonic and the Cartesian visions. It did not, like the former, construct a transcendent, immobile and authoritative vindication of the organizational and belief patterns of stable agro-literate society. It did not, like the latter, codify an individualist opting-out of culturally enshrined prejudice, an exile which makes possible the instrumentally effective explanation and manipulation of the world. Unlike either style, it accepted and stressed the diversity of cultures, and saw (hazily) the contrast between Platonistic and Cartesian societies. It tried to formulate an overall vision which placed each type in a grand scheme. This scheme would simultaneously explain *and* justify diversity and, above all, confer authority on its general direction. It would vindicate the culmination of this process, which Western man either believed he was already exemplifying, or was due to attain shortly.

The philosophy of Progress was formulated under two successive and separate impacts: that of history, and that of biology. The two could also be combined. The perception that history seemed to have an overall upward pattern initially inspired a general theory of Progress; later, the Darwinian news from biology, to the effect that this upward motion was something true of all life and not only history, generalized and confirmed the lesson.

If this upward surge was the central fact of life, it lent itself admirably to satisfying, in a new and acceptably secular manner, the need which had previously been catered for in large portions of humanity by the great generic salvation faiths. This was the need for a solution to the problem of evil, the reconciliation of man to his world. The world, it seemed, no longer needed an *extraneous* saviour, redeemer and guarantor. It constituted, provided and guaranteed its own salvation. It was saved by processes drawn from within itself and by criteria emanating from and validated by itself. The religion of Progress does indeed provide a superb solution of the problem of evil. Evil is overcome in the end by a basic principle operating *within the world*. But in the short run, evil also provides a kind of necessary spur or obstacle. Without it the achievement of the later good condition would lose much of its flavour, and perhaps not occur at all. So it was a necessary and functional evil after all.

Thus, by means of conceptual resources now drawn entirely from within the world, the old unification of fact and value was temporarily, though rather precariously, restored. The most important version of this kind of theory, in the worlds of both thought and of politics, turned out to be the Hegelo-Marxist one.

World history, it taught, had meaning, direction, and purpose. Change was not mere disruption. The old value/fact fusion would be maintained and completed (Hegel), or alternatively, though it had been spurious in the past, it would at long last be replaced by the genuine article (Marx). The coming condition of humanity would fuse them even more intimately.

In its Marxist form, this vision was destined, of course, to become one of the major world religions. It blends a number of ideas. The most important of these are that the various social forms which mankind has known and is yet to know have a terminal point, which is also morally normative; the various preceding stages are determined primarily by their productive base; they correspond to its development, to its continuous augmentation throughout history; and the terminal stage will be free both of coercive institutions and of private property. Thus, in a curious way, a materialist typology of societies and theory of social dynamics were jointly used to formulate a political messianism, which promised the end of both coercion and illusion.

It was, of course, not the only theory of progress. In France and elsewhere, the Comtian tradition was also prominent. Darwinism inspired a whole new crop of theories, of which Pragmatism was probably the most important. Pragmatism taught that the process of adaptation and elimination, which had begun in a nature red in tooth and claw, was, in principle, perpetuated by mankind in its later cognitive and ethical striving. No overarching unity was needed as a premiss or guarantor or unificator, for these piecemeal adaptations were perfectly self-justifying, or were justified by their success. The Pragmatist dismissal of unifiers, and the passionate commendation of petty adjustments, ironically itself became a great and exceedingly abstract unifier. It is probably the most important indigenous North American philosophy. The Pragmatist vision of sustained and continuous progress was made possible by crediting, most implausibly, primitive man with fairly single-track cognitive activities. Tacitly it retrojected the modern division of labour. It was well suited to a culture endowed with little genuine recollection of an *ancien régime*, from which that division had been absent.

The generic, overall fate and weaknesses of Progress philosophies is what concerns us here. One of them has of course
become the state religion in a very large part of the globe. In
regions where thought has remained free, progress visions have
in the end not fared too well. In the agrarian age, belief systems
could *seem* to give hostages to fortune by their claims, but they
were seldom if ever actually and effectively called to account. The
social and logical protective mechanisms which kept them stable
were aided by the failure of the cognitive capital of the society to
grow significantly. The entire ethos of the society was simply
averse to any sense and expectation of cognitive growth. So the
central and sanctified doctrines were not frequently contested.

Now, all that is changed. The social, historical or biological
neo-metaphysics of the nineteenth century can still, when they
become official belief-systems, benefit from social or outright
coercive protection. They can still evade all contestation as belief
systems always have done. They are well equipped with devices
for doing so. But the merciless growth of knowledge and the
pervasive spirit of criticism expose them to relentless erosion. No
stable faith can be extracted either from the patterns of history or
from those of biology. Such patterns are too precarious to sustain
such a load of moral authority.

This last great generation of metaphysics, of the systematic
underwriting of this world, was a hybrid breed. These systems
still underwrote our order by something Higher. But this time
that Higher Validation was, more or less ambiguously, merely
the deeper and permanent currents of *this* world. These alleged
currents were sufficiently of this world not to be dualistic in the
old religious way, and not to offend our sense of the unity of
nature. At the same time they were meant to be sufficiently deep
and permanent and distant from the humdrum daily issues to
address us with authority. These systems have, of course, not
disappeared altogether; at least one of them seems destined to
remain as a major historic presence for a long time. But their time
has gone, and they have lost their bloom. Our current ideological
perturbation springs not from the death of God, but from the
demise of these nineteenth-century God-surrogates.

CHAPTER 6

The Coercive Order and its Erosion

Patterns of Power

We have followed the transformation of the first great sphere of human activity, cognition, across the crucial stages of the division of labour: from hunting/gathering to Agraria, and from Agraria to industrial capitalism. What, meanwhile, was happening to coercion? How did patterns of power relate to the developments in man's cognitive world? How, above all, did the agrarian age, in which coercion or predation was the central theme and value of life, give rise to the industrial age, in which production took over as the dominant theme and changed the whole organization and ethos of society?

In pre-agrarian societies, devoid of stored wealth, no very clear sense can be attributed to power and domination. A man who does not provide for his own future, and who possesses no means for safeguarding the future, has only limited incentives for suborning others. Domination for immediate, non-delayed ends and for acquisition of status obviously can and does occur; but to what extent can it engender a permanent and impersonal stratification of power? The small scale of the society reinforces the barriers set up by the lack of permanent, storable resources.

The situation changes drastically with the emergence of agriculture. Storable goods constitute a surplus. With the existence of stored value, power in a serious sense becomes not merely possible, but mandatory. Plato noted that it was the existence of a surplus which made defence and order-enforcement unavoidable. Basically, you own what you can defend, physically or socially. Property and power are correlative notions. You can defend property by direct force, or by invoking social rules which are themselves sanctioned by force. Domination in a propertyless society is not inconceivable. But there is clearly a limit to the persistence or elaborateness or scale of such domination. But there is no such limit, once material wealth makes its appearance.

The agricultural revolution gave birth to extensive storage and wealth and thereby turned power into an unavoidable aspect of social life. No set of rules for the distribution of a surplus can be either self-evident or self-implementing. Mechanisms must exist for protecting resources, and for enforcing the "equitable" or approved distribution of their fruits. So Power is born, and becomes the inescapable accompaniment of social order.

Roughly speaking, power can be divided into primary and secondary. Primary power is exemplified by a man directly coercing another by a physical threat. Secondary power occurs when a man uses a socially imposed rule to bend the will of another, say by threatening to publicize an accusation which will lead to some kind of punishment. In this second case, the effectiveness of the threat depends on the reliability of the implementation of the social rule. A social regularity is used as a lever. The lever itself depends only indirectly (if at all) on the threat of actual force. A violation of the rule itself may be sanctioned by force, or may in turn depend on further social conventions. It may be that such a circle of mutually reinforcing rules is never put to the test by systematic defiance.

Primary coercion is fairly rare, and pure primary coercion, in which nothing but the immediate balance of force comes into play, is very rare, though it is important. Social rules and the reliance on them can be assumed to be present and important in all human societies. If it were the case, however, as used to be maintained by some anthropologists, that primitive man stands in utter awe of rules which he holds to be supernaturally sanctioned, it would follow that reverence for rules had been quite specially important in the lives of early men. There are, however, some grounds for doubting such a theory: even in simpler societies, rules need to be sustained by social mechanisms as well as by faith, and the breach even of sacred rules is not unknown. Internalization of norms, and material sanctions, are *both* present. The manner in which the use of force, and the invocation of automatically respected rules, interact and complement each other varies a good deal in different types of society.

Once the concrete problem of power arises, there are two extreme, polar solutions: the concentration of power, or a balance of power. The logic of each of these solutions is fairly obvious.

The path which leads to the concentration of power is simple: if two or more men are potentially in conflict, because one or more of them possesses resources which the other could usefully seize, it is very much to the advantage of either or any participant to take pre-emptive action. He should make use of any advantage he may temporarily possess. Unless he does so first, it will eventually be done unto him. This knowledge, shared by all, escalates the conflict. After all, if you know that your opponent will reach deeper into the armoury if he is in danger of defeat, you might as well anticipate him and use your own armoury to the full, from the start. You cannot lose thereby, and you may win. This mechanism presumably accounts for the fact that most agrarian societies are authoritarian.

The logic of the situation imposes a kind of ruthless eliminatory struggle on the participants. One can see this re-enacted in any society in which a revolution destroys the old recognized centre of legitimacy and the old circle of mutually reinforcing convention: competing new self-proclaimed authorities emerge, none of which is yet hallowed by age. The one which can destroy or intimidate the others most effectively eventually concentrates power in its own hands. The Reign of Terror is not a corruption, a betrayal, a "distortion" of the Revolution: it is its natural corollary. A time-hallowed regime is clearly distinguished from its would-be supplanters, and may need no extreme measures to affirm its authority. A new centre of power has nothing to elevate it above its rivals, other than its capacity to intimidate more convincingly. The re-establishment of order is generally far more violent than its mere maintenance. Minor participants have the option of either taking part in this lethal conflict, or making their submission to whoever seems likely to end as the victor. These submissions to the victor fortify his position, and may snowball until one authority really does become unassailable.

The unpredictability of outcome of violent conflict hinges on its being genuinely total in its violence and unmindful of rules. Much *seemingly* violent conflict, on the other hand, though blood may be spilt, is in fact heavily ritualized, and not genuinely total. Some tribes, for instance, observe a feuding season, selected so as not to interfere with the harvest. The pervasive rules ensure that there is much joyful conflict, with relatively little loss of life. Nonetheless, genuinely violent and rule-defying conflict is always a danger, and occurs often enough. In such conflicts, unpredictability of outcome becomes very significant. Either party may prefer to refrain from conflict or escalation, given the uncertainty of outcome; better give up the hope of victory than risk the danger of defeat. In such cases, a balance-of-power situation may ensue.

Unpredictability may, however, be increased by a larger number of potential participants and the fluidity of alliances. New allies may flock to the winning side; the winning side is identified by its capacity to attract allies. It may attract them because it is "in the right", and because it is endorsed by the legitimation-specialists of the culture in question. This then leads to a Single Victor situation and a concentration of power. The party with the more meritorious case may attract allies/supporters not because all the other members of the society have a deep thirst for righteousness, and an unwavering faith in the verdict of the clerics or shamans, but because they know or suspect that other waverers are also eager to be on the winning side. Attention to endorsement by the official legitimators may be the best way of picking winners. The endorsement crystallizes the collective support which transforms mere contestants into winners. This is of great importance when considering the relative power of warriors and clerics.

There is, however, the alternative possibility, another path to relative equilibrium. Two opponents may be fairly evenly matched or highly uncertain of the outcome of any possible conflict, and may prefer to abstain from attacking each other, by virtue of a tacit or an explicit truce. Thus communities may grow up within which a more or less – far from complete – stable balance of power is maintained.

Intermediate or mixed situations can of course arise. Escalation/elimination with a single final victor, and an even balance of power between participants, are the two polar extreme possibilities. Complex situations can arise which combine elements drawn from the extreme situations. For instance, a total concentration of power may arise in the relation between two communities – a kind of Spartan/helot relation – while at the same time a balance of power may obtain *within* the dominant group. Or again, a unique central authority may dominate local communities and expropriate their surplus, but prefer to grant them a certain autonomy: it may be easier to let them administer themselves. Direct rule might be arduous and actually diminish output. So, while the central state may possess a sharply defined power apex, the local communities it dominates may be fairly egalitarian internally. They may practise an internal balance of power which is wholly absent from their collective relation with their overlords.

One might accept as a provisional hypothesis that concentration of power will generally obtain, unless special countervailing factors operate. The balance of power is precarious and, once disturbed, will not be re-established. It would be madness for the beneficiaries of a temporary advantage not to push it to the point where it becomes permanent. Why give a defeated rival the chance of a comeback? The majority of agrarian societies do indeed exemplify great economic inequality and a jealous, exclusive concentration of power. What kinds of factors are liable to operate against this usual coagulation of power in a single centre?

Pastoral societies, especially (but not exclusively) when nomadic, provide a milieu within which centralization of power, though not unknown, tends, when it does occur, to be short-lived, ephemeral, and to lead, after a fairly short time, to a return to the initial, uncentralized situation.[1] The explanation is not far to seek: though pastoral societies possess storable wealth, it is *mobile* wealth, and those who own it may escape the dilemma of the pre-emptive conflict. They do not need to become either oppressors or oppressed, and they can flee those who would oppress them.

Something similar is true of peasant societies in difficult terrain. Generally speaking, peasants are tied to their fields and therefore eminently exploitable: they cannot run away. Nevertheless, if their fields are located in terrain that is difficult of access, then the imposition of domination may be too arduous to be worthwhile. In such circumstances autonomous, fairly egalitarian and uncentralized peasant communities are not uncommon.

Another example of power diffusion arises from upper layer fragmentation. The central authority may be capable of subjugating distant regions, but, having done so, is faced with the problem of their ongoing exploitation. Ideally, it could do so by temporarily delegating authority to revocable local representatives. This is the bureaucratic solution – i.e. rule by temporary nominees, whose delegated authority springs from the centre, and can be terminated at will.

But this ideal is not always practicable, and is often corrupted. Just as rulers may prefer to govern whole peasant communities, who simplify the task of administration by taking on local duties, so the central authority may also prefer to rule through locally recruited nominees, who already possess a power base in the area. Alternatively, men who began their careers as central nominees are liable to acquire and develop a local power base with time. Central authority is faced with a virtually insoluble dilemma: if its local representatives are weak, they will not be able to defend their fief against external enemies or internal rebellion. If, however, they are strong, they will acquire an independent power base, and will eventually be able to act independently.

When this latter process goes far, it reaches a situation in which the ruling stratum of local warrior/administrators has become fragmented, with its individual members fairly independent of central authority and totally independent of each other. When this situation becomes formally recognized, and ratified by an ethos, formal rituals, and a set of rules and laws, we have the phenomenon of "feudalism".

Or, again, there are urban communities, and, in particular, trading towns. Not all cities are inhabited primarily by traders or other non-agricultural producers, and most certainly cities do not in general constitute exceptions to our baseline hypothesis, i.e. the presumption of the concentration of power. But some do; and they are, perhaps, the most important single phenomenon within the agrarian world, for they appear to constitute the one and only exit point from agrarian social organization.

Pastoral communities may exemplify widespread political and cultural participation, but they are certainly incapable of transforming themselves into something else, let alone transforming themselves and retaining those virtues. The same is true of independent peasant communities, though they may, in alliance with trading towns, make their contribution to social transformation. Feudal diffusion of power and formal ratification of privilege may also have made its contribution to accountable, law-bound government, by inculcating the notion of rights and of contractual government.

But most of these social forms share a certain negative trait. They may oblige their participants to be simultaneously producers and warriors (tribal and independent peasant communities), in which case the heavy load of *social* duties inhibits the division of labour: this kind of society is indeed characteristically given to despising the trading or artisan specialist. Alternatively, such societies may polarize their members into severely distinct producers and warriors. Neither oppressed populations, nor men imbued with the participatory military ethos and a contempt for specialists, are likely to become economic innovators. And the same is true of those who combine violence with production. What seemed to be needed, for a radical breakthrough and an escape from the agrarian impasse, was men who were producers and who did not double up as coercion-specialists, but who nevertheless escaped oppression. Is that possible? Generally speaking, it goes against the logic of an agrarian society.

Egalitarian, participatory communities manage their internal affairs, and ensure their external defence, by requiring and instilling a strong sense of loyalty, generally organized in a series of nested, "segmentary" units and sub-units. These are frequently, though not universally, self-conceived as kin groups. The obligations of loyalty are generally seen as arising from shared *blood* or *bone* (the myth of the physiological incarnation of shared identity varies). The kin links may or may not be genuine and, contrary to what is sometimes supposed, tribesmen often know them to be fictions. But in a cultural sense, such "republics of cousins" are as constraining, albeit in a different way, as oppression by a central ruler. Much of mankind faces the dilemma of being constrained by either king or cousin, and some men are oppressed by both. The question is – is there a way of escaping both kings and cousins?

Towns can simply be administrative centres, or ritual religious centres, or combinations of the two. Even when they are centres of trade and artisan production, they are not necessarily independent. Even if they are independent and trade-oriented, protection of their own trade may make them trade-protectors as much as traders, and this may lead to a concentration of power. When all these possibilities are set aside, there remains an important residue of urban societies which are production-oriented and not politically over-centralized.

An authoritarian single-ruler trading centre is not inconceivable, nor without historic exemplars. In fact, it is a common form in certain early stages of commerce between a barbarian hinterland and a more developed centre. Both early medieval northern and eastern Europe, and parts of black Africa on the periphery of Arab and European expansion, developed ephemeral trading mini-states of this kind. This is all the more likely to happen when the trade is not in diverse manufactured goods but in a few valuable luxury commodities – slaves, precious metals.[2]

But diversified trade which handles multiple goods, is related

PATTERNS OF POWER

to production, and copes with changes in a complex market, cannot easily be run in this manner. The complexity of the operation requires autonomous activities of numerous and independent traders. The relationship of such traders to each other is in some ways at least similar to that of fellow pastoralists or mountain peasants. They will incline towards a political balance of power rather than to escalation and pre-emption.

In fact, they have an even stronger incentive towards such a solution than do egalitarian tribesmen. The latter may find themselves in a zero-sum situation, in which the material gain of one can only be at the cost of the loss of another; but, owing to the unpredictability of the outcome, each side agrees to refrain from aggression. They also benefit from the mutual insurance against outside aggression which they provide for each other. In conflicts between traders, these considerations – uncertainty of outcome in internal conflict, mutual help in external conflict – also apply; but on top of that, there is the consideration that the game is *not* zero-sum. If the trading town prospers, each citizen does not prosper merely in proportion to the destitution of some other citizen. They can prosper *jointly*. The prosperity of some can be the basis for the prosperity of others.

Egalitarian tribesmen retain their freedom and their equality through a very high Military Participation Ratio, in S. Andreski's useful phrase.[3] They all have the duty, or the proud privilege, of taking part in inflicting and resisting violence. In fact, they tend to keep their hand in by fairly continuous feuds, just as the feudal warrior class keeps its hand in by petty private wars between each other, and by bloodthirsty games.

Urban trading communities may call on their citizens to take part in the common defence of the city, and will in extremity do so. Nonetheless, they will be less eager to do it continuously, and make less of a song and dance about it. The practice of violence will not pervade their ethos. Quite often, they will not be averse to employing mercenaries. The reason is simple: excellence in trade or production, like excellence in most other activities, requires concentration, and a really good performance may well take up most of the practitioner's time. A pastoralist does not mind giving up much of his time to practising violence – minding the flocks leaves him the required leisure. In any case, minding flocks against depredations by wild animals or, above all, by other shepherds, in any case constitutes a permanent training in violence. But if you wish to concentrate on subtle movements of the market or on your ledger, taking off too much time on archery practice or the TA may turn out to be tedious. Excellence calls for specialization, and specialization has its price.

So some urban trading communities will have a balance-of-power type of government (which can of course be very far removed from a general egalitarianism and wide and full participation). They may be free from that complete commitment to glorification of violent "honour" which otherwise often pervades the agrarian world. It is this type of society, and apparently this type of society only, which seems to be capable, in very favourable and possibly unique circumstances, of becoming the agent of a breakthrough out of the agrarian world. It can terminate the domination by the Red and the Black, the Warriors and the Clerics.

Conditions of the Exit

Agrarian society is doomed to violence. It stores valuable concentrations of wealth, which must needs be defended, and the distribution of which has to be enforced. The wealth is never reliably sufficient: agrarian society is Malthusian, impelled by the need for productive and defensive manpower to expand its population close to the margin. It values offspring or at least male offspring, and periodic famines are more or less inevitable. Then the grain-store citadels *must* be defended, whatever form they take. Malthus did not perhaps stress sufficiently the political consequences of social strategies of distribution *and* the existence of a store, which Plato saw clearly. The Malthusian picture suggests a free humanity, starving at the social margin. England in the early nineteenth century may have been such a society. But during the agrarian age, most of mankind was not free and on the edge of starvation. It was oppressed and half-starving. It starved in accordance with rank. The ranking was enforced, but it also constituted an instrument of social control. Men were constrained by the desire to retain or improve their station.

The logic of the situation is reinforced as well as reflected by the pervasive ethos of the agrarian world. It very seldom places a high valuation on work: it would be strange to do so, given that work is what is imposed upon the lower orders of society. Work is sometimes commended for others, so that they should deliver tithe or tax to their betters; it is seldom proudly acclaimed in the first person. The dominant values are the values of the dominant class. The Marxist formula, not always valid for the sphere ("ideas") where it was originally formulated, has some plausibility when it is applied to the normative ethos. The agrarian world cannot but commend the life style of its dominant strata, and it does so by enthusiastic precept as well as by example. It tends to have an exemplary class if not an exemplary state.[4]

It does not always place violence at the summit of excellence, though the Western equation of nobility with military vocation does so. Sometimes it places the scribes/legitimators above the swordsmen, though we must remember that it is the scribes who write the record and formulate the principles. On the other hand, they are often not above pandering to the vanity of their more forceful masters. They do not always, like Plato or the Brahmins, endeavour to sell a social programme which elevates their own class to the top. The Brahmins persuaded the warriors to accept a lower ranking, though in practice the ruler-warriors controlled the details of caste-ordering.[5] The Brahmins, incredibly, persuaded conquering herders to accept the sacredness and inviolability of the cow. It is said that overcome revulsions make the greatest pleasures: by the same token, the prohibition of the greatest pleasure may be the most potent expression of moral ascendancy. When beef-eaters were turned into cow-worshippers, the authority of priests was well and truly demonstrated.

Agraria does on occasion invert values. They may conspicuously defy, rather than mirror, the social hierarchy. It may commend ascesis or humility rather than display, conspicuous consumption, and assertiveness. These inversions of values, of the utmost importance in the history of mankind, can be seen in part as devices employed by rival elements within the wider clerisy. One way the legitimators gain influence and power is by being outside the formal system, by opting out, and ascesis or humility constitutes a kind of conspicuous self-exile. The logic of the agrarian world, however, does not allow such values to be implemented consistently and universally. The one occasion on which a deviant set of values did indeed become generalized over a society was also the occasion when mankind escaped from the constraints of agrarian civilizations.

The sword is mightier than the plough. Those who habitually, professionally, acquire and maintain an expertise in handling the sword can normally be expected to be more proficient at handling it than ploughmen who only handle it intermittently and *in extremis*. Sometimes, of course, in free peasant communities, ploughmen are also swordsmen, as was the case in early Rome. Hussite farmers in fifteenth-century Bohemia beat the hell out of the feudal crusaders sent against them. But that is exceptional.

The equilibrium situation seldom lasts. The swordsmen prevail, and have little incentive to allow the henceforth defenceless producers more than is required to keep them going and producing. In the early Ottoman Empire, a simple and elegant political theory was formulated which sums up, lucidly and adequately, the general condition of agrarian society. The rulers are there to keep the peace, so that the producers can produce. The producers, who benefit from the peace, must pay taxes so as to keep the rulers and their apparatus going. This is the Circle of Equity. This doctrine preceded and differed from the Labour Theory of Value, by claiming a share for peace-keepers as the just price for their contribution to value-creation. Sociologically it was far more profound. A theory of value which concentrates exclusively on the labour which is "mixed with" the product, and ignores the coercion which is also inescapably mixed into it, does so at its peril. The Ottoman Empire was more typical of the human condition than was nineteenth-century England, and its theorists understood the relation between force and value better than did Marx.

In these general conditions the question of how much the ruled should grant to the rulers, the specification of a just or a minimum price for keeping the peace, hardly arises. Any views the ruled have on this matter are of largely academic interest. They are not consulted. The rulers are free to take what they can or what they wish.

No doubt there is a great deal of variety in this matter. Cunning, custom, and alliance may conspire to enable members of society other than coercion specialists to retain more than the minimum which they would retain in virtue of the simple balance of power. One of the most important roles of religion in agrarian society is, precisely, to enable the ruled to hang on to a proportion of the accumulated wealth. The rulers need religious personnel for legitimation or cohesion or arbitration, and hence the ruled can then also use the prestige of religion to protect some wealth from confiscation. Competition between rival rulers may help the ruled: rival contestants may vie for support by offering better terms. All in all, however, these various devices and stratagems do not modify the basic situation very much. In general, agrarian society is marked by a concentration of wealth amongst the coercion-and-salvation-monopolizing rulers, and by poverty amongst the ruled.

Can some cunning members of the ruled classes not occasionally dissimulate the possession of wealth, employ it to hire swordsmen, and displace the rulers? Certainly this can and does happen. But when it does happen, there is no incentive whatever for the new rulers, the erstwhile ruled, not to behave precisely in the same manner as their ruler-predecessors. Why on earth continue to toil in the production of wealth? It is arduous and perilous. The management and deployment and enjoyment of power is incomparably more attractive. In medieval Spain, it was affirmed that warfare against the infidel was both a quicker *and* a more honourable path to wealth than productive activity. And so it is. If a reversal of fortune, a turn in the political wheel, does occur, it merely rotates the personnel, but does not modify the overall structure or ethos.

Our problem is to understand how, on one occasion at any rate, the entire structure can be modified, as opposed to a mere change of personnel within it. How can it happen not merely that the weak, the swordless, overcome the swordsmen, but that the whole organization and ethos of society changes, that Production replaces Predation as the central theme and value of life? Everything in the standard condition of agrarian society militates against such a miracle. Yet it did happen. In consequence, the world became transformed out of all recognition. How could it happen?

There are various candidate explanations which, perhaps in some combination, may provide the answer.

1 *Feudalism as the matrix of capitalism.* Under the feudal system, a small stratum of professional warriors, each with a local base, monopolizes warfare and government, but owes loyalty, nominal or other, to a central monarch. The relationships between members of various levels in this stratified structure are, however, ideally and in principle, contractual. Though governed by status and not contract, feudalism nevertheless allows and even affirms a curious free market in loyalty, with land leased in return for a commitment to loyal service. Status determines what kind of contract is open to a man, but allows him some leeway in choosing his contractual partners from a given status group. This model of contractual and binding relationships sets an important precedent.

Urban trading and artisan centres grow up, under the protection of local or central rulers. They develop autonomy, because it is easier and more expeditious for the tax-gathering ruler to make a compact with such communities, allowing them to collect their own taxes. This may mean he gets less, but it may also mean that he gets it sooner and with less trouble. He may in fact get more in return for granting greater liberties, and more still if the beneficiaries of the liberties prosper in their enjoyment. Conflict eventually arises between central ruler and local barons.

The central ruler allies himself with the burghers who have acquired a weight of their own, breaks the power of local barons, and effectively centralizes the society. The question, however, remains: when he has done so, what prevents him from re-establishing a centralized version of the old domination of force over wealth?

2 *Church/state dualism.* During the medieval fragmentation of power, a dual system emerges, in which a centralized clerisy acquires a monopoly of legitimacy, at the cost of abjuring (in most places) direct temporal power. The fragmented temporal power selects its ruling personnel by *legitimate* birth, whilst the Church acquires the monopoly of legitimating procreative unions.[6] Though the Church possesses relatively little military power, its diffusion among many temporal domains makes it at least an even match for most of them in isolation, and, on occasion, even for the largest and strongest among them. Canossa can occur. The separation of ultimate legitimacy and immediate political authority sets limits to the rapaciousness of the state. Note that, once again, this explanation on its own is of little avail. A re-affirmation of the power and independence of the Church in the Counter-Reformation had effects quite different from those we seek to explain.

3 *The restrained state.* For various possible reasons, the successful centralizing state which followed feudal fragmentation was law-abiding rather than confiscatory. It may have been due to a cultural survival related to the Roman legal heritage.[7] It may, more plausibly, be connected with the fact that the new commercial and eventually industrial wealth is confiscation-elusive or fragile. Unlike a sack of potatoes, it cannot easily be seized, and, if interfered with, it withers.[8] The rulers may have found that the tax-potential of their subjects diminishes if they are brazenly or arbitrarily oppressed. A state of this kind is in military competition with other similar states. Its strength depends on financial resources. Presiding as it does over a partly commercial society, its fiscal income is greater if the subjects prosper. Prosperity depends on a measure of security and liberty.

Excessive tax demands or arbitrariness are counter-productive, as those who manage the state realize. The law-abiding state may in such circumstances become stronger than an arbitrary one.

4 *The restrained burghers.* In the traditional situation, the rulers are oppressive and pre-emptive not merely from rapacity, but also from perfectly rational caution. If they do not dispossess the *nouveaux riches*, the *nouveaux riches* will dispossess them. But those endowed with the Protestant work ethic not merely ploughed back profits, but also had a tendency not to turn them into conspicuous display, prestige, power. Admittedly the English Protestant extremists did have a go at an ideological revolution; but when it failed, they turned to pacifism, and contented themselves with demanding toleration rather than aspiring to domination. This bourgeoisie at least was not revolutionary, and thus made it possible for the old rulers to make an accommodation with it.

5 *The permeable aristocracy.* An aristocracy which was not a severely circumscribed caste or estate, but which on the contrary was given to primogeniture and the elimination of its own younger sons, may have been amenable to fraternizing with the new wealth, rather than combating it. An eagerness to locate younger sons in productive activities may well go with a willingness to absorb wealth in the form of dowries. The widely held thesis of the permeability of the English aristocracy has been challenged,[9] but the issue remains open, and the idea retains its plausibility.

6 *The availability of an expanding bribery fund.* In the early stages, the new production-oriented order needed to bribe the old rulers to keep them happy; in the later stages, it had to bribe downwards rather than upwards, and placate the new urban poor.

A mere shift to commercialism, even if favoured by the sudden opening of new markets, and favourable political circumstances internally and externally, would not have possessed the means for buying off opposition, if total resources had not been expanding. It is difficult to imagine the emergence of the new order in conditions approximating to an economic zero-sum game, or even in conditions where the diminishing increment was turning it into a zero-plus game.[10] What made this expansion possible?

7 *The rising ceiling of discovery.* The precondition of the expanding bribery fund was the lifting of the ceiling of available technical discovery.

Any given society has a certain technical equipment. Given this, one could construct the range of innovations and improvements which are plausibly within the reach of the society in question. A society possessing one kind of tool can, one must assume, devise a tool which employs much the same materials and principles, but in a more effective manner. The specification of this hypothetical, counter-factual "ceiling of available discoveries" is of course a bit tricky. This notion could easily become circular. If we include "unwillingness to seek or deploy a given innovation" amongst the constraints, we could easily end up with the conclusion that, for every society, the ceiling is set firmly on its head: the society can have no equipment other than the one it actually has. Equally, one could place the ceiling too high, and credit the society with an excessive potential. But there is no need to use the notion in either an over-restrictive or an over-liberal way. Notwithstanding an element of arbitrariness, one might roughly specify such ceilings of possibility in given societies.

The contention is that, for most societies, this ceiling is located rather low, only just above their heads. They can conceive of and utilize innovations, but they lack a sense of the possibility of sustained and radical innovation. This spirit, the emergence of sustained scientific and technological growth, coincided with the march of producers towards social domination. It provided them, eventually, with that expanding bribery fund without which they could hardly have prevailed.

One may refine this argument by saying that the ceiling had to be relatively *low* in the early stages of the transition; and moreover it rose and had to rise – if the miracle was to occur – at the right moment. *It had to be fairly low at the start* if it was not to have excessively dramatic and presumably counter-productive political repercussions.

An excessively early and sudden surge of technological power would presumably have had one of the following consequences: it would have alerted the beneficiaries of the *ancien régime* to the need to take pre-emptive measures. It could also have tempted them, or those who controlled the new power, to use it to impose an easy political domination. This would then have removed the incentives to further economic and cognitive growth. Something of this kind does indeed happen when backward societies are dominated by states which borrow techniques of coercion from outside. It was an important feature of the early stages of growth that it did not (yet) either frighten or attract those who think primarily in terms of power. However, the eventual conquest of the world by the new social order was contingent on a dramatic acceleration of the growth of new technology in the nineteenth century, which enabled the producer nations to dominate the old predators without even trying very hard. They did so in a state of absence of mind, as the famous phrase goes. At the same time they could use it to mollify the internal discontent which, according to the most celebrated analyst of the new order, was doomed eventually to destroy it.

8 *Free peasants are alive and well.* Within the agrarian world, the trend to the concentration of power can, on occasion, be avoided by communities of more or less free and equal producers, who succeed in running their own affairs. They do so by preserving an intra-communal balance of power. But this kind of society does not constitute a possible path, an exit, from agrarian stagnation. Cousins are as stifling as kings. These societies tend to have a strongly anti-individualistic, communal ethos, valuing loyalty to clan above other virtues.

Societies of this kind are implausible catalysts of modernity. One may admire the brave stand of the Swiss mountain cantons against Habsburg autocracy, but one may well doubt whether it contributed significantly to the emergence of modern Europe. Freedom may indeed have two voices, but that of the mercantile sea was heard more clearly than that of the mountains. As for other semi-autonomous, participatory, feud-addicted mountain tribesmen who managed to survive late in European history, whether in the Scottish Highlands, Corsica, the Abruzzi or the Balkans, it is distinctly hard to enlist them as soldiers of Enlightenment. They have a marked tendency to fight on the wrong side, as they do to this day in the Yemen. David Hume, who knew what the Enlightenment was about, and who its enemies were, described the five thousand Highlanders who followed Bonnie Prince Charlie to Derby as the bravest and worst inhabitants of Britain. It is possible, indeed almost irresistible, to romanticize such people, but only when they have first been safely neutralized.

In its general form, I find this argument convincing. Nevertheless, a case has recently been put forward which in a way enlists free farmers on the side of modernity.[11] In abbreviated and hence inevitably simplified form, it runs roughly as follows. In crucial parts of northwest Europe, within which later an individualistic and production-oriented civilization emerged, fairly free and individualistic agricultural producers survived, never fully losing their independence. They were not really reduced to servility; strangely, they were not over-socialized into kin groups either. They somehow escaped the dilemma of being imbued either with the spirit of clan-loyalty or with servitude. Their kinship pattern was surprisingly individualistic.[12] The contrary assumption about the medieval situation in this region is, on this view, at least in part the fruit of the nineteenth-century assumption that pre-modern peasants in this area *had* to resemble the backward peasants found in the nineteenth century in Eastern Europe, India and elsewhere.

On this view, the peasants of the privileged parts of northwest Europe weren't, strictly speaking, "peasants" at all – they were tied neither to land nor to kin units, nor were they supinely submissive to an upper stratum of monopolists of violence or faith. This thesis claims for this privileged super-peasantry a liberty *both* from rulers and from kin units.[13] The greatest difficulty this thesis faces, perhaps, is that it merely pushes the question one step further back. Just how did it come about that this privileged set of people developed, and were allowed to develop and maintain a spirit which, in the context of wider history, is so very unusual? How did they escape the logic of the agrarian situation, which prevails in most other parts of the world? In a subsequent work, an explanation is suggested: the Christian hostility to the flesh is superimposed on a relatively loose bilateral kinship system. This confers social respectability on celibacy. By bestowing honour on the unmarried state, it frees men from marriage as a means of reinforcing and perpetuating the kin group. Men who marry from calculation, not obligation, in a voluntaristic way, are better accumulators, can escape from or diminish Malthusian population pressure, and their "rational" spirit is liable also to spill over into their productive activities.[14]

Despite the difficulties it faces, the case has been powerfully argued and has not been demolished by its critics. This of course is not the same as saying that it has been positively established. So the possibility that an endogenous former individualism has made a direct contribution to the emergence of productive, non-predatory society deserves serious consideration.

9 *The clerical origins of individualism, I.* An interesting theory of the emergence of individualism has been put forward by Louis Dumont, arising from his comparative work on South Asian and European societies. Dumont works with a double opposition: hierarchy/equality and holism/individualism.[15] Only the West ended with a society that was both egalitarian and individualist. India was hierarchical and holistic. The question is – how could one move from one pole to the other? India, on Dumont's argument, was a social order in which an individualist escape from a rigidly ascribed place in a hierarchical and king-dominated world was possible, but only at the price of isolation. It is possible to escape from the dictates of caste, but only into religious ascesis.

The first deviant step away from this stark dilemma was taken by the European tradition when the Church centralized and controlled such opting out. It replaced monk/hermits by monastic communities. The second crucial step took place when this organization of centrally administered escapees from the social world was deprived of monopoly, and became universalized by the Reformation. You might sum up this story as follows: first, dissidents out (of society); next, all dissidents into well-supervised rule-bound hostels; third, with the reformed generalization of priesthood, everyone may be a dissident, and opt out of prescribed and ascribed roles. No further supervision or restriction on individualism. In this way, an unrestrained, socially pervasive individualism is born.

The entry of the Church into the world had modified the situation: a kingly priest, on this view, was basically different from the previous priestly kings. Despite the political involvement, the ideal of an individual directly related to the deity was preserved. When the politically involved Church, upholding this vision, in some places disbanded itself by the Reformation, an individualist society became possible.[16]

The trouble with this theory is, of course, that the second step is in no way restricted to the Western tradition. Monastic communities are very common elsewhere. The doctrine that the monastic condition should be generalized, an aspiration in that direction, can also be found elsewhere. On occasion, monasticism in fact expands in a cancerous manner and absorbs an astonishing proportion of the total society. What *is* lacking elsewhere is not an aspiration towards reformation, but its successful and *unreversed* implementation. Islam too preaches the direct relation of individuals to the deity. But generally attempts at reformation are quickly followed by a reversal, a backsliding to the earlier condition. Social pressures making for a clerisy distinct from civil society are too strong. So the success of one particular Reformation, the presence of a bed on which the seedlings of individualism could flourish, needs to be explained. Perhaps this account presupposes, rather than explains, the idiosyncratic individualism of the West.[17]

10 *The clerical origins of individualism, II.* An interesting alternative individualism-engendering role is ascribed to the

Church by Jack Goody.[18] The barbarian tribesmen who overran Europe at the collapse of the Roman Empire are assumed to have arrived as self-perpetuating kin groups. Much the same may be assumed to be true of many of those whom they conquered, and with whom they eventually melded. So, the social organization of early modern Europe did not yet differ significantly from what is found in other parts of the agrarian world.

But, at a certain period, the Church began to impose a wide variety of marriage restrictions on the faithful. The curious thing about these restrictions was that many of them lacked biblical warrant. Why should the Church see fit to interfere with custom-hallowed patterns of preferential marriage, which helped to maintain kin units? Why should it invent new rules and prohibitions? Why should it feel called upon to extend the range of God's laws?

The answer may be found in the consequences of the imposition of such rules. What if the break-up of the kin group was not an accidental consequence, but a (semi-conscious?) function of such prohibitions? Unable to seek brides along quasi-tribal lines, individuals became isolated. The links that bound them to their more distant kin became eroded. Such kin links are kept alive by the need for joint defence and by the requirement of brides, by the exchange or rotation of women. Joint violence by peasants was curbed by the nobility anyway, except for outlying and ill-governed regions. But the nobility was presumably unconcerned with the patterns of peasant mating as such.

For the Church, on the other hand, the atomizing of the kinship structure had important consequences. The argument hinges on the coincidence of the imposition of the new restrictive rules, and the growth of the Church as a European landowner. Atomized, isolated individuals, unbound by kin obligations to units, when faced with approaching death, are rather more likely to leave some or all of their wealth to the Church. They might refrain from doing this if they have direct offspring of their own, but the accidents of disease and demography must have ensured that in any one generation a significant proportion of those about to die were not blessed with progeny. They were now faced with the alternative of seeing their lands go to people about whom they cared little, or of having them re-assigned by political superiors, or on the other hand of enhancing both their own spiritual status and their post-mortal prospects by bequeathing them to the Church. The last option must often have been the most attractive. Thus, a kind of individualistic society could arise in consequence of the restrictive marriage rules, which at the same time enormously benefited the Church.

The Church may perhaps be free of any special animus against the *Gemeinschaft* of kinship, but not to be indifferent to its own enrichment. In agrarian societies generally, the authority of religious institutions provides one possibility of protecting property against depredation by the powerful. The linking of property to religious endowments is a widely used device for protecting it. By making any subsequent act of confiscation simultaneously an act of impiety, eager would-be confiscators may be restrained. So, the clerisy and civil society may be in collusion and limit political arbitrariness. On this argument, however, the Church on this occasion secured an enormous transfer of landed property to itself, by means of imposing a new set of marriage restrictions.

The irony of this account, if valid, lies in the manner in which the Church helped dig its own grave, by indirectly engendering an individualism which later helped to dismantle the Church itself. The account, of course, faces difficulties: why did the Church fail to erode kin groups in those southern areas where it also later maintained itself best? However, if the Church undermined its own position by success, perhaps it is not puzzling that it also survived best in regions where its kin-atomizing mission succeeded least.

11 *The direct Protestant ethic thesis.* This is the most celebrated of doctrines concerning the emergence of modern society.[19] The economic miracle of Western civilization is a political event rather more than an economic one. What requires explanation, perhaps, is not so much why production expanded, as why it was allowed to do so, why it was not thwarted by political forces,

why the golden-egg-laying goose was not devoured, as normally happens.

In addition to the structural prerequisites, which were also present in other parts of the world, where capitalism did not develop, the emergence of an important class of rational producers required a certain spirit, a devotion to orderly and productive activity. On this view, they emerged in consequence of some characteristically Calvinist theological doctrines, not directly, as a result of what was positively preached, but indirectly. In a determined world, in which salvation was already decided, there was no longer any point in the old attempts at manipulating or propitiating the supernatural. A man's duty was simply to fulfil his "calling". But if he believed that his success at that calling was an indication of his "saved" status, would he be able to resist the temptation to cheat unwittingly, and try to bring about the evidence of his own salvation? In this way artisans and traders became committed to their work rather than to its material rewards, and ploughed back their profit. Their magic-free vision of an orderly world also led them to that rational linking of means to ends, which is the essence of modern entrepreneurship.

12 *The negative Protestant thesis.* On this view,[20] the Reformation did not itself engender anything unique and distinctive. What accounts for the dramatic shift of economic and intellectual dynamism from southern Europe to the North is not the positive benefits of the Reformation in the North, but the baneful and disastrous effects of the Counter-Reformation in the South. The Counter-Reformation restored and strengthened that political-clerical domination which is the prevalent condition of agrarian society. A centralized Church and a set of centralized states, terrified of forces of change dangerous to them both, imposed a long sleep on southern Europe.

13 *The plural state system.* The fragmentation of Europe into a number of genuinely independent yet internally effective states had a profound effect. Its obvious consequence was that it prevented a general freeze, a general return to the characteristic

late-agrarian high level equilibrium trap. This did indeed happen in some parts of Europe. But it did not happen everywhere, and was very unlikely to happen in all places at the same time.[21] A plural state system enabled enterprising minorities (Jews, Moravian Brethren, Huguenots) to migrate to areas that allowed them to display their energies and talents.

14 *An internal as well as external balance of power.* A plural state system as such might not have been sufficient, had each of the autonomous states been internally centralized and authoritarian. Internal chaos and constant conflict would, of course, not be helpful either. But a situation may arise in which a fairly strong state, effectively keeping the peace internally, and capable of defending the society externally, is nonetheless restrained by an internal balance of power from excessively arbitrary or oppressive action. The internal balance was one both between institution and interest groups, and between ideologies. The conflict engendered by attempts at domination by one participant or another eventually persuaded many of them to accept and, in the end, positively to internalize a pluralist compromise. Toleration became an ideal rather than a regrettable necessity.

The internal and external balance may also be interdependent. A state precariously involved in an international balancing act may be disinclined to push internal attempts at establishing homogeneity to their limit, for fear of the international implications. A complex balance of this kind did, it seems, come into being in parts of northwest Europe in the seventeenth and eighteenth centuries.

15 *A national rather than civic bourgeoisie.* Generally speaking, when commercial, participatory, uncentralized sub-societies emerged in the agrarian world, they took the form of city states. A city could live by crafts and trade, and depend on its rural hinterland for an agricultural surplus. In pre-modern times it is hard to imagine an entire country doing so. At the same time, if the instrumental, production-oriented spirit was to take over the world, it is hard to imagine a mere city providing a sufficient

base. It is true that one city state did once conquer the entire Mediterranean basin, but it did so through its martial rather than commercial spirit. An island society, served by the sea in the office of a moat, and enjoying civic liberties granted not to individual towns but to a national parliament – a country with a national rather than a merely civic bourgeoisie – was perhaps uniquely fitted to constitute the launching pad for the new order. Holland, an association of urban republics, also played a great part; but it may be significant that the central locus of the transformation was England.

General Summary

It is unlikely that we shall ever know with precision the precise path by which we have escaped from the idiocy of rural life (Karl Marx's phrase). An enormously complex, multi-faceted historical process took place: the record is fragmentary and at the same time overburdened with data. Many factors are inherently inaccessible, and the practical and conceptual problems involved in disentangling the threads will in all probability remain insoluble. We cannot re-run the experiment. Nonetheless, our understanding of the outlines of the process, of the main possible alternatives within it, will be advanced if we clarify our questions.

Our no doubt very incomplete catalogue of candidate-explanations does offer a framework. Each of these items, and no doubt many others, are, in varying degrees, possible elements in an explanation. It is unlikely that any one of them could have been operative or sufficient on its own. For instance, political fragmentation on its own is not an inducement to anything: it is frequently found in other parts of the world, without being in any way fertile. The combination of effective but law-bound government, the presence of an entrepreneurial class neither wholly disfranchised politically nor eager to become dominant, and endowed with some inclination to continue in its calling beyond the point of satisfying its needs; the presence of opportunity, not merely through a geographically expanding world, but also through a rising ceiling of available potential discovery – all these clearly did have their part to play, and could only play it jointly.

For connected reasons, it is unlikely that the great transformation could have been, on its *first* occurrence, anything other than both unconscious and individualistic. The transformation was too profound, and too contrary and indeed offensive to the established patterns of thought and values, to be understood in advance. Had it been grasped in advance, however hazily, surely the threat it implied to most established interests would have led to a more determined attempt to thwart it. By the time the understanding came, it was too late to try and throttle it.

CHAPTER 7

Production, Value and Validity

The Economic Transformation

Our contemporary theoreticians of cognition are, most of them, devoid of any sense of radical change. They may have some sense of the manner in which data reach us in the context of other *cognitively* relevant data. What in the main they lack, however, is a sufficient sense of the way in which cognition is enmeshed in the context of *non*-cognitive activities and considerations. They take *our* cognitive situation – roughly speaking, an individual faces a basically homogeneous data base, composed of equal, unprivileged elements, in abstraction from his social involvement, and assumes them to be fragments of a unified, orderly nature. They credit early man with a similar state of mind. For instance, Thomas Kuhn talks[1] as if pre-scientific man *lacked* a "paradigm". In fact, he has a more compulsive paradigm, though one of a radically different kind.

Thus a vision, which is the fruit of a rigorous separation of questions, is projected backwards onto forms of thought which knew neither the separation of questions nor a proper division of labour. Now it is of course trivially true that an organism cannot survive if its reactions to the environment are such as to make its own survival in that environment impossible. From this it follows that organisms which do survive do in some sense embody valid appreciations of the nature of their environment. They must not, so to speak, be built on misguided assumptions about external conditions. But it in no way follows that these successfully adaptive reactions exclusively or primarily function "proto-cognitively", i.e. that they *only* encapsulate tacit information about the environment. Their design also serves multiple internal

172

ends. Multi-strandedness, poly-functionality, is the order of the day in nature as well as in most human societies.

There are of course others, romantics, who positively prefer the multi-stranded, un-atomized, or, as they may prefer to put it, un-desiccated form of thought. In such a style, diverse questions remain conflated, and engender a total, "meaningful" unity. But these fashionable romantics, who are very much with us, do not help us too much with the understanding of social and conceptual change either. For if the insouciant pan-modernists tacitly suppose that cognition was ever modern and specialized, the romantics think and feel (they prefer feeling, really) that there always was or ought to be man-in-the-round. They much prefer a being unmutilated by the neat separation of questions and the division of labour. The erstwhile functionality of the multi-purpose style of thought is treated as conferring validity on itself. If it is gone, it can be revived. This viewpoint makes nonsense of any cognitive advance, by treating all belief systems as equally valid. If these romantics have any sense of change at all, it consists of the recognition that, of late, the amount of regrettable mutilation has been increasing. They feel it ought to be stopped, and the trend reversed.

When we turn to the theory of economic life, the situation is similar. Perhaps it is a little better; the debate, which has striking analogies with the cognitive one, has received a far more thorough airing. The insouciant pan-modernists are of course still very much with us: they comprise the majority of professional economists. They assume that economic theory is concerned with the economic life of all mankind, not just a segment of it. Hence they have some considerable difficulty in even grasping the question about its range of application. But among non-economists concerned with economic issues, plus a few perhaps untypical economists, the question has been vigorously and persistently debated.[2] With the conspicuous and disturbing arrival on the scene of economies highly successful in the *modern* world, but operating in a society markedly *unlike* the one familiar to economists (notably, Japan), we may expect the question to be raised more insistently.

There are basically two ways in which such an attribution of economic rationality and single-mindedness can be carried out. One of them really is a kind of outright, unlimited expansionism on the part of economic concepts. It consists of seeing *all*, in any sphere whatever, as the application of means–ends rationality. This theory is not partially true: in a very lefthanded sense, it is wholly true. It is a tautology. It can easily be forced onto the data so that any facts whatever are made compatible with it.

Try to imagine conduct which would contradict this thesis. Suppose a man immolates himself at some shrine. In what conceivable way can he be furthering his own interest, as opposed to, possibly, that of the shrine? Our economic rationality theorist is unabashed. The interest of the man in question happened to lie in furthering the glory of his revered shrine. Or take a man who seemingly defies rationality by living out some rigid role, come what may, in total insensitivity to all other opportunities and menaces. He surely cannot be claimed for the means–ends rationality thesis! His conduct would seem to exemplify systematic indifference to such efficiency calculations.

Once again, our pan-economist is unabashed. He had, after all, never circumscribed the area of possible human aims. Aims arise from human tastes or choices. They are in no way prescribed by his theory. They are accepted as given. It was never suggested or implied that human aims must be restricted to satisfactions of man's physical sensitivity. Nor were they restricted to the attainment of ends expressible in quantifiable terms, such as money. Such a restriction would be highly unrealistic, and our theorist is fully aware of the wide diversity of human aims and aspirations. He merely claims that, given some aims (which for him are a strictly extraneous datum), men pursue them to the best of their ability. He asks no more. If some man is dominated by some bizarre aim, or the rigid enactment of a role, well, that is perfectly compatible with the means–ends rationality model. All ends, however logically complex or abstract, however much endowed with a holistic, Gestalt quality, are equally grist to his mill.

And so it is. The thesis has a marked affinity to that of

psychological egoism, the doctrine that all men are and must needs be egoists. After all, whatever aim they pursue (however other-directed), it is still, after all, *their* aim. On the appropriate interpretation of these terms, we can escape neither egoism nor rationality. But, of course, either thesis, when it becomes so omnivorous and devours all facts, also becomes vacuous. Such formal, all-embracing schemata are sometimes quite useful; but this one is not. The point is that we need a selective, discriminating concept of rationality, as something which grows and augments with the progress of human history. After all, something *has* changed in the course of human history. We need terms which can seize the *differences*.

The other argument, not always clearly enough kept separate from the first, is empirical. It is indeed the case that many (though not all) populations, previously constrained by kin and custom in their economic activity, learn to understand and apply the principles of market behaviour with alacrity. Within a restricted sphere of their lives, they may have already practised them in the past, before circumstances allowed and encouraged them to expand the area of purely economic rationality. This does rather suggest that single-end rationality may not be quite such a difficult and rare accomplishment. Need it really be the fruit of a long, complex and arduous evolution, which took place within one particular historical tradition? (That is, on the whole, the viewpoint argued here.) Could it not be ever latent in all mankind?

On this view, *Homo economicus* was ever hidden inside social man, signalling wildly to be let out. He emerged with glee at the very first opportunity. Man was born a maximizer, yet was everywhere in social chains. Calculating rationality did not need to be invented. All that was needed was that the chains be struck off. Not all those who revere economic rationality believe this (the best contemporary spokesman of this position, Hayek, does not). But it is a possibility which must be borne in mind.

There is an obvious parallel here with the suspicion that cognitive, referential, single-strand rationality is also latent and strong in all men, seeking or waiting for the first opportunity of liberation. An important support for such a claim lies in the very fact that so many societies deploy the absurdity of ritual assertion as a means of highlighting the solemnity of an occasion. If a man weren't already latently rational, would he even notice the signal? Would it alert him to the solemnity of the occasion? The ritual impact of irrational affirmations is an unwitting compliment of unreason to reason. Reason must have been very strong in us, if we can get so much of a kick from unreason.

But whether latent in us and waiting to emerge, or whether painfully acquired as a by-product of an obsessional and unusual theology, instrumental rationality as a pervasive and dominant way of life and production was not always with us. Production was largely submerged in other concerns, notably the maintenance of social order. It needed first of all to be disentangled from the strands with which it was previously intertwined. The problem of how this was achieved remains with us.

Production and Coercion

There is a fundamental distinction between production and coercion. They have a radically distinct logic. They cannot be treated as parallel. The political and economic histories of mankind, though intertwined, are not carbon copies of each other.

It is useful to begin with a very stark and exaggerated contrast between the logic of coercion and the logic of production and exchange. This will subsequently require a good deal of refinement.

Economic advantage is divisible, calculable and negotiable. Coercion is not. It operates in a context of incommensurate, stark, yes/no absolutes.

Economic exchange is the sphere of fine adjustment. The operating sanction or incentive is *advantage*. Advantages can be finely weighted. Very small adjustments can be made to bring a deal closer to equilibrium, to a point where each of two participants comes as close as is feasible to an optimal situation.

Coercion is totally different. The final sanction of coercion, the *ultima ratio regis*, is the infliction of death. Death is incommensurate with other things. Life is the precondition of the enjoyment of all other benefits. On occasion, the loss of other things dear to him can bring a man to a point at which he prefers his own death; but this is rare. In most circumstances, his own death cannot be balanced out by anything. Thomas Hobbes tried to make this point into the basis of binding secular legitimation of all political order. You cannot be a little more dead or a little less dead; there cannot be any fine tuning of advantage. As de Maistre put it, the executioner is the foundation of the social order.

The difference between the economic and political orders is pervaded by this difference between the ultimate sanction within each. Within one, what is at stake is minor gain or loss; in the other, everything.

It may be objected that the contrast has been overdrawn, and, more important perhaps, based on a limited range of evidence. Within stable systems, political and even military haggling does take place. Eighteenth-century warfare, for instance, was a professional affair with something of the quality of chess. Neither the overall social order, nor even either of the warring parties, was very much at risk. Calculable gains were secured at the cost of calculable risks. Warfare really was the pursuit of political ends by other means.

Tribal feuding is also frequently a far from total affair. After the harvest is safely in, a lot of ritual shooting goes on, one or two men are killed, the scores are checked and added, blood money is paid. Then everyone waits for the next season and discusses the finer points of performance of both sides. It is said that in Kathmandu valley the peasant caste went on working their fields, quite unconcerned with a battle between two rival sets of warriors, fighting it out in the next field. Caste boundaries of basic activities were respected.

Despite the total, yes/no quality of the difference between life and death, and despite the fact that coercion in the end operates through killing or the threat thereof, societies often succeed in taming, ritualizing, restraining violence and coercion. A society *is* a group of people, endowed with a mechanism which inhibits pre-emptive escalation of conflict.

The mark and supreme achievement of effective political systems is precisely this: they avoid the escalation of conflict. Somehow or other, they create a situation which inhibits the thought that it is advantageous to strike first. Disagreements may be finely negotiated, re-negotiation is possible. Participants do not feel, nor are led to feel by the objective situation, that escalation of conflict is preferable to accepting a less than advantageous solution. A political system *is* a collectivity in which escalation does not take place, either because one party has secured control, or because a balancing mechanism is available, inhibiting escalation.

Conversely, it may be argued that on occasion, quite often, perhaps, economic bargaining, with all the elements of bluff that enter into it, can also be played out in a total spirit. Economic negotiations only become a matter of sliding-scale haggling when basic sustenance is assured. The reason why a genuinely poor, primitive economy cannot be a market one is that its surplus is so small and the minimum required for subsistence cannot be handed over to the vagaries of a market. When starvation is close, economic decisions become like political ones. They are in any case enmeshed with political ones, with the self-maintenance and defence of the social unit.

Great success or total destitution may on occasion depend on single economic decisions. These in turn may have to be leaps in the dark, for lack of adequate available information. Major investment decisions, commitments of large resources, are often preceded by an elaborate ritual of research and documentation. Anyone attending a committee at which decisions of this kind are reached arrives equipped with a heavy bundle of papers. These contain impressive-looking collections of figures and analyses of the situation. It would be quite unprofessional, nay unethical, to arrive without such preparation and to be swayed by the toss of the coin. But, in fact, there are semi-modern or even modern economies in which astrologers are consulted, and whatever defects these economies may have, I doubt whether it is the astrological intrusion which is to blame. Advocates of rival policies can always find their own astrologer or economist. Everyone involved in such decisions knows that the uncertainty of crucial factors, the questionable assumptions on which the data were gathered (not to mention outright unreliability), the weighting of incommensurate considerations, all jointly ensure that decisions in the end retain a leap-in-the-dark quality.

All these qualifications do hold. The contrast between the sphere of power and coercion on the one hand, and that of production and exchange on the other, is not quite as simple as that between sliding-scale, calculable advantages on the one hand, and the total opposition of victory and death on the other. Calculability does often enter politics and war, and absoluteness, total backing of one amongst several incompatible and incommensurate package deals, can and does occur within the economy. But for all that, the ultimate and underlying principle of coercion is yes/no, life or death; and the ultimate principle of the market is – a bit more or a bit less.

Concretely, in serious military and political struggles, victory and defeat are irreversible, and infinitely distant from each other. *Vae victis*: a real victor does not allow the vanquished to have another go next season. That would be utter folly. The vanquished of this season, if allowed another try next year, would not be so foolish as to indulge in similar generosity. The logic of deterrent nuclear strategy is that neither victor nor loser will be there when the next season comes.

From the calculable, negotiable character of trade it follows in a way that trading practices are only adopted where either an overarching order, or a balance of power, prevents robbery or piracy. Perhaps it is not so much that violence is absolute and commerce given to calculation, as that, when forced into total yes/no situations, we are violent, whereas in an affluent or an orderly context, we may negotiate fine advantages. We may then do so even when the venue is nominally a battlefield. The incalculability/haggling opposition and the violence/parley opposition can cut across each other. Sometimes we parley about the incalculable, and sometimes we haggle about violence.

Early traders doubled up as pirates or conquistadores; trade was practised when the alternative was too perilous. Trading means the recognition that the rates of exchange are to be settled at some point of a continuous spectrum. Violence, when not restrained and ritualized, means a recognition that one will end up at one of the two extreme points of the spectrum. On the whole, mankind has lived in predominantly non-negotiable, political situations, with negotiability restricted to a ghetto, and the ghetto specializing in the negotiable. The rationally negotiable style has on one occasion only conquered first one society and then the entire world. In all probability, it is now contracting once again.

The Three Stages of Economy

The neatest and simplest typology of economic stages is that of Karl Polanyi, the sequence of Reciprocity, Redistribution and Market.[3] This does not altogether correspond to another very natural classification, that of Subsistence Economy, Partial Markets (for luxury and strategically crucial goods), and Generalized Markets.

Reciprocity clearly predominates in pre-productive societies in which there is very little *to* trade. Though redistribution is presented as a type of economy, it is just as natural to consider it a type of polity. It corresponds to a social order in which a political centre is strong enough to extract a sizeable surplus from producers and then distribute or keep it at will. A generalized market economy, in which the overwhelming proportion of goods consumed passes through the market, and only an insignificant proportion is consumed and produced in the home, clearly has a double precondition: one, that the productive forces are so great that food-producers can become a minority (and yet supply enough food for the entire society), and two, that the political centre allows, or is obliged to allow, a very substantial proportion of production to be freely traded in the market.

These two conditions are largely, but not completely, tied to each other: great and growing production is conducive to good government, as Hume and Smith noticed, but of course also requires good government. But they do not remain rigidly tied to each other. Once a powerful technology exists and is known to exist, a productively powerful society without much of a market also becomes possible. Whether it then *inevitably* engenders a hidden market ("the double economy"), or networks of reciprocity, is an interesting question.

It is in fact very difficult to specify successive models of the economy without in effect speaking of patterns of coercion, or abstentions from coercion. The general pattern of redistributive agrarian society is one of domination by violence, even if it is generally indirect and secondary. The sword-domination of agrarian society needs of course to be qualified by allowing for the role of the clerisy in the organization of coercive groups. The men who longed to strangle the last king with the bowels of the last priest rightly noted that the clerisy should receive its due recognition in the scheme of things.

The generalized market was made possible by a mild technological expansion which in turn, initially, favoured a further expansion of the market and technological growth. But the very powerful technology eventually also came to presuppose an enormous, indivisible, inherently shared and collective infrastructure. This in turn reduces the social role of the market. During the first economic miracle, the required infrastructure happened to be ready and available, by an historic accident. This is no longer so: the infrastructure that is now presupposed has grown so enormously, and can no longer be generated spontaneously. Nor can it itself be run or maintained in a market manner, and it cannot be set up without conscious design.

It can only be run "politically", i.e. by global, centralized and multi-purpose decisions. So we are about to return to a more political, less economic world. The make-believe return to atomic individualism cannot conjure away the dependence of a modern economy on an enormous, indivisible and inevitable politically controlled base. We return from contract to status; just what the system of statuses will be this time, we do not yet know. For the time being, it seems to be an egalitarian and bureaucratic status system. A baseline egalitarianism is combined with a generation-by-generation reallocation of hierarchical roles. Whether this egalitarianism will survive a diminution of mobility, whether in turn mobility will survive the diminishing return on additional wealth and innovation, and whether indeed such a diminishing return will make itself felt, are the crucial questions facing us.

The Ideological Transition to the Generalized Market

The agrarian world is oriented towards stability and hierarchy. Its ideological apparatus endeavours to confer stability on its institutions. All this is reflected in its attitude to economic activity. Just as, for instance, Aristotelian physics envisage a rightful place for objects, towards which they tend to move, so the characteristic economic theory of the age which hailed Aristotle as the Master of those who know was naturally attracted to the notion of a "just price". In a later age, this idea was much decried.

But the notion is not absurd: in a stable order endowed with a static technology, a fixed price – enforced and hallowed by an aura of fairness – may be a sensible way of settling economic issues. In a stable world, there may be no place for "economics" on the map of knowledge.[4] We sorely miss the notion of a fair and morally imposed price, and we may yet return to it on a more general scale. In a society which permits collective organization and bargaining by segments of the work force, and within which some such segments can on occasion paralyse the entire economy, the re-imposition of the concept of a "fair wage" may be the only alternative to either mass unemployment or perpetual inflation (or, indeed, to a conjunction of both).

An expanding unstable economy with an innovative technology, on the other hand, can hardly work with such an idea. What it needs is varying prices which, as its own favoured theory loudly insists, act as a system of infinitely subtle and sensitive signals, indicating the points at which human endeavour must be expanded, and the points at which it must be retracted, if human satisfaction is to be increased. An expanding economy and a market, variable-price mechanism went hand in hand.

An economy can of course expand without such a market mechanism, if the driving power of the expansion is a single or at any rate a limited discovery, whether of a new resource, a new territory, or a new technique, or if the technology is imported by the central authority. The crucial initiation of agriculture itself was such a single-shot innovation.

The great archaeologist Gordon Childe suggested that it was slavery which inhibited innovation, by undermining the motivation for seeking easier ways of doing things. Slavery proper may be defined as the treatment of atomized individual slaves as genuine chattels, as opposed to either their insertion in a lowly place in households, or the enslavement of entire communities, whilst allowing them to retain their internal organization. Such genuine slavery may in fact have the opposite effect: a slave-owner, who has to buy his slaves and keep them alive, does in fact have good reasons for welcoming increased productivity. Slavery proper is curiously rare in world history.[5] Specialists have suggested that the number of societies which practised it can virtually be counted on the fingers of one hand (two of them occurring in the ancient Mediterranean, and three in the post-Columbian New World). "Real" slavery uses individual slaves as simple labour power, with unrestrained sales or transfers of such anonymous "talking tools" (a Roman phrase) according to economic convenience. "Real" slavery looks like an anticipation of "rational" capitalism and the single-purpose allocation of labour power, unhampered by multiple social considerations. One can speculate about why it did not or could not lead to capitalism proper.

What is far more common in other societies is the forcible

incorporation of captured or purchased individuals in an existing community at a low level, or of course the reduction of entire communities to servile status, or indeed the deployment of "slaves" of high status. This is, in effect, but a special terminology which confers a certain status on bureaucrats. It helps to ensure that all their perquisites and their position itself are revocable at will. Any modern bureaucrat takes it for granted that the power which flows from his position in the organization is not his to use and keep, that he can be dismissed from his position; in traditional societies, it may have been necessary to call him a slave to ensure that this should indeed be so. Even then, it was generally difficult to enforce such a condition for any length of time. The state might own the slaves, but the slaves could own the state.

So the true explanation of a low level of innovation may be more general: agrarian social orders lead to servitude which in turn inhibits innovation. Those of servile status have little reason to innovate, and those who dominate them tend to have an ethos favouring the virtues of aggression or of stability rather than those of enterprise.

Those deeply imbued with the merits of a free market mechanism tend to scorn what seems to them the spurious moralism of the just price and just wage concept. R. H. Tawney, interestingly enough, shared this vision sufficiently to call Karl Marx the last of the scholastics. The suggestion was that the labour theory of value, and above all the moral inspiration which underlay it, is a continuation of the pursuit of a "fair" determination of economic rewards.

The denigration of the "fair price" concept is part and parcel of the general rejection of metaphysics and superstition by the Enlightened mind. The whole idea, it is suggested, had clearly been based on the infantile expectation that God, or Nature, or some other Authority, sends objects into the world with labels attached, specifying their price. It is all clearly part of that vision of the world as a "cosmos" rather than as nature, a vision which generously projects purpose, hierarchy, inherent value everywhere. Its world is suffused with value, which is too deeply blended into the nature of things to be subjected to the sordid and perverting indignity of market determination. The labour theory of value was a curious compromise. It was traditional in seeing value somehow inhering in objects, rather than being a volatile function of their enjoyment. At the same time, the manner in which it was injected into objects was one which credited human agency, human work, and not some outer authority, with the power to bestow value. It was both objectivist and man-centred.

But we have learnt to separate distinct questions, and to see things as they are. We separate that which is in them and that which is our construct or projection, and we recognize that things do not have any such value place in the scheme of things, there being no such scheme. When men believed in it, there was little innovation. We, however, live in a world based on innovation, and on the separation of questions and tasks, on the cold dissection of the world. The new view claims that we have liberated ourselves from the old superstitions. Our flexibility, and the volatility of value, are closely linked.

So prices, and rewards generally, are not prescribed. They reflect the satisfaction things and services give, and their scarcity, and their negotiable flexibility is precisely what encourages innovation, progress, growth. "Fair price" was not just a metaphysical error and a superstition. It was the very paradigm of the most damnable kind of error, the unwarranted freezing of the world into a set mould. This mould was then endowed with an aura of sacredness and authority which it never merited. So it was not just a theoretical error, but constituted a crucial impediment to human progress and satisfaction. The revival in modern times of an aspiration in that direction then appears as an inexplicable striving to go back, reactionary in the fullest and worst sense. It becomes explicable only as the expression of the psychic weakness of individuals who wish to return to the old cosy stable social womb, because they cannot stand the freedom, the responsibility of living in an emancipated open society.

The "market" theory of validating value is the crucial point at which the economic and cognitive transformations of mankind meet. The new economy is to be justified in terms of notions which assume a homogeneous, atomized world. Value or merit attach to things only as a function of the satisfaction they give. Neither aims nor means are fixed. They are empirically established. Aims are given by our desires, and means by the connections objectively prevailing in the world. Thus only does value enter the world.

Unfortunately, the truth of the matter is somewhat more complex. It does not lend itself to this simple black and white characterization, it is argued. It cannot all simply be described as the confrontation of superstitions, rigid objectivism, with enlightened, flexible empiricism. The Enlightened mind was not quite as enlightened as it complacently supposed: it committed and exemplified the very error which it castigated.

Certainly, the notion of a just price, inscribed into the nature of things, is a superstition. There is indeed no nature of things, and it is not given to assigning value-labels. But, alas, there is no market price either. The apotheosis of the market price, its endowment with an aura of independence, authority and legitimacy, is simply a more subtle repeat performance of the very same old superstition. Enlighteners, enlighten yourselves. The more-enlightened-than-thou spirit in which you preach your vision is a little comic, for thou art a damned sight less enlightened than thou confidently supposest.

The market can only determine the price within a given institutional/coercive context. That context is not *given* either, any more than a "just price" could be given. Inevitably, it is historically specific. Such contexts vary a great deal, and are the result of imposition or of a particular historic compromise. The illusion of a self-maintaining market as an objective oracle arose because the particular institutional/cultural context into which it first emerged *seemed* fairly self-evident to those who lived within it. It had emerged spontaneously, and came to feel "natural" to those who lived within its ambiance. It seemed to illustrate the human condition as such, rather than a very specific historical constellation.

Those who analysed it had some measure of sociological sophistication and imagination, but not quite enough. They knew that conditions were favourable; they did not realize clearly enough that they were *unique*. They thought these conditions liberated generic man; they did not realize that these conditions had created a new and rare species. They were grateful for the favourable political climate. But they did not fully appreciate the specific cultural and technological preconditions which also made it possible. The availability of this minimal and uniquely favourable social infrastructure they were too inclined to credit to humanity as such.

A political and cultural framework is necessary for the market. It is not only a matter of the peace being kept, important though that is. It presupposes a minimal physical and social infrastructure, and a cultural atmosphere, the availability of suitable personnel. Early industrialism and an early extended market economy were relatively modest in their infrastructural and technological requirements compared with developed industrialism. At the same time, the satisfaction of these requirements was extremely unlikely in the agrarian age. Those requirements were met on this occasion, without deliberate planning and policy. They could consequently seem to be parts of a reasonably natural, and not too idiosyncratic, order of things. A natural illusion perhaps in its context, but an illusion nonetheless. Later industrialism is altogether different: its infrastructural requirements become enormous, conspicuous and contentious. Emulative industrialization is often imposed in conditions that are not so favourable to economic activity, and which themselves need to be *imposed*.

Once it is fully clear that the market operates only in a political context, and that these possible contexts are extremely diverse in kind, and *not* given, it also becomes obvious that the verdict of the market, the price, is not issued by the oracle of "the market" alone. In fact it can only be the ventriloquist's mouthpiece for the particular political situation which happens to underlie it. In the eighteenth century, it still seemed to make sense to formulate a kind of specification of the "correct" political background. If such a unique specification could in turn be validated and justified, then what the market decreed within its terms of reference could be credited with a kind of legitimacy.

In any one given political context, the market will give a unique verdict. If the legitimate political context can also be uniquely defined, the oracular market verdict is also unique. It stands at the end of a chain of reasoning, untarnished by arbitrariness at any point, so it can be revered.

One could specify the "correct" political background by saying that the political interference should be minimal; this was the famous theory of the minimal, "nightwatchman" state. The theory has actually been revived in our time, when in fact the tremendous size of the required infrastructure renders it absurd. The theory had its plausibility then, because the state really could be rather small. The society in which a generalized market order emerged was so well equipped with the kind of culture and institutional framework required for the expanding market that initially the state was not required to help out a great deal. The relatively feeble technology of early industrialism could thrive on the base provided by a particular advanced agrarian society. This relatively feeble technology also failed to disrupt the society within which it emerged. Twice over, it was compatible with its own social matrix.

Now all that has changed. Highly developed productive technology requires an enormous, centrally maintained infrastructure. Its cost, in developed societies, has come to be somewhere in the neighbourhood of half the national income. Without such an infrastructure, both the production *and* the consumption of a modern industrial machine would seize up. A modern motor car industry could not dispose of its products were it not for the fact that the political agencies of society ensure the existence of an enormously elaborate and expensive system of roads.

Once the political framework of the market is so conspicuous and large, and is seen to have so many different possible forms, it can no longer be dissimulated as a kind of neutral or innocuous minimum. It can no longer be presented as a mere necessary precondition, one which merely enables that impartial oracle to function, without interfering with or prejudging its verdicts. Such an illusion is no longer possible.

Once this is plain, and it ought now to be plain, the pronounce-ments of the oracle lose whatever aura they may once have possessed. They cannot be presented as coming objectively from outside the system, without prejudice, reflecting nothing but the tastes and preferences of men, and the manner in which, given the distribution of resources, they can best be satisfied. Once the enormous weight of the political input into the alleged verdict is seen, we are no longer free to use the market as our economic and neutral arbiter. *We* make the political order. Hence we are responsible for its verdicts. The market verdicts are but its echo. All this is not in conflict with the claim that, within a politically chosen framework and set of principles of distribution, all further details are best left to "the market".

So the objectivity of market prices is as much a metaphysical illusion as the "just price". We had started with the just price, and replaced it by the market price. Now we must similarly replace that in turn – by what?

The Re-Entry Problem

The basic liberal story of the legitimation of prices was simple. But its erosion has left us, ideologically, hanging in thin air.

This story is not unique. On the contrary, it is the very model of a very large number of similar stories, all of which display a similar plot, the same logical structure. The justification of prices was the first example of the new style of legitimation and its problems. But it is only one specimen of a whole genus of problems. This should be called the Re-Entry Problem.

Strictly speaking, it is not a re-entry problem, but rather, simply an *entry* problem. But the name chosen reflects the way in which it is conceived by many positivistically inclined people. The implicit and very seductive story runs as follows. Animals are good positivists, they can be assumed not to have any metaphysics (they don't think at all). They simply interact with their sensory data, and that's that. When man emerges, for some obscure reason, he misuses his newly acquired faculty of thought: he thinks not merely about the data which he genuinely possesses but also wilfully invents a lot of Extra, perhaps just because he has not yet fully mastered this new instrument, *thought*. The extra is of course fiction, invention, largely useless, though possibly containing some useful hint about how to use and interpret real data. It may also give him confidence, confirm his social order, encourage him to conduct himself well, though all this is cognitively irrelevant. However, with the emancipation and liberation of the human mind, he at last realizes that the Extra is but fiction. He then *re-enters* the world of genuine reality, the single and unique realm of nature. It is interesting that both positivism and Marxism revive a detour or fall theory of man. He is assumed to have been sound and whole at the start, but in need of rescue from a fallen condition.

During the days of his Babylonian exile in fantasy, the argument proceeds, man had acquired the habit of legitimating all contentious values and principles by invoking the authority of the fictitious Other. As it was fictitious, those in power could always manipulate the Other so as to make it say what they wished. The dominant fictions were the fictions of the dominant class. But the days of this kind of trickery and delusion are over. Henceforth, all validation, all legitimation, will have to be based on intra-mundane materials. It might seem less solid than those illusory absolutes of the beyond, but is really that much more genuine, and much worthier of mature humanity.

The thinkers of the seventeenth and eighteenth centuries busied themselves with finding earthly bases for human values. They sought the ultimate, guiding, court-of-appeal principles of our diverse intellectual and social and other activities. *That* is the re-entry problem: the return of mankind to this world, to nature. It follows a sojourn in fantasy, stretching presumably from the earliest beginning of humanity to the Age of Reason. If, however, the separation of issues is a unique and late accomplishment, then what we really face is entry, not re-entry. Early man had never lived in a positivist Eden, nor could have done so.

Re-entry or entry, the process takes place in parallel forms in a wide variety of fields:

Government and Authority: once sanctioned by God, now based on consent, or calculation of self-interest, or sentiment.

Right and Wrong: once divinely selected or rationally established or inherent in the nature of things, now fóllow from social convenience, or sentiment, or some combination of the two.

Knowledge: truth was once determined by the normative essence of things. Now, the arbiter of truth is – *our* sensations or perceptions.

Beauty: criteria of perfection were located in rules of proportion etc. inscribed into the nature of things. Now – hedonistic or functional or similar theories of aesthetics.

Economics: price, once prescribed by independent natural justice, now determined by the amount of labour-input, or by the market interplay of supply and demand. These in turn depend on the pleasures of consumption and the arduousness of production.

With variation in detail, the same pattern can be found in any important and contentious human activity. Once upon a time, during the Platonic age, the crucial principles of legitimacy or excellence were held to be inscribed into the nature of things, or to spring from the will of a deity. They were in the keeping of the guild of revelation-storers, or disclosed to special, elevated faculties. In fact, their rigidity was rooted in the ritual-instilled authority of concepts, as Durkheim saw. The formal doctrine of the Other was only appended when this way of running a social order reached a measure of self-consciousness, thanks to a literate clerisy.

Now, however, the field of activity in question finds itself endowed with governing principles whose authority lies in something mundane and publicly accessible. Rooted in human choice, convention, sentiment, enjoyment or experience, the verdict is available to all. It gives rise to no cognitive privilege or hierarchy, nor is indebted to it.

And the weakness of the new position, which has not yet fully dawned on all of us, is much the same, in outline, in each of these and similar fields. The new allegedly independent sovereign, strictly internal to the world or to man – this new supreme court of appeal turns out not to be genuinely independent after all. It has strong, intimate links to the very litigants whom it is meant to judge. The old judge was a fiction, a fraud, and a figment of human superstition. The new one, by contrast, is simply corrupt.

Our choices or decisions, which are to be the basis of a new social order, can only assume an intelligible form if made by men *already* shaped by a social order. This would be all very well if that order were unique, or could for any other reason be treated as given. But what if this is not so? Our tastes and desires, intended to be the foundation of a new ethics and to mould a new society, are formed by *a* society; our experiential data, which are to sit in judgment on all theories, are themselves theory-saturated; and so forth. The verdict of the judge is pre-judged by a prior culture. How can it tell us what culture to have?

From a world which believed in transcendent norms, we inherited the assumption of a given and fixed identity. Having shed the assumption of the accessibility or existence of a Transcendent, we turn to ourselves as the new sovereigns, the lords of all we behold. We need to confer direction on a world which is no longer stable. With pained surprise, some of us have now noticed that the identity which was to carry this burden of decision is simply no longer available to perform the task. It has gone with that stable world which had found its own mythic vindication in its own shadow up in the clouds. Neither ritual nor the Other nor the Inner constrain us. The same transformation which led us to seek legitimation and foundation *inside*, and abjure the Other, has also deprived us of that fixed and given identity, which alone could have borne such a burden.

The Circularity of Enlightened Reasoning

The circularity of the new vindication can be illustrated by the principal enlightened theories of politics, of morality, and of knowledge.

Enlightened politics have a tendency to be democratic, or at any rate to invoke the sovereignty of the people or *Volk*, even when they are in fact authoritarian in organization. Agrarian, Platonic politics were proudly and avowedly hierarchical and authoritarian: the values built into the nature of things and their inherent norms were to be implemented. Consent was not sovereign, but, on the contrary, only valid if in conformity with the norm. Wisdom, not consent, was what mattered. Wisdom was identified by criteria not chosen by mankind itself, but imposed on it.

As a modern restorer of one version of the agrarian vision, Imam Khomeini, has it: true democracy is the implementation of divine law, and not the codification of a merely human will. The higher orders of society were exemplary, their authority was rooted in their status, and their task was to enforce the values which they incarnated. An exemplary state, caste, text or church was there to guide us. But now we claim to know better. It is *our* consent, and our consent alone, which legitimates a political order, a system of coercion. Legitimation can only spring from the governed community itself. The rulers are delegates, not models.

This is all very well *if* our consent does indeed exist independently of a social order. In some measure, and in the short run, of course it does. Situations in which a society collectively wills one thing, but is coerced into enduring another, are not uncommon. Consent is not automatically and easily at the beck and call of anyone in control of the current apparatus of coercion. In that sense, consent is indeed endowed with an independent existence.

But in the longer run, the situation is not so simple. What one consents to depends on what one *is*, and what one is, in the end, springs from the society which has formed one. Could a vote have been taken, in the late Middle Ages, on whether mankind was to move onwards to a secular and industrial world? The question would have been unintelligible. Those who were capable of thought at all endorsed the world they knew. They *knew* it to be right and proper, and they knew radical changes to be accursed. The changes which have taken place since then have given us a humanity which, in the main, prefers itself as it now finds itself to be. But which third man, encapsulated in both, or independent of either, could possibly choose *between* them, and endorse that transformation "democratically", by consent? There is no such third man. He cannot possibly exist.

Fundamental changes transform identities. Yet without a single, persisting and somehow authoritative identity, there is no one available to give his full consent to a radical transformation. No one is available who could confer the democratic sacrament, blessing and vindication on it. Small changes, within a preserved identity, can of course be endorsed, or repudiated, by consent. The notion of democracy, of government validated by consent, does have a meaning, and is possible, within an overall cultural situation which is more or less stable and taken for granted, and which confers identities on its members. But when applied to the making or validating of fundamental and radical choices, the idea of consent quite literally has no meaning.

Critics of actual democratic systems like to say that they only work where their basic organizational assumptions are not challenged. The charge can be strengthened: it is only then that the idea of democracy has any meaning. When truly radical options are faced, there simply is no one available to give that overall consent. You cannot consent to a change of identity. There is no "you". The very notion of a change of identity precludes it. The pre-metamorphosis self is no longer, and the post-metamorphosis self is not yet. But the real subject of philosophical history is, precisely, our collective change of identity.

Take the most important and typical Enlightened moral philosophy, Utilitarianism. The basic idea is admirably simple: values maketh man. The seal of approval which society grants to institutions, ways of conduct, character traits, etc., must be governed by but a single criterion – namely whether, on balance, the institution or practice best contributes to human contentment. What the theory repudiates is the Platonic idea that merit is attached to institutions etc. independently of us, by the nature of things. By repudiating that notion, the new vision liberates us.

The theory hands over the choice of values to *our* desires, our preferences. This would constitute a solution if those desires were indeed *given*. Some Utilitarians knew, of course, that we could cultivate our tastes, and, strangely enough, invoked this when it suited their book. Within reasonable limits, the theory can accommodate some human control over tastes. But what if tastes are being radically transformed? What if our desires depend on our values, and our values on a rapidly changing society? The malleability of our desires and values is not a tangential feature of our situation. It is the central trait of our pliable, manipulative, technological, knowledge-based social order.

The model on which utilitarian reasoning relied was that of a given, isolable pleasure or satisfaction. This was to sit in judgment on values, much in the same way as an isolable given fact sits in judgment on theories. We are familiar with the problem which arises from the realization that facts are theory-saturated: what we perceive depends on our background expectations, the general equipment with which we apprehend it. How then can our perceptions sit in judgment on theories? But our pleasures too are concept-saturated. The system of concepts within which a man conducts his life is known as a culture. But cultures are no longer given: they are optional, rapidly changing and manipulable, and the options are subject to political contestation. We cannot judge rival cultures in terms of what gives us more pleasure, for our pleasures are culture-bound. They do not emanate from some pre-cultural, extra-social human being. So, once again, that which is to be judged turns out to be the judge. . .

In the sphere of knowledge, the Enlightened vision would seem to be somewhat less at risk than in other spheres, such as morality or politics. The ultimate court of appeal for cognitive claims is assigned to "experience". But experience in turn, according to a very popular and persuasive theory, is meretricious and malleable, just like consent and desire. We cannot, we are told, experience anything without a prior framework, a "paradigm", which pre-moulds it and saturates it with theory. But if there is *no* experience without paradigms, without theory-saturation, how can one use experience to adjudicate between paradigms? Answer comes there none, and, on the premises of the argument, there simply cannot be one. Once again, of course, the theory does not preclude experience from acting as arbiter *within* a stable system. The problem does arise, and seems insoluble, when we come to deal with global totalities and with radical discontinuities.

The paradoxical situation we face is that we use and invoke an extraneous, extra-social arbitrator ("nature", "experience", "pleasure"), without at the same time ever encountering it in a pure form. We only know things or events in nature as predigested by a cultural set of concepts; these, however, are impermanent and subject to further revision. Nonetheless, the set of practices, techniques and principles loosely known as "science" is based on the assumption of an orderly, homogeneous, unified external system, endowed with no fixed baseline ontology, accessible through its fragmented manifestations, and never directly approachable as a totality. This procedure does seem to work cumulatively and consensually. The activity governed by the single aim of apprehending the laws of such a system, and using them to predict and extrapolate, does work, and involves no internal contradiction. This is a supremely important datum of our collective situation.

The division of labour and the submission to single, clearly formulated aims has made us what we are. In the sphere of cognition, there seems to be nothing to stop us continuing to practise it. It is not so in other spheres. Coercion and the maintenance of order knows no criterion such as would permit endless growth, endless "progress". The yes/no quality of this realm is incompatible with any open-ended, interminable progression. All we can say is that affluence, the size of the new

holistic, indivisible infrastructure, the complexity and interdependence of modern society, have transformed the rules of the
game, in some ways for better, in some for worse. Coercion has
certainly become both easier and possibly less necessary.

In the sphere of value, of the specification of the good life,
instrumental rationality does end in a contradiction. There is and
can be no single aim that we can pursue. A single-strand philosophy works in science, but not in ethics or in politics.

Objectivity or Not?

Our argument may seem to be going in two contradictory,
incompatible directions. When concerned with the overall pattern of the role of cognition in society, we have endeavoured to
trace the path along which the objective, unified, referential style
of cognition eventually came to see the light of social day and
became dominant. On this account, mankind had begun with a
multiplicity of disconnected quasi-empirical sensitivities, each
deeply meshed in with its own set of quite *un*-referential, non-
empirical, social controls. These diverse conceptual "senses",
apertures onto the world, were neither able to combine into one
single global picture, nor able to pose any threat to the socially
oriented but referentially feeble conceptual systems of the time.
Those were presumably in large part governed by the requirements of social cohesion. In any case, they were certainly *not*
governed by any need for cognitive growth.

These disconnected sensibilities owe their first unification not
to being made more referential, but to being made *less* so.
Literacy; scholastic unification into a system; exclusive and
jealous monotheism; the shining model of truth-maintaining
rigorous inference in geometry, logic and perhaps in law; a
centralization of the clerisy; a strict delimitation of revelation
and a narrowing of its source, excluding easy accretion, a
monopolization and bureaucratization of magic by the clerical
guild – all these jointly somehow gave rise to a unified, centrally

managed, single-apex system. At any rate, something close enough to such an ideal emerges, causing it to become familiar and normative. It only required the apex of the system to let it be known that He did not interfere in the detailed manifestations of His creation, but preferred to maintain its lawlike pattern, and to withdraw into an infinitely distant hiding, for some of His devotees to seek for His design in the regularity of His creation, rather than by privileged short cuts, and to fuse this endeavour with the deployment of precise and content-preserving mathematics – and an objective, referential, world-unifying science was born.

Our endeavour has been to explain how such referential, socially neutral and blind, objective cognition, in other words science, *could* conceivably arise and be implemented in the productive life of society. The full story was no doubt immeasurably more complex; nevertheless, this is a schematic account which is not internally incoherent, and, as far as I know, compatible with the known facts of the history of thought and science.

One possible objection to the argument might arise from the fact that in the early period in Ionian Greece, cosmological theorizing had arisen without the benefit of the unificatory impulsion of a jealous Jehovah.[6] Conversely, the demotion of the deity to the orderly system of a single Nature is a development which did occur in China but does not seem to have led to a cumulative theoretical science.[7] Another important difficulty arises from the fact that during and immediately preceding the period of the birth of modern science, magical tendencies had been extremely prominent in European life. Frazer had postulated the sequence magic–religion–science. The study of sixteenth and seventeenth century thought suggests instead the series religion–magic–science.[8] Far from being puritans who eschewed magical manipulation and avoided a hermeneutically significant and readable and manipulable nature, the founders of modern science seem, many of them, to have been much tempted by and involved with magical techniques and ideas.[9] The Royal Society seems to have been closer to the spirit of magic-seeking

Faustus than to an intellectually rigorous puritanism.[10] This seems especially true of the great Newton himself, the supreme symbol of the new vision, whose voluminous and largely unpublished mystical writings, in quantity at least, outweigh his physics, and continue to embarrass the Royal Society.

Is this cabbalistic and hermetic outburst of the Renaissance to be discounted or explained away as the last attempt of the human mind, already awake to the prospect of an intelligible nature, to secure a cheap short cut to quick rewards? Was this the last feverish attempt at magical manipulation, before a final resignation to the more arduous cognitive path which we now considered proper? Or does this important phenomenon destroy the present argument? I cannot answer the question. It seems worth putting it on record. Suffice it to say that the new vision *was* reached: perhaps by the path indicated, perhaps by some even more devious route.

We have striven to explain how one society, and one only, had, by a series of near-miraculous accidents, attained this kind of world; and also to explain how at the same time it was endowed with productive and political systems which allowed this world to expand: an unusual productive style did so by succouring it materially, and an unusual polity, by refraining from stifling it at birth.

Yet we also argue that the philosophy by which it has tried to explain and validate its own achievement to itself is circular and fatally flawed. In essence, it claims to possess a big unitary aperture onto reality, called experience, which answers the crying question: what shall we think about the world? (Whatever sensory data permit.) What shall we value in social life? (The arrangements that are found experimentally to satisfy our collective wishes best.) What authority shall we obey? (The one which we collectively agree to obey and to which we delegate power, because it is found to serve us best.) How shall objects and activities be valued and priced? (By the price they can command on the free market.) And so on. You name your problem, and some bit of *experience*, and naught else, will be your answer. No need to revere some oracle and its vapours, no need any longer to take some self-appointed revelation at its own valuation, as was the old habit of earlier societies. Now we go to a universal and public oracle, transparent, without vapours and mysteries, for all who have eyes to see. Our epistemology is clear, honest, and egalitarian.

Yet we query this answer. This oracle is in its own way as self-appointed as the others which have preceded it. It has its social roots, as did the others: it springs from a unique culture, one in which the division of labour and instrumental rationality have flowered fully, and which it reflects. Can it, without circularity, vindicate itself? Circular self-validation seems to be back in a new form.

The fact that the answer cannot be accepted on its own terms does not mean that we may discount and fail to recognize the phenomenon itself. Scientific/industrial civilization clearly is unique, if only in the number of men it allows to subsist on Earth, and also because it is, without any shadow of doubt, conquering, absorbing all the other cultures of this Earth. It does so because all those outside it are eager to emulate it, and if they are not, which rarely happens, their consequent weakness allows them to be easily overrun. The prevalent eagerness in turn is so strong just because the new order plainly "works", i.e. it is the key to a technology which confers unparalleled economic and military power, incomparably greater than that ever granted to other civilizations, to other visions.

So its superiority, in one sense, is not open to doubt. The question is – can that superiority be explained and vindicated by its own favoured theory?

Its own theory, as we have shown, consists of applying the division of labour and the separation of questions, which is but an aspect of that division, to human activities in general. Thereby it separates out what in most human societies is fused, namely reference to some extraneous system or systems on the one hand, and internal organization and social validation on the other. Moreover, it insists that the system be in the singular: there is but one extraneous system, not many.

The basic elements of this vision are the separation of the

referential *and* its unification into a single system. It is endowed with a turnover ontology, i.e. there are no permanent world-bricks: the items out of which it is constructed are open to frequent revision. The only thing which is permanent is that the system is unified (no entrenched privileged points in it, no guaranteed discontinuities and chasms); that it is not under social control, but that it *is* subject to something else ("experience", "nature") which, though we can never see it in a pure form, nonetheless can and does communicate its verdict to us. The consequence is "Nature", i.e. a unified, yet revision-prone world which cognitively makes sense and which morally, socially, fails to do so. By contrast, mankind had hitherto lived in worlds which were cognitively stagnant and morally comforting. We have tried to highlight the mechanics both of our own disenchanted vision and, generically, of the enchanted visions of old. It all hinges on just how you operate the division of labour.

Now is there, or could there ever be, a neutral way of deciding which of these two visions is correct – the morally satisfying and cognitively stagnant one, or the cognitively expansive and morally mute one?

Note that, *from the inside*, each of the two visions ratifies itself. As in Lessing's story of the ring, in which the representatives of the three rival Western religions compete to vindicate their own faith, each ending by endorsing his own, the charm only works *inwards*:[11]

> Do the rings work only inwards and not outwards?
> Does each but love himself?
> Then each of you are deceived deceivers.
> None of your rings is genuine.
> The true ring has been lost.

Both the Platonic and the empiricist or naturalist arguments home in on themselves. Circle for circle, what's the odds? Indeed, latterday irrationalists delight in this *tu quoque* argument.[12]

The only way we have of justifying our own vision is an inelegant conflation of two incommensurate considerations: the internal plausibility of our own model of how, fundamentally, cognition works, *and* the external consideration that it leads to great control, power, and hence, pragmatically, that it prevails.

What is most appealing in the empiricist vision is not the questionably persuasive story about "experience" teaching us, but the deep insistence that a cognitive system must in the end be judged by something outside itself, and outside social control. Whether that X be called Experience or Nature or anything else perhaps does not matter too much. Though experience is never pure and free from theory-saturation, nevertheless persistent probing, the refusal to countenance self-perpetuating package deals, does in the end lead to a kind of referential objectivity. For the attainment of the impressive cognitive performance of the new vision, what mattered was not the particular nature of the External, but the fact that it was not under anyone's control. Empiricist philosophy sometimes sounds subjective; it makes private individual experience into the ultimate base of knowledge. This only expresses the fact that the vision is both individualist and free of social closure.

From the viewpoint of a sociologist or philosophical historian who attempts to explain it all, the really rather surprising fact is that the world *is* indeed amenable to this cognitive strategy. It has in the end generously rewarded those who knew not what they did but, by an historical accident and perhaps from bizarre motives, came to practise it. From our viewpoint, all that is simply a datum. We cannot explain why the assumption of an orderly unified regular Nature, accessible to investigation by a rigorous, truth-preserving notation, is so stunningly effective. That must remain a mystery. We can only try to explain, schematically, the social mechanisms which led us to stumble on it, and which allowed a society to practise it. The assumption of the existence of such a Nature and adoption of the appropriate cognitive strategy is historically eccentric. It is not part of the equipment of most societies. The one society which did stumble on it *and* was in a position to deploy it, in production (and, rather absent-mindedly, in war), conquered the world.

It is natural to try to explain the cognitive and technological effectiveness of the "scientific" vision by saying that the world "really is like that". There "really is" a single and orderly, unified Nature: hence the exploratory strategy which assumes that this is so comes to be successful. This position can be named "realism". Such realism is psychologically very attractive, and quite irresistible for some of us: how could our science work so well, were it not for the fact that the system to which it refers "really is out there"?

Note, however, that this realism in no way genuinely explains the success of this cognitive strategy: it merely re-affirms it. We shall never have some genuinely independent *additional* fact or information, telling us that a unified orderly and indifferent Nature really does exist. Our own atomized, piecemeal, corrigible cognitive style can only give us further data. It precludes, prohibits, a so-to-speak penetrative, global and final access to the underlying totality, which alone could then vindicate, guarantee, underwrite the vision as a whole. It alone would constitute an independent confirmation of our cognitive style (and not a mere covert re-invocation of its success, so far): but just such a confirmation is incompatible with the very style which it would vindicate. The prohibition of such penetration and final cognition is the first principle of the new method; indulgence in it was the crucial feature of the old cognitive styles. So the new spirit is inherently debarred from vindicating itself in a really reassuring manner. All we can ever have is further individual successes of the strategy based on the assumption that this is how things do stand. If you wish to treat this as an "explanation" of the success, and call it Realism, feel free to do so . . .

The sociologist or philosophical historian is not obliged to ponder this question. As far as he is concerned, the fact that mankind eventually turned towards this kind of division of labour and that it works is a datum. Why "Nature" is such as to make this work is not a question he either can or need answer. I do not believe that anyone else can do so either. It is quite enough for him, however, that Nature, at any rate so far, has been obliging enough to make that strategy work brilliantly. The motives of the lady, if she has any, are not his concern. Historically, the lady conferred her favours on us at just the right

moment: a bit sooner and they would have been used to dominate us politically; and had they come a bit later, the economic
revolution might well have foundered through those very internal contradictions which its most famous critic attributed to it.
The new economy would not have been able to bribe its way out.
The political throttling of freedom by the new technology may of
course still come to pass.

What is the sociologist's concern, however, is to explain the
circuitous and near-miraculous routes by which agrarian
mankind has, *once only*, hit on this path; the way in which a
vision not normally favoured, but on the contrary impeded, by
the prevailing ethos and organization of most human societies,
has prevailed. He must counter the ethnocentric narrowness of
those thinkers who, born among latterday beneficiaries of the
unique situation, naively take it for granted, and talk as if it had
been ever with us as a human birthright. It was not: on the
contrary, it is most untypical. It goes against the social grain. It
requires explanation, and we have tried to offer one.

The present position is only very distantly related to Pragmatism, which it may resemble superficially. It does indeed appeal to
success; but only to one particular instance of it – not as a generic
and permanent principle. Pragmatism naively supposes that
selection for *cognitive* effectiveness took place throughout
human history, and of course before that, in nature.

Our kind of pragmatism, should our position be so characterized at all, is altogether different. It merely asserts that the one
radical, traumatic shift to unified, single-purpose, referential
cognition does, when completed, irreversibly confer far greater
power on the societies in which it occurs. The way back is
blocked.

CHAPTER 8

The New Scene

The Concept of Culture and
the Limits of Reason

Cognition has some of the attributes of coercion and some of trade. It has *come* to resemble trade: once it consisted of qualitatively distinct elements, blended into wholes which eluded all bargaining; it has of late shifted to a single idiom, a single measure, a universal logic. The single currency then permits replacement of parts, in the light of convenience. In fact, production itself also only became negotiable, became *trade*, when real penury was overcome. Initially it too tended to be absolute, unnegotiable. But the great switch to a single conceptual currency in cognition is itself, like the acceptance or repudiation of an ultimate threat, something that goes far beyond either haggling or calculation. But it has taken place. And once it has taken place, *within* it, within the new dispensation, innovations are rationally negotiable. They do not impose total and trans-rational choices on those engaged in investigating nature.

There is, however, a curious consequence of the specialization, the insulation, the hiving off of cognition proper from other activities. Once upon a time, concepts were affirmed only in some very small measure as a means of communicating empirical information. Their affirmation was primarily the reminder, the reinforcement, the implicit ever-renewed loyalty-oath to a way of life, to a community, to shared expectation and values, to a recognized system of roles. It was not so much the daily plebiscite, in Ernest Renan's phrase, as the daily ritual of re-confirmation, of membership, of re-initiation.

Yet those functions must still be performed. If no longer

carried out in a way which conflates them with cognition, they must be fulfilled in isolation from it. Modern society may indeed be less tightly organized than traditional societies had been; nonetheless, it still needs some verbal and conceptual rituals, markers of status, of occasion, of membership, of bounds of expected or proscribed conduct. If these tasks can no longer be either performed, or legitimated, by the now severely segregated cognitive deployment of language, they must be performed by other aspects of discourse.

There is a generic term for this set of performances: *culture*. Just as civil society is in effect society minus the state, culture has now become conceptualization minus cognition proper. Just as the notion of civil society is hardly usable unless the state is neatly defined and circumscribed and delimited, so the notion of culture does not really make much sense until the strictly referential, growth-oriented knowledge has hived off under the name of "science". In a simple society, order-maintenance is barely separated from other institutions, and hence one can hardly speak of "civil society". Similarly, when there is no segregated science, and cognition meshes in with all the social markers, there is hardly any point in speaking of a culture as distinct from science.

In a post-Axial society endowed with a storable surplus, a clerisy and a literate codification of doctrine, quasi-cognitive doctrine stands in judgment *over* social practice. Later still, in the crucial development which has transformed our world, cognition detaches itself both from authority and from society, while retaining the unification and orderliness acquired previously. At that point, culture is rendered visible. It also becomes possible for men to become knowingly loyal to *culture*, rather than to a king or priest.[1] The age of nationalism arrives.

What scientific cognition leaves behind is a kind of cultural buttermilk, remaining over after the extraction of the butter of referential knowledge. There are, in fact, many varieties of such buttermilk. The old theological high doctrine may formally continue to claim to be referentially true, though inevitably also conceding, whether with emphasis or evasively, that its own truth is "different in kind" from that of science. A distinction is invented which had been absent before, and would previously have seemed absurd. Alternatively, high theology is dropped or ignored or played down, allowed to fall into the empty space between referential science and non-referential social markers. In that case, the more folksy elements of the previous blend are stressed or even accorded exclusive loyalty. "Populism", a mystique and adoption by educated classes of a folk tradition, or what is believed to be such, arises when societies are unable to maintain faith in the old local high theology, or remain loyal to its institutional carriers, and yet are also unwilling, through national pride, to defer excessively to an alien rationalism.

The central fact is and remains – we must needs live in and with the help of *some* culture (even a syncretic or sliding-scale one, i.e. one taken seriously to a varying extent, according to context). No social gathering, no meal, no establishment or perpetuation of a human relationship, is conceivable without some idiom to set the scene, limit expectations, and establish rights and duties.

Culture now not merely becomes visible, almost for the first time (men now notice that they talk prose); it also becomes, self-consciously this time, an object of reverence, even of worship. Durkheim thought that men revered their own society and culture and made its perpetuation possible, through their worshipful attitude to ritual and, later, to doctrine. We no longer respect the old rituals or doctrines, but we still need social order. So some of us come to revere culture, but this time directly, with new rituals, and in full awareness of what it is we do.

Doctrines which ratify culture and enjoin respect for it were common in the nineteenth century. The fortifying, confirming major premiss no longer claims a transcendent object: it is a theory concerning the role, the function, of culture within the world. Durkheim's own doctrine was one example: religion was to be respected not because it was true (in the straightforward sense assumed by the old theologians), but because it was "true" (i.e. essential and functional within the social order). Durkheim let it be understood that "truth" was just as good as truth, in fact the same thing, really. This general attitude might be called auto-functionalism. It is influential in a very wide variety of forms, in historicist, biological, literary, *kulturgeschichtlich* and other idioms. The auto-functionalist stands outside all cultures to affirm the major premiss: cultures are functional. The minor premiss is stated from inside: I *am* my culture. Conclusion: my commitments are valid (in a sense left deliberately ambiguous).

These self-vindications of culture are generally spurious. The medieval Muslim thinker Al Ghazzali observed that the genuine traditionalist does not know that he is one; he who proclaims himself to be one, no longer is one. Cultural prose ceases to be innocent when Monsieur Jourdain proclaims it to be prose. When culture was genuinely authoritative, men either took it for granted or, later, vindicated it by means of a theology which they held to be true in a literal sense, and which they genuinely respected. The dogmas and imperatives which constituted those doctrines were taken very seriously; they placed enormous burdens and strains on believers. It seems that some of these strains were the catalysts which brought forth our world. Had those beliefs only been held in the double-think, auto-functionalist spirit, they could never have had such a powerful impact. The sleight of hand perpetrated by various typical contemporary ideologies consists of insinuating the contrary: we need (some) culture, so the faith and morals of (this, our) culture are binding on us. Respect so based is seriously flawed. They will hardly take a man through a serious crisis: men may die for their faith, but will they die, or suffer even mild inconvenience, for their "faith"?

There is one respect in which the romantic notion of an embracing culture-cocoon, within which a man lives and finds fulfilment, does indeed score a point against the cult of orderly division of labour. The division of labour is so effective, because by endowing each activity with a single aim, a single criterion, it makes it possible to judge, assess, and hence improve efficiency.

But what we call satisfactions are seldom if ever isolable things or experiences. We live our life in package deals, known as roles within a culture. Isolable sensory or material pleasures enter into these, but in no way exhaust them. Our pleasures and satisfactions, like our sensations and perceptions, are concept-saturated;

and the relevant concepts are those of roles and positions in a *culture*, in a complex way of life, which does not and cannot serve a single end. Whatever plausibility attaches to a single criterion ("happiness", "pleasure") springs from its abstractness and ambiguity: indirectly, it leads us back to a valued way of life, an identity. This inevitably takes us back to the inescapable irrationality of multi-purpose, incommensurate choices, not eligible for an insulation of aims. This is one important, cogent and entirely valid point in the romantic counter-charge against the rationalistic, single-criterion philosophy, which had tried to universalize and generalize the type of thought linked to the effective division of labour, and which tried to see all life and its purpose in an instrumental spirit.

This is a point of great importance both for the social organization, and for the principles of legitimation, of a complex society. Take these spheres in turn.

At the level of social organization, it manifests itself in various ways, of which some of the most important perhaps are the selection of policies and personnel *at the top*, and the way we select deep personal relations. In modern organizations, "rational" (explicit, publicly testable) criteria can be applied to subordinate roles, just as they are to subordinate tasks. In a certain underdeveloped country, the story circulated about a prominent father who was worried that his son, propelled into a senior job in a ministry by his father's influence, was being led into bad habits by his large salary. The father approached his friend the minister, and begged him to re-allocate his son into a more junior post. The minister expostulated: "But my dear friend, if your son is to have a junior post, he'll have to pass exams!"

Occupants of subordinate posts are meant to do a definite job, with clear job specifications. Hence, clear, publicly checkable criteria for performance and suitability exist. If these criteria are not applied, we feel that we are in the presence of *corruption*. Our efficiency depends on *fair* selection of persons for posts, and we believe in meritocracy. But at the top? Or in choice of fundamental policies? Big decisions face issues which are inescapably complex, with incommensurate and multiple criteria entering into the assessment of success. No single criterion being available, we cannot but make do with a less than "rational" and intuitive evaluation. No Delphic oracles for small issues, where reason prevails; but for really big questions, oracle-surrogates remain in use.

The same point also has important implications for private and intimate life. Various observers of modern life have commented on the increased affective importance of the nuclear family and household, and indeed on the cult and mystique of intense personal relations. The erosion and diminution of importance of intermediate, middle-size communities in large, mobile, anonymous societies leads, at one end, to the cult of the large, education-sustained cultural community – in brief, to nationalism; it also leads, at the other end, to the importance of those residual but important personal relations which are not ad hoc, single-shot, instrumental. No rational criteria can sensibly be proposed for a choice of spouse, or any kind of permanently close partner. The criteria entering such a choice are too multiple and incommensurate to be formulated. The cult of romantic love and the *coup de foudre* is presumably in part a cover-up for the inability to give good reasons for either a Yes or a No in these situations. The possibility of invoking the uncontrollable, unpredictable, unaccountable, but – by common consent – authoritative voice of our psychic deep lets us off the hook. We need not explain. As in other contexts, the invocation of an oracle (internal or external) covers up the impossibility of rational decisions in complex situations. It mitigates the offence which such decisions must frequently contain. Our rationalistic background beliefs compel us this time to invoke *internal* oracles, the mouthpieces of the inner dark gods.

If this argument is valid, the days of oracles at the top, for global decisions ineligible for rationality, will never be over. The rationality dependent on the division of labour has transformed our world, but will never reach those all-embracing, inherently multi-strand choices between incommensurate alternatives.

Egalitarianism

A marked feature of modern societies is their egalitarianism. Tocqueville's belief in the secular tendency towards an equalization of conditions is, on the whole, conspicuously vindicated by the facts. Passionate egalitarians dispute this judgment, and complain of the failure of modern societies to live up to the egalitarian ideal. There are indeed enormous differences between men in fortune, power, influence, respect, life prospects.

Modern society is indeed inegalitarian when judged by its own aspirations, but it is markedly egalitarian if compared to the larger-scale and complex societies which have preceded it. Anyone surveying the history of human societies can only conclude that with their growth in scale and complexity, they have also become increasingly more unequal internally – until some fairly recent point in time, when this trend has become reversed.[2] Why did this happen?

It is not enough to invoke modern egalitarian ideology as an explanation. There are profound social reasons why that ideology should have such an impact. The new social reality acclaimed as Liberty, Equality and Fraternity in fact turned out to be Bureaucracy, Mobility and Nationality. The newly emergent order assigns rank more or less by rationally assigned function, it makes status changeable and status-differences gradual, and links the sense of brotherhood and belonging to shared and literate culture, rather than to corporate groups.

Even if equality were not implemented, which at least in part it is, the sheer proclamation of an egalitarian ideal strikingly distinguishes modern society from others.[3] Moreover, in certain ways the ideal is actually implemented. Modern society does not separate out its population into different species, into different *kinds* of human being. It either lacks political or ritual specialists, or tones down their role, and it opens access to these specialisms. Its stratification is continuous and finely graded, without, in the main, any great chasms and discontinuities. If sharp social boundaries do survive or emerge, they engender severe, deeply felt and intolerable frictions and tensions. They are held to be scandalous. Past societies could and did accommodate themselves to radical differentiation of their members. Their functioning, far from being hampered by it, was manifestly eased by profoundly internalized, formally endorsed and severely sanctioned inequalities. The opposite is true of modern society.

Modern society is not mobile because it is egalitarian. It is egalitarian because it is mobile. The degree of its mobility varies, but basically it is destined to remain mobile as long as persistent economic innovation keeps the occupational structure in flux. A fluid occupational structure would, if combined with anything resembling a caste system, engender endless friction. It cannot accommodate itself to the attribution of status independent of occupation and preceding it. Any attempts to do this have led to great strains. Which is to trump which in a given encounter between two men, the permanently ascribed status category, or the rights and duties inherent in the occupational position? Human beings can and do accept profound inequalities, and strangely enough seem to enjoy them, even when they find themselves at the unfavourable end. But they can only do so if they are stable and unambiguous. Under modern conditions, however, the inevitable ambiguity and instability of any profound inequalities could turn them into intolerable irritants. When, as a result of racist sentiment or legislation, a caste-like set of relationships is established, it can only be upheld with very great difficulty and by a sustained deployment of violence. A society making such an attempt is internationally stigmatized.

This is not the only reason why modern economic organization has an inbuilt bias towards the equalization of conditions, or at any rate towards a shared, universal baseline of rank. What passes for work in a modern society is not the application of brawn to matter, but the communication of messages between people – a large number of context-free messages, and a large number of anonymous people. The flow of such information would be hopelessly inhibited if the rank of the carrier were, as habitually it is in more context-sensitive cultures, incorporated in the message.

Whether modern egalitarianism would survive the restabilization of the occupational structure, and whether such a restabilization will occur, we do not yet know. If it is to come, it will not be soon: it is not yet discernible on the horizon. In the meantime, we can expect modern societies to remain egalitarian, in the sense that they espouse the egalitarian ideal and recognize but one kind of human being. Inequalities, however great, will remain statistical and anonymous, rather than formally congealed. They are linked to power positions or wealth, spread out along a continuum devoid of sharp breaks, and only contingently attached to their owners, rather than attributed to some deep ascribed essence.

What Next?

We have followed in rough outline the transformation of the three great spheres of human activity, cognition, production and coercion, across the crucial stages of the division of labour. What can we expect from the future? Simple extrapolation from existing trends is a pointless exercise. Trends in history do *not* follow the past slope of the curve. But there is some point in carrying out the exercise which is the theme of this book: if we argue back to the factors which seem to determine the paths so far, we can see what possibilities of combination and recombination they now face.

Cognition: one strong possibility is that mankind, or a significant portion of it, will continue to live with a permanent tension between cognition and culture. Cognition will remain the domain of serious, socially neutral and disconnected exploration of nature, unpredictable in its outcomes, volatile and hence altogether unusable for the chartering or marker-provision of social life. It will remain inherently technical and discontinuous from the discourse of daily life. This means that the symbol-system used for daily social life is deprived of the kind of validation it had in the agro-literate age. The world we seriously *think* in and the world we *live* in, will remain distinct.

Clearly there is a price to be paid here. Ordinary life, life as lived, has its crises and tragedies. When men face these, they need to be succoured by ideas they take seriously and hold to be cognitively valid. Men can attend carnivals without necessarily endorsing the theological or magical beliefs which had inspired them. "Ironic cultures", which are not granted serious cognitive respect, are perfectly practicable over a large part of life. Many of us live within them, often comfortably enough. But it is hard to be content with them when something very dear and important is at stake, or when tragedy strikes.

One must distinguish between specific problems and generic salvation. Concerning specific ailments, men will no doubt turn to putative or genuine bits of science which offer help, or promise to do so. When it comes to generic salvation, the need to endow life as a whole with an acceptable meaning, they will continue to face the current options: they may hope to extract an overall vision from serious cognition (some men will continue to seek this); or they may turn to (usually bowdlerized and selectively re-interpreted) faiths surviving from the agrarian age, or from the transition period; or they may, perhaps, be satisfied with a candid and brave recognition that the age of cognitive validation is gone for ever.

There might even be a triple fragmentation in developed liberal societies: serious cognition, legitimating ideologies, and the culture of daily life. Serious cognition will of course have direct repercussions on technology, and have its echoes both in ideology and in daily life. Ideological thinking may become stabilized on the analogy of constitutional monarchy, providing continuity but losing much of its authority. It might also become volatile, with a rapid turnover. Whether such a condition will eventually make a society ungovernable, and whether it will be terminated when liberalism is replaced by a faith imposed as a political necessity, or whether there can be a spontaneous out-burst of a new faith (as Max Weber seemed to think), is something we cannot foretell. We can watch the straws in the wind.

Such is the state of the ideological market in developed liberal societies: largely secularized, socially, "symbolically" held historic faiths; a few overtly secular counter-faiths surviving from the first flush of the transition; some more or less lucid recognition of how things actually stand. There is also a fringe counter-culture indulging in an overtly irrationalistic use of both old and new forms of magic and consolation.

There is of course another developed world, namely the Marxist one. In Raymond Aron's admirable characterization, these societies are ideocratic. One might just as appropriately say that they are caesaro-papist. The head of the church is the *de facto* ruler of the state. Church and state possess parallel and intertwining hierarchies, with personnel moving between the two, and the church dominant overall. The doctrine around which the church is organized is one of those nineteenth-century counter-faiths, heavily messianic and oriented towards a collective version of total salvation. It contains not merely a promise of deliverance for all mankind and a theodicy, but also an overall theory of, in effect, *everything*. No aspect of life is untouched by it. The faith has the advantage and the weaknesses of being articulated, more or less, within the recognized idiom and assumptions of serious cognition of its time. It also has the very great and conspicuous advantages of being centred on some of the major problems of its time, notably the problems of economic inequality, social conflict, and the relationship of economy and polity.

Whether on balance all this really is a benefit is arguable. The continuity of the idiom with current cognitive discourse, the fact that the belief system contains propositions about issues which are still objects of scientific inquiry, means that the faith can also be taken seriously as genuine cognition. Its claims certainly overlap with those entertained by scholarship. But it also means that items in the doctrine are perpetually under risk and open to challenge. It would of course be an absolute miracle if all the bits of contemporary science dredged up and incorporated by Marx and Engels in the middle decades of the nineteenth century continued to hold good at the end of the twentieth. The crucial themes are abstract enough to make it ever possible for skilful theologians of the system to adjust them to current need. Such theologians are available, and some of them are gifted. The sustained disconnecting of society-defining myth from current science, so pervasive in the West, is difficult (though perhaps not impossible) for this system.

The situation on the ground in Marxist countries is of course complicated by very diverse local political conditions. In some of these countries, the doctrine is connected with a strongly resented alien domination. It is, for instance, doubtful whether there are any genuine Marxists left in much of Eastern Europe. In countries where a Marxist victory was endogenous and not imposed, the matter is more complex. In a somewhat routinized, semi-secularized, but none the less socially influential way, these societies continue to live "under the banner of Marxism".

In the Third World, one of the great religions as yet shows no signs of weakening under the impact of allegedly general secularization. The socio-political clout of Islam has been enormously enhanced rather than weakened. An explanation is available for this unique, most remarkable and, in the West, not fully appreciated phenomenon. The West has noticed it in connection with the Iranian revolution, but has barely perceived its extent.

Traditional Islam possessed a high theology and organization, closer in many ways to the ideals and requirements of modernity than those of any other world religion. A strict unitarianism, a (theoretical) absence of any clergy, hence, in principle, equidistance of all believers from the deity, a strict scripturalism and stress on orderly law-observance, a sober religiosity, avoiding ecstasy and the audio-visual aids of religion – all these features seem highly congruent with an urban bourgeois life style and with commercialism. The high theology and the scholarly social elite associated with it were traditionally found in the trading towns, which were prominent in Islam. But the upper strata of commercial cities did not make up all of the Muslim world. There was also a countryside, much of it tribal rather than feudal. There, order was maintained by local groups with a very high military and political participation ratio, to use S. Andreski's phrase.[4] So military/political activity was not monopolized by a small stratum, but rather widely diffused. Pastoral/nomadic and mountain groups in particular had a strong communal sense and maintained their independence from the central state. Central authority effectively controlled only cities, and some more easily governable peasant areas around them.

The wholly or partly autonomous rural groups needed religious mediators and arbitrators (as did, for quite different purposes, the urban poor). Thus, quite distinct from the lawyer/theologians who defined and maintained high Islam, there was also a host of semi-organized Sufi, "maraboutic" or "dervish" religious orders and local living saints. These constituted an informal, often ecstatic, questionably orthodox unofficial clergy. It really defined popular Islam, which embraced the majority of believers. For many centuries, the two wings of Islam co-existed, often in tension, sometimes peaceably. Periodically, a (self)-reformation, a purifying movement, would temporarily reimpose the "correct", scholarly version on the whole of society. But though the spirit be willing, the social flesh is weak: and the exigencies of social structure would soon reintroduce the spiritual brokers, mediating between human groups in the name of mediating between men and God. So, even if the formal urban Islam was "modern", the Islam of the countryside and of the urban poor was not.

With the disruption of the Muslim world by an economically and militarily expansive West, a new wave of reformism swept Islam. But this time, it prevailed; and it would seem that it has prevailed for good. Its "protestant" features made it compatible with the modern world, the newly found strengths of urban life gave it a wider and more stable appeal. Above all, it could define the Muslim community in the name of something which had dignity, by modern standards, but which at the same time was genuinely indigenous.

In most countries of the Third World, struggling with an exogenously initiated industrialization, the ideological *ancien régime* had become indefensible. At the same time, the unqualified acceptance of a Western model and ideology meant a humiliating self-rejection. One favoured solution was the invention of a local folk model, and idealizing virtues of the local little tradition. Only thus could one refrain from either endorsing the old local high theology, or fully accepting some Western system of ideas. But Islam was spared this dilemma. The old high culture was carried by scholars more than by political authority, and so could detach itself from the latter and (except in Turkey) remain relatively untainted by its debacle. In this way, the old high culture would become the pervasive culture of the entire society, simultaneously defining it against the outside and providing the impetus for regeneration and self-correction. The consequence is that, at present, both socially radical and socially conservative Muslim regimes are in the throes of a fundamentalist revival, which appears to have a powerful hold over the newly urbanized masses, and even over a very large part of the elite. There is little sign, as yet, of this religious ardour abating.

It is too early to say whether, eventually, this system too will undergo secularization. In the one Muslim country in which secularism has been politically imposed, Turkey, the attempt has proved markedly unsuccessful. Rather, it has greatly accentuated and sharpened social conflict. So it is conceivable that, eventually, Islam will show us a society which is "modern" by other standards, but rigorously organized around a seriously upheld and imposed pre-industrial faith.

The rest of the world as yet presents a motley pattern. India is characteristically dualist: the ideological tradition had possessed a stability which the old Indian *political* structures markedly lacked. The contemporary political central institutions have British (or possibly Muslim) roots, and the high culture is now eclectic and disconnected from the folk culture which perpetuates the old order. Both its fragmentation and its communalism presumably aid the survival of a non-authoritarian, non-military central regime, a survival which is itself something of an oddity in the Third World.

The mystery of the Japanese success in industrialization is far from solved. Some of its features, notably stability of employment and a communal ethos, conspicuously contradict much of the erstwhile conventional wisdom concerning the preconditions of industrial society.[5] On the ideological side, one element, however, is conspicuous, and will presumably have to figure as an element in any adequate account: Japanese culture was on the periphery of China, and was ever pervaded with the sense of the authority of Chinese cultural models. This collective other-directedness presumably made it easy to adopt *another* model, when another model had demonstrated its technical effectiveness. The present effective blend of emulation of Western technology and a good measure of cultural continuity may perhaps be a good example of that separation of culture on the one hand from cognition and from production on the other, which may be the destiny of all industrial societies.

Some regions – Latin America early in the nineteenth century, sub-Saharan Africa in the late twentieth century – acquire political independence in a fragmented form while not yet very far advanced towards industrialism. This means that the state is in a position to acquire means of coercion out of all proportion to the strength of civil society.[6] The balance between power-holders and wealth-producers, in any case generally tilted in favour of the former throughout agrarian society, is tilted even further. The consequence is a strong tendency towards military dictatorship, accompanied by ideological eclecticism and opportunism. In such societies, the superiority of coercion over production, characteristic of the agrarian age, is accentuated rather than diminished by partial borrowings from the new world. They favour the state more than they do civil society.

To recapitulate: at the ideological or cultural level, a number of social forms can be observed at present.

1 Western pluralistic. A free market in ideas and faiths. A widespread recognition, a tacit conceptual concordat, between genuine, nature-explorative cognition, and moral-orientation belief systems. A pre-industrial religion survives, and sometimes

retains an official status, a connection with political ritual and so forth, but is upheld in a rather semi-cognitive spirit. It is maintained along a kind of sliding-scale of bowdlerization, ranging from literal fundamentalism to a complete lack of all cognitive content. It is part and parcel of the situation that the precise location along this spectrum is left ambiguous; the ideological consumer is free to slot himself in at any point.

Some belief systems survive from the age of rationalistic counter-doctrines, though their influence is limited. There is a fairly widespread sense of "disenchantment", a lack of a satisfying world-story. A large part of the intellectual life of the society is taken up by a flourishing re-enchantment industry, a provision of ideological products purporting to reverse all this and endow life with "meaning". The products of this industry have a very high rate of obsolescence. Fashions rotate at considerable speed, almost decade by decade.

The society engenders an active counter-culture, much larger in times of prosperity than in periods when genuine fear of (relative) penury concentrates the minds of potential converts. This counter-culture is sometimes rather chaotically revolutionary and violent, at others quietistic and given to peaceful withdrawal from the world. It is recruited in large part from the young and the less successful members of the more prosperous strata of the society. When affluence becomes even greater, and the memory of its absence ever more distant, and genuine satiety sets in, one may well wonder whether a counter-culture of this kind could become virulent enough to cause genuine disruption.

2 Marxist societies. These are built round a well-integrated nineteenth-century system, within which theoretical accounts of the world and moral/political prescription are fused into one more or less coherent whole. The political order could not survive the defeat of its faith on the open intellectual market, and it does not tolerate any such market. In the short run this is an advantage for the system: able intellectuals, facing the option between expressing themselves within the official idiom and not

expressing themselves at all, often choose the first option. In many cases they may find it psychologically preferable to talk themselves into doing it with subjective sincerity. The internal ambiguities of the system facilitate such a procedure. There is at present a marked diminution of ideological ardour.

3 The Muslim model. Here there is a traditional faith, which in its high culture variant is highly compatible with the requirements of modernization, and whose genuine local roots make it ideally suitable as an expression of a new national identity. There could be a genuine revival of faith and orthodoxy. This certainly appears to be the present situation. Whether this is merely a transitional phenomenon is something only the future will tell.

4 Societies in which paternalistic modernization-from-above is combined with a toleration of the old folk culture, sometimes shared in their private lives by the elite, sometimes politely ignored by it. The uneasy pluralism perhaps has some resemblance to that of the West, even if the elements that go into it are different.

It may of course turn out that the pluralism will not be uneasy. The rationality which had engendered the birth of the modern world pervaded the minds of those who brought about the economic and cognitive miracles. It was a kind of disinterested, un-opportunistic, unconscious or at any rate uncalculating, and in an important sense, *irrational* rationality. It was not instrumental, even if a few thinkers, such as Francis Bacon, seem to have preached it in that spirit. Had it been calculated, opportunistic, instrumentally rational, it probably would not have worked: rewards would have been sought or garnered too soon. Neither honesty in business, nor orderly procedure in cognition, pay off in the short run. They rewarded entire collectivities in the long run, but those collectivities were somehow impelled in that direction by other motives.

Take cognition: a man following traditional ideas is at least deploying something unlikely to be wholly false, and will at least fall in with the social proprieties of his culture. By contrast, given the infinity of possible truths, a man experimenting with new ideas is unlikely to be successful (cognitive success is a miracle), and at the same time is likely to be socially offensive. The impulse to what we now, with hindsight, know to be the correct path, would hardly have been, in any calculating instrumental sense, rational. The transformation of the world had to happen inadvertently.

The obverse of this point is that the only cultures which adopted economic, cognitive and technological rationality "rationally", i.e. instrumentally, did so because the pioneer societies had already shown these to be effective. But for that very reason, they need not be pervaded by the rational spirit in other aspects of their lives. They chose economic and technical rationality as a *means*. It did not in their case emerge as a by-product of a general cast of mind. Men had always been capable of so to speak isolated rationality: they could always apply levers which were already known to work. The first miracle had occurred when men for obscure reasons persisted in working a set of levers not yet known to work. Their fruits were not yet obviously forthcoming. (A characteristic seventeenth-century criticism of the new natural science was its lack of practical value.) Those who adopt the new ways in the opportunistic emulative spirit may maintain or develop cultures quite different from those of disenchantment. The computer and the shrine may be compatible.

This point might even become valid generally. Consumption gadgets tend to be so constructed as to ensure that their employment becomes facile, intuitive. As the balance swings in favour of consumption and against production, a "rational" i.e. orderly, mentality may recede. A technically rational productive economy, requiring little labour, may be compatible with an expressive and anti-rational culture, instead of being, as has been claimed,[7] in a stressful contradiction with it.

5 Backward societies, in which relatively strong states dominate

weak civil societies, and where ideological life is opportunist and largely a function of utilizing the international competition between blocs. *Cuius military aid, eius religio.*

CHAPTER 9

Self-Images

Economic Power (Wealth as Lever)

The basic fact about the contemporary world is the imminent possibility (barring nuclear disaster) of an inverse-Malthusian society: one in which output grows markedly faster than population.

The termination of scarcity must obviously change both society and culture out of all recognition. The whole notion of "wealth", of "goods", is inevitably transformed. The logic of our conduct, the aims we can meaningfully have, are bound to be modified. This has no doubt occurred at least once before, at the point of transition from a gathering to a productive economy: material objects, for a nomadic hunter or gatherer, are, beyond a certain minimum, simply pointless loads. They do not yet become, generically, assets, levers of power. What now?

My belief is that, contrary to the assumption of some economists, human *material* needs are rather restricted and exiguous. They are *not* liable to indefinite expansion. Short of adopting the Roman practice of using emetics at dinner parties, what a man can actually consume is rather limited. A man can also only wear one set of clothes at a time, and be located in only one habitation or vehicle. In an economic situation in which all these minima are easily satisfied, what is the meaning of "possessions"?

The answer is, of course, that they can lead to power and status. They can determine or express the nature of a man's relation to his fellows. It is in this region that our aspirations are located. In this sphere, a man whose literally physical needs are satisfied, may still wish to improve his condition. In this sphere, the end of material scarcity does not imply the end of competition.

But this sphere, on the other hand, does not look as if it were amenable to general growth. On the contrary: it seems condemned to something like a zero-sum situation. One man's gain is another man's loss.

The link between material assets on the one hand, and status and power on the other, is not self-evident or given by the nature of things. The links are socially created, and what we need to think out is what those links can become under the new dispensation. Material goods do still lead to power and status, but they are not the only path towards it. The allocation of position depends on the social system and not the economy.

In the agrarian age, possessions are important for at least three reasons. (1) Scarcity is genuine. Men starve, or die from exposure. (2) Because of this, control over goods is power and leads to more power, as well as requiring power. He who controls objects can induce others to obey him. In so far as agrarian society is – because of the scarcity which is inherent in it – inescapably competitive, violent and coercive, men need to seek power, if only to protect themselves against others who likewise seek power, and who will deprive them of sustenance if they secure it. (3) Partly because of the preceding two factors, possession and display of goods generally is a sign of prestige and status, and thus goods are much sought after. (There are exceptions. Ascetic aristocracies, clerisies or religious virtuosos may on occasion use the inverse way to prestige.)

It would be an exaggeration to say that in an affluent, post-Malthusian age, possession of more or better goods as such never makes any difference to wellbeing. An expensive claret may actually be better than a supermarket Rioja, an individually booked hotel on the Riviera may be better than a package deal on the Costa Brava. (But don't be too sure.) More significantly, expensive medical treatment may on occasion be more effective than treatment available on the National Health Service. (Though, once again, the opposite is not unknown.) Bought education is often much better than that which is freely provided, though, once again, some of it may be markedly, conspicuously worse. Nonetheless, we *are* entering a situation in which the whole concept of wealth assumes a new and perhaps surprising meaning.

There is as yet little evidence that technology has reached a point of diminishing returns. On the other hand, it is difficult to see how further advances, beyond a certain point either reached or soon to be reached by broad strata in advanced societies, make any further contribution to the *material* wellbeing of men. If men continue to compete for increments in material wealth, it must be either from inertia or because such "wealth" is really a means towards status and/or power.

Some further assumptions may be appropriate: one hopes that a certain moral climate will prevail, which damns genuine, objective deprivation as morally scandalous. In conditions of plenty, it is widely felt that it is utterly repugnant that anyone should unnecessarily be deprived of nourishment, medical attention, shelter, and cultural incorporation through education. These moral assumptions are in fact broadly shared, even by those who hold ideological premises which may be in conflict with them (e.g. extreme and rigid commitment to *laissez faire*). There are various reasons why these more or less minimal-humanitarian views are warmly endorsed: men are not ungenerous when it costs them little, and in conditions of affluence and growth, the elimination of genuine poverty imposes few sacrifices on the rest.

Provision for the genuinely indigent is in line with what very many societies have practised in the past within the context of the local and intimate community. The inclination to generalize this attitude to a large and anonymous society is reinforced by the fact that under modern conditions, with atomized and mobile populations, it becomes extremely hard for small, intimate units to fulfil this role. A village could tolerate a village idiot, and help him live an acceptable life; an extended family had no great trouble in carrying one or even a few persons suffering from a long-term disability. By contrast, in a modern nuclear family, where adults tend to be in full-time employment outside the house, and the young in full-time education, the support of such a person becomes a very serious, if not an intolerable predicament.

Given that such tragedies strike unpredictably, an affluent society (including its extreme and doctrinal economic liberals) is inclined in favour of adequate welfare provisions, and will implement them when economic growth makes it possible to do so without visibly taking away anything from anyone else.

A large proportion of the population of the advanced developed countries (i.e. prosperous working class upward) has reached something like affluence, i.e. a condition which, in material terms, surpasses by far the condition of the wealthy in earlier times. Genuine deprivation in these societies occurs only in special cases: (1) the overlap of economic poverty with isolation and other forms of personal disaster, incapacity, inadequacy, illness, etc.; (2) minority groups excluded from full cultural participation in the society; (3) periods of economic stagnation or recession, when resources are canalized into buying off hostility of powerful groups in the society, such as the well-organized parts of the working class, and when services intended for groups devoid of political clout inevitably suffer.

Let us make the optimistic assumptions of a return of growth, and of a solution of the problem of conspicuously identifiable minorities. (The former assumption is not a very strong one; the latter is more problematical.) In other words, assume a fully affluent and reasonably homogeneous society, permeated by ethical assumptions about the inadmissibility of destitution, and one growing or capable of growth, and thus capable of staving off discontent where it is rooted in material deprivation only.

In simpler terms, we assume a society without material scarcity. That does not mean – and this is the crucial point – that it will be free of other forms of scarcity or competition. It is perfectly possible that such non-material conflicts may become more, not less, acute.[1] But the point is that in a situation in which we have assumed everyone to be supplied materially with a sufficiency, conflict or competition will have to be not about wealth in a narrow sense. It must, in effect, be about prestige and power.

It may seem implausible to suggest that wealth as such will cease to be a matter of concern. Perhaps it is indeed an unrealistic expectation, but the matter is far from clear or obvious. The experiment has not yet been carried out. If the suggestion seems implausible, it may be so because in our society, and in the societies most men have lived in since the neolithic revolution, wealth, power and prestige have remained strongly linked.

It is not inconceivable that once wealth ceases to be necessary as an insurance against material deprivation, an adequate minimum being generally assured, the link between wealth and power and prestige will become different in kind. Affluence already in some measure undermines the power of wealth: the extreme difficulty of recruiting staff for servile domestic posts in affluent societies (even during periods of unemployment) strongly indicates this. Mankind will crawl under the whip of hunger, but not in response to mere bribery.

In a fully affluent society, men can really only compete for "positional" goods, for relative social position. They are not struggling to fill their stomachs: they are struggling to improve their position, by whatever means are made available by social context and convention. The question then is – will material goods remain an effective way of acquiring such positional goods?

Note that an important form of industrial society exists – contemporary communism – in which the answer to this question is largely in the negative. High positions, within what is in effect a single hierarchy, carry material goods – car, servants, *dacha* – as a corollary: but the obverse is not true, or only very seldom and marginally. It is seldom the case that a man who has made a lot of money on the grey or informal market can thereby buy his way into the party hierarchy. Power engenders wealth, but not vice versa.

The discussion of an analogous development in non-Marxist societies may seem artificial and implausible, given the notorious and much-castigated, feverish and deeply engrained consumerism of Western societies (which communist societies would eagerly emulate if they were allowed to do so). It is, however, reasonable at least to explore the implications of the supposition that this will not go on for ever. There is the possibility that it is only a transitional phenomenon, perpetuated by three factors:

1 Material needs proper are still not fully satisfied. A further increment in material welfare may still genuinely reduce domestic drudgery, or even improve the quality of consumer goods.

2 The recollection of genuine scarcity is still so vivid, whether as a personal memory or as something engrained in the culture, that people continue to seek material goods beyond any necessity. (An émigré from a socialist country whom I know insists on keeping his giant fridge overful and bulging, on the misguided assumption that goods may soon disappear from the shops – an assumption valid enough in his home country, and one which has ineradicably entered his soul.)

3 In liberal pluralist societies, wealth can genuinely buy a man position and power. Though the texture of sand and sea is the same on a cheap package holiday and in an exclusive and expensive resort, the ability to go to the latter can carry with it membership of a powerful elite. In the sphere of education, the possibility of buying a favoured, preferable identity is particularly important. This is inequitable and as such offensive to modern egalitarianism.

The possibility of purchasing power also has marked beneficial political consequences: in a society in which all perks are attached to occupancy of a single hierarchy, the struggle for control of that hierarchy inevitably acquires a ruthless winner-take-all quality. In such conditions, tolerant liberal politics, free of the escalation inevitably engendered by winner-take-all conflict, and of the pre-emptive suppression of losers by winners, is scarcely conceivable. At any rate, it has not as yet occurred, despite various attempts in this direction. In a society in which wealth *also* constitutes a form of power, and so pure power has no monopoly, pluralism and the possibility of buying off losers is at least available. Hence it is possible to limit the stakes (and hence the ruthlessness and totality) of political conflict.

In liberal societies, the residue of pre-industrial status systems also introduces a valuable pluralism into the system. Many positional goods, e.g. honours for achievement, cannot be purchased through wealth (or only in a limited proportion of cases). It was really the crucial sign of the transition from the rule of thugs to the rule of producers, when those "in trade" could be richer than those in power, and did not need to hide or dissimulate their wealth. They did not need to transform it into power at the first opportunity. When trade became more profitable than robbery, a new world was born. A great change occurred when wealth became conceivable without power; another such transition may take place when position becomes attainable without wealth.

In so far as the drive to useless wealth is motived by the pursuit of position and status, it may be arrested by inventing new marks of position and making them effective. Possibly the material status-markers will lose their magic, precisely by devaluation through abundance, and through their frequently self-defeating character. (In a small town, when every family has a number of cars, no one can drive or park anywhere.) The mood of a counter-culture, which may be ephemeral and which is minoritarian, may become more general, though there is as yet no indication in Western society of a determined breakaway from the use of goods as signs of status. Yet it is widely recognized that their production is environmentally disastrous and socially self-defeating. Cultural inertia or a stalemate of interlocking interests?

Perhaps the breakaway will eventually come. The alternative is a society of permanent potlatch, where competitive status-seeking by consumers leads to an inherently pointless production and destruction. Something similar may have happened in late Rome. The large landowners managed to push free farmers off the land and make them go to Rome as proletarians, while they manned their estates with slaves as a result of Roman conquests.[2] With the slaves they produced corn which fed the city of Rome and its proletarians; the city acted as arbiter in a curious political selection system, in which feeding the populace played its part. To feed the populace, corn had to be bought from the land-owners, who produced it with the help of the slaves who had replaced the proletarians ... One feels that the whole circle was somewhat pointless: could not some other political procedure be found, dispensing with a useless consumption city, leaving farmers on the land, and not importing slaves? But there was, it seems, no way of breaking out of the interlocking constraints, and something similar might yet turn out to be true of status-consumerism.

The question whether affluent liberal society is doomed to remain a perpetual potlatch society or whether it can convert itself into something else, is indeed one of the most intriguing of issues. Some Western societies can confer positional honours by sheer ascription: knighthoods in Britain, the Légion d'Honneur in France. Conferring either of these does not either use up scarce natural resources or pollute the atmosphere.

The trouble is that these symbols only mean something at the top of the society, where there is a kind of metropolitan village, with mutual familiarity and a great concern with relative ranking and pecking order. *La place à table ne ment jamais* (Mauriac). In a thoroughly anonymous and mobile suburb, on the other hand, how can one convey status other than by material symbols which do waste resources and cause pollution? Would it be conceivable for local councils to confer, let us say, municipal mini-knight-hoods? Of course it is conceivable, but would they be taken seriously enough to dissuade both the recipients of the Borough Ks, *and* their unsuccessful rivals, from purchasing unnecessarily large cars?

There really seem to be at least four options: perpetual potlatch; a universal Bohème arising from a victorious, generalized counter-culture; an artificial re-ritualization of society, such as was in part practised by European right-wing dictatorships earlier in this century; or the Soviet caesaro-papist system, in which a single unified hierarchy confers both power and wealth, can control pollution but is incapable of extending liberty (which would destroy that single hierarchy).

The first continues the chase for an inherently pointless further augmentation of material goods, by using them as tokens in the pursuit of status. At the same time, this system is pluralist and favours liberty. The second option would generalize the repudiation of wealth in the manner pioneered by Bohemian counter-cultures since the very beginning of industrialization. The third way would remove the now rapidly expanding leisure time from the private world and restore it to organized, communal activities. To do so, however, it would have to invent and create such ritual-sustaining communities in a world which at the moment is not well endowed with them.

The individual, socially unorganized use of leisure is hard to conceive when leisure becomes truly widespread. Blaise Pascal noted the desperate need for *divertissement* felt by privileged members of society who have leisure thrust upon them. In Pascal's opinion, they danced so as to escape the ultimate despair inherent in the human condition. When leisure is thrust on us all, how shall we dance? Could it possibly be a series of individual, uncoordinated dances? Most of what we know about the human psyche makes this implausible.

We are familiar with the social forms engendered by a pervasive need for work and coercion. Can we as yet imagine the patterns possible when these needs become attenuated?

The New Coercive System

The coercive system of a modern complex society operates under conditions and constraints which are radically different from those prevailing earlier. Direct coercion is rare, and only occurs in certain exceptional circumstances. Men are relatively seldom obliged to do things by weapons held at their throats. Some of those circumstances are:

1 Revolutions and civil conflict can occur. The Iranian revolution has demonstrated that in a partially modernized country, a wave of strong urban feeling can de-legitimize a regime, can sweep it away and overcome even a large, well-equipped, un-defeated and disciplined army. It can destroy a state machine

which is anything but bankrupt. The once widely held view that military defeat and economic bankruptcy are required for a successful revolution has been dramatically refuted.

2 Urban areas can become ungovernable and unpoliceable, at any rate for a state restrained in ruthlessness. Sizeable populations go into a kind of internal dissidence. This may overlap with terrorism, which in turn is greatly facilitated by various aspects of modern technology and the anonymity of mass society.

3 This kind of semi-political urban violence can overlap with urban criminality and government-by-mafia. Ruthless organizations can prevent or inhibit the effective use of legal procedures against themselves.

4 The astonishing case of the Lebanon deserves to receive greater attention. It contradicts many of the most plausible generalizations about modern commercial society, notably the idea that their functioning presupposes the maintenance of public order. The Lebanon is now in effect a territory without a state. The so-called state is the locus at which sub-community leaders negotiate truces with each other. Nevertheless, the level of production and general economic performance, at least for quite a time, probably remained superior to those of many "developing" societies with relatively effective states. The Israelis, with a strong state, cannot control inflation; the Lebanese, without a state, could or at any rate did control theirs. (This argument ought perhaps to be invoked by extreme anti-etatist protagonists of *laissez faire*.) The Lebanese case may be so exceptional that, when properly scrutinized, it does not really contradict the plausible generalizations about the need for public order for a functioning economy; but it should perhaps receive such a scrutiny.

5 Direct and immediate coercion obviously were deployed in the large concentration camps and gulags of Hitler and Stalin. These cases prove that direct and brutal coercion can still be applied. They do not prove that it need be. It is not obvious that either

233

system would have failed to work (by its own criteria) had it refrained from using this method as extensively as it did.

These exceptions apart, the generalization with which one may begin is that the maintenance of public order in complex modern societies is relatively easy. Blatantly unpopular regimes do survive; liberal regimes, with astonishingly mild and unrepressive police and judicial methods, also survive. A complex division of labour does turn out to have some at least of the consequences which Durkheim attributed to it. Society is at least cohesive enough to enable those who control the centre to stay there, without fearing anarchy and disintegration. The interdependence of society's diverse parts seems to make it susceptible to conformity. Systems of authority can survive both extreme unpopularity and great permissiveness, though not perhaps both at the same time.

In some ways, modern societies may yet become ungovernable, given the unavailability of rational legitimations and loss of faith in irrational ones. Nevertheless, the imposition of order by the central state does seem easy, and it is widely imposed without excessive difficulty. Political structures are surprisingly stable. Arguably a liberal modern state interferes in the lives of its citizens far more than a traditional pre-industrial despotism. The complexity and interdependence of society, and its dependence on an overall infrastructure, makes its members docile and habituated to obedience to bureaucratic instructions. In one way, the striking thing about Nazi-dominated Europe is not the brutality of its camps, but the amount of obedience it could extract without even deploying such brutality. People cooperated in the various stages of their deportation and eventual annihilation. Submission to bureaucratic orders is habitual, normal and inevitable. If the final step of a series of conformities to instructions leads to the gas chamber door, it is then too late to resist.

Another very profoundly significant instance of the order-maintaining potential of modern society, whose implications deserve our most attentive study, is the "normalization" of Czechoslovakia after 1968. A regime which corresponds neither to the wishes nor to the economic interests nor to the general culture of a population, and which was publicly and passionately denounced and despised by the majority at its inception, was eventually imposed, without – and this is the truly staggering fact – a single execution or political murder. The manner in which it was achieved is interesting. The argument of the lesser evil, the threat of "lest worse befall", can induce liberals to moderate their struggle with the conformists, and to tone down their resistance. Once a plea of this kind is effective, opponents can be insulated, and "salami tactics" applied. The majority is suborned by the fear of, quite pointlessly, suffering the same fate as an already penalized minority.

The professional middle class is tamed by threat of deprivation of what it holds dearest – education for its children, and meaningful work for itself. This kind of pressure can be astonishingly and depressingly effective, if no simultaneous collective, large-scale defiance crystallizes. If collective opposition does retain its cohesion, it is difficult to cope with it, as the Polish Solidarity period shows. But even there, central authority maintains itself, notwithstanding the open contempt in which it is held by a large part of society.

All this does indicate something about the balance of power prevailing between state and civil society under contemporary conditions. It may be argued that in some of these cases, the imposition from above was perpetrated on populations sadly lacking in a recent tradition of resistance. I do not think this point should be given too much weight. Mass liquidations under Hitler also affected Russian and other prisoners of war; the imposition of detested regimes in Eastern Europe also occurred amongst populations with strong traditions of political turbulence and of romantic, even hopeless, resistance.

It is interesting that whilst the imposition or maintenance of order by anyone in possession of the central machine seems easy, the imposition and internalization of faith is not. Given the importance, pervasiveness and sophistication of modern mass media, and the centralization of education, the opposite was to be expected. But the Communists have conspicuously failed to emulate the Jesuits. The Communist counter-reformation in Eastern Europe has in no way succeeded in repeating the performance of the original Counter-Reformation in southern Europe after 1648, which sent half a continent to sleep for centuries. This too is something we should ponder.

What general propositions can one make about the coercion system or state apparatus in modern society?

First, the units over which it operates will seldom be smaller than those of a nation state, and they will in the main contain culturally homogeneous populations. The nationalist imperative, the requirement of "one state, one nation", will by and large be implemented. The cultural heterogeneity which was so characteristic of and even useful to large agrarian states leads to considerable difficulties in mobile and near-universally literate and educated populations. Cultural pluralism goes well with insulated rural communities, and with stable and hierarchical occupational systems, with profession and status transmitted from generation to generation. It goes exceedingly ill with mobile populations dependent on a state-supervised educational system for their culture.

Second, modern societies will inevitably be centralized. The importance of the shared infrastructure, its tremendous cost, and the need for its homogeneous and even maintenance over a reasonably large area, all ensure this. Given the importance and power of this centralized system, and the fact that it is at least an important (though not necessarily the only) source of the perks and prestige attaching to *positions*, it will continue to play a large part in the lives of men.

One important nineteenth-century sociological theory which has also become a world religion does seriously, and disastrously, contest it. But the notion of a complex industrial society, with its all-pervasive infrastructure, restricting itself merely to an innocuous "administration of things", is absurd. Given that the state is bound to exist and to be powerful and important, the question we must ask about the state is not *whether*, but *of what kind*. One option is a state which leaves the economy relatively autonomous and thus opens avenues to power other than political. Hence it can be liberal, though possibly at great ecological cost. If the state is the *only* real source of privilege, this automatically escalates the seriousness of political competition. That in turn makes liberty virtually impossible. The nature of the modern production process erodes effective local, non-economic institutions. (Raymond Aron used to say that there were only two real institutions in France – the state and the Communist Party.) The maintenance of order and of the global, indivisible infrastructure cannot but be the concern of the central power. If the independence of economic institutions is *also* destroyed in the name of "socialism", it is impossible to avoid a single-hierarchy society, and all that this implies.

Third, the weapon systems in the possession of fully developed industrial societies are so powerful and so expensive, so difficult to build up, that open and outright resistance by civil society against the state is barely conceivable. The period in which market and industrial society emerged was quite different. Twice in two successive centuries, the monarchy presiding over the most crucial society was decisively defeated by its own citizenry, once in its home country, and once in its transatlantic colonies. Yet this monarchy presiding over a pluralist and commercial society could also repeatedly defeat its continental, far more centralized and wholeheartedly military rival; but it could not do the same to its own subjects. The military equipment which could be improvised by a rebelling population was not significantly inferior (if inferior at all) to that in possession of the central army. This kind of balance of military strength is not something that we shall ever see again. And here of course we come to the crucial question – how frequently, how generally, can we expect power to be liberal rather than totalitarian?

The totally new economic base of society obviously affects the situation, though it is not entirely clear in which direction. Agrarian states are generally impelled in an authoritarian direction by the exiguousness of resources and production. On the other hand, the removal of the economic whip may lead to the emergence of wilful counter-cultures, or a general unwillingness to occupy the less prestigious positions in the system. The logic of the type of cognition which underlies the emergence (though not perhaps the emulation or maintenance) of modern technology tends to deprive the state of the absolutist legitimation of the kind that agrarian states habitually invoked. This has also removed one temptation to authoritarianism: modern power holders are less likely to be authoritarian from a sincere sense of religious duty.

It is less than clear whether there is an economic impulsion towards liberalism. In the short or middle run, liberal societies tend to do markedly better, economically, than over-centralized ones. In the middle-long run, both may do well enough, and expansion of output may matter less than internal maintenance of order. One thing seems certain: the liberalism which accompanied the initial emergence of a technological and scientific society is no longer necessary (though it may still be advantageous) for its emulative reproduction. It is conceivable that inertia will be decisive, and that advanced societies will perpetuate the system they possessed, for whatever historical accident, at the point of attaining prosperity.

The Two Running-Mates

The transition to industrial society has stimulated the emergence of two great rival but intimately related ideologies: liberalism and socialism. Neither is seriously conceivable outside the context of industrial society. Each contains a theory of how society does, and how it should, function. Both were perhaps over-impressed by the explosion of wealth. Each is open to the suspicion that it underrates politics and coercion.

Liberalism is inspired by the conspicuous contrast between the old agrarian-predatory societies, stagnant, oppressive, and dominated by the sword and superstition, and the progressive, prosperous and relatively free societies which followed them. A miraculous transformation has occurred which has for once transferred power from the predators to the producers. The transfer was accompanied by vastly improved government, growing wealth, growing knowledge and cultural enrichment, a softening of manners. Anyone perceiving this change could hardly fail, or so it seemed to those smitten by the vision, to make it the central fact of his thought. In its simple, elegant and extreme form, the conclusion then runs as follows: the lesson is plain. Government, constraint of men by other men, is at best a necessary evil. It should be restrained to the minimum. (Ibn Khaldun's definition of government probably remains the best: it is an institution which prevents injustice other than such as it commits itself.) This achieved, men freed from fear will, through the free pursuit of their own interest, lead mankind to material and intellectual riches, in peace and freedom.

The picture has an enormous appeal. Anyone comparing, towards the middle of the eighteenth century, as Adam Smith did, the burghers of Glasgow with the barbarism still prevalent a small number of miles to the north, could not easily resist being swayed by such a vision. This basic picture has retained a great appeal to this day, and has recently enjoyed a certain revival.

The rival vision insists that the hump of industrialization led to a severely polarized society, with acute poverty for the new industrial working class. This may or may not have been more acute than the rural squalor which had preceded it, but at any rate it seemed such, and perhaps actually was worse. It was certainly far more conspicuous and dramatic. This situation will not improve or will even deteriorate, and this is inherent in the basic logic of the system. All this is sufficient to lead one to reject the entire system, and seek an alternative.

Over and above the polarization and poverty, there was also the romantic objection to the new and acute division of labour. The worker was separated, "alienated" from both the tools and the product of his work. He had to sweat away at an isolated and inherently meaningless task, in order to gain the pitiful minimum which would enable him and his dependents to survive. The vaunted liberation from oppression brought by commercial/industrial society was but a fraud: all that had happened was that coercion had assumed a new and more inhuman form. Secondary, indirect coercion had at long last become pervasive and dominant.

Even as in the old agrarian order, the thug rulers did not need to hold the sword to the peasant's throat all the time, but could content themselves with guarding the entrance to the storehouse, so now the new-type thugs contented themselves with enforcing the *rules* of the market (as indeed their manifestoes proudly proclaimed). No need for them to extort wealth with direct menaces, as had been the old amiable custom. An entirely impersonal economic mechanism, free of visible or conspicuous coercion, was quite sufficient to ensure that, under seemingly fair rules, the oppressed were powerless in face of their exploitation. They could be deprived of the fruit of their labour, without ever needing to look into the muzzle of a gun.

To the liberals, it was and remains unthinkable that mankind should be capable of such ingratitude and folly as to fail to be thankful for the shift from thug rule to producer rule. The lemming surge towards a return to the rule of force and dogma, the eager rush along the road to serfdom, accompanied by eager moralizing and messianic zeal, is something which can only inspire the liberal with horrified puzzlement. It leads him to depth-psychological speculations, concerning how this bizarre *Sehnsucht* for slavery can have such a hold over the human heart. Mankind has hardly been liberated from the millennia-old rule of thugs and humbugs, when large portions of it, led by a significant segment of the intelligentsia, rush towards a re-establishment of authoritarian and ideocratic rule. They do so in the name of an alleged new millennium which promises to correct the defects of that very market system which had liberated mankind. But these defects might be corrected far more effectively, without possibly irreversible return to a new and more dangerous set of kings and priests. Thinkers such as Schumpeter had noticed this odd and moralistically complacent self-destructiveness of a free society.

The socialist vision has its answer to all this. From one viewpoint, it is but a version of the typical romantic reaction to the new mobile, industrial world. The romantics, who dislike the new ways, generally cannot opt for a return to the *ancien régime* which had preceded the modern developments. The *ancien régime* is remembered too well and is known to be repugnant. So what they do instead is to seek a return to a simpler, pristine social form, exemplified by an even earlier condition and possibly surviving in some measure amongst relatively untouched rural communities. The populists who feared the impact of the West did not rhapsodize about the Czar, but about the muzhik.

Marxism, curiously enough, did much the same, *nur mit ein bisschen anderen Worten*. It never said – we wish to repudiate the intellectual and political achievements of the Enlightenment. The assumption was that man's original generic essence was collectivist, cooperative, and that it had been temporarily corrupted and obscured by a series of exploitative social formations, of which both the various agrarian stages and industrial capitalism were but successive sub-species. The alleged collectivism of early man was a view taken over by Marxism, and made into the essence of humanity. Not the Russian muzhik, but a universal pan-muzhik was hidden and encapsulated in us all, signalling desperately to be let out.

In a curious way, Marxism is also an extremist exaggeration of liberalism. Liberalism dislikes coercion and recommends that it be minimized. Marxism goes much further and anticipates that it will be abolished altogether. Is this feasible? The strange doctrine that indeed it is, follows from the postulation of a basically cooperative, harmonious nature of man. Conflict and violence are inherent neither in his nature nor in his general situation, but merely in a specific (though alas fairly widespread) kind of situation, engendered by the division of labour and differential control over the means of production. Once these are abolished, coercion, and in particular the entire coercive apparatus known as the state, become redundant and will, in the famous phrase, wither away.[3]

There is a curious element of truth in this: the agrarian human condition, though it certainly did not invent violence, did make it mandatory and pervasive: the stored surplus in a Malthusian society must needs be guarded, and those who control it are the rulers. The curious inference is that both the division of labour and coercion can be abolished on the basis of affluence, and that

241

a social form is available, imminent, and indeed somehow self-generating, in which coercion and enforced specialization both will be absent. It remains to be seen whether we have the slightest reason to anticipate such an end of coercion.

So, the perception of the great transformation, of the replacement of predators by producers (or, if you wish, by exploiters), engendered two ideological poles, two extreme positions concerning the rightful ordering of society: there are those who, perceiving the institutional features which had brought us wealth and liberty, codified them and want to turn them into the entrenched features of our social constitution. They argue this on the eminently questionable assumption that the unique conditions of the emergence of industrialism will persist during its maturity. They are opposed by those who repudiate them as frauds, and wish to institute a social order even better, which retains all the merits of the liberal ones, but in even more extreme form, and is freed of the erstwhile fraudulence. It remains to be seen what merit either of these general diagnoses and programmes possess, when applied to our real condition.

The Right-Wing Alternative

Although liberalism and Marxism may be the most striking and obvious reactions to the new age, they are not the only ones. The centre and the far Left do not exhaust the political and ideological spectrum. The Right, and rather diverse forms of it, is not devoid of importance and interest. It is as well to remember that as far as continental Europe is concerned, an ideologically eclectic but politically confident version of the right-wing reaction was securely in command in the early 1940s. Continental Europe would have accommodated itself to the New Order. Large segments of it would have done so without excessive reluctance. The philosophical stock of ideas of the continent would have found little difficulty in providing the status quo with a vindication, had it remained victorious.

It was a geographical and historical accident that an offshore island and two essentially extra-European powers eventually destroyed this option. The outcome of the war was not a foregone conclusion and, but for complacency, folly and politically pointless excesses on the part of the temporary victors, it might well have gone the other way. It may not have been *the* destiny of Europe, but it certainly was *a* possible destiny.

It is salutary to consider this option and its intellectual bases. It is idle to pretend that it was an aberration, which had somehow appeared on the scene from outer space. Some celebrated commentators have come close to claiming something of the kind.[4] In fact, this option was present on the natural agenda of European development. It is complacent and unwise to ignore this. The elements which went into it were not fully coherent, and the particular version which was vanquished in 1945 may hopefully be assumed to be dead. It would be wrong, however, to conclude that none of the elements which went into it deserves our attention.

A central thread in our argument has been the consideration of the implications of the re-naturalization of man. The cognitive explosion, which made possible a society based on growth and affluence, also fatally eroded the old systems of legitimation by supra-terrestrial authority. The consequence was discussed: new systems of legitimation arose, which placed the ultimate locus of authority not in the Other, but in *man*.

So far so good. But in this kind of approach, an enormous, indeed a decisive, weight is placed on the conception or image of man which is at its base. Man rules OK: but what *kind* of man is it that rules?

The Enlightenment naturalized the bases of legitimacy and the vision of man. But naturalized man as presented by the eighteenth century was astonishingly innocuous and benign. The thinkers of the Enlightenment were perhaps not totally starry-eyed, but they were exceedingly optimistic.

The eighteenth-century naturalistic view of man was based primarily on a rather innocuous empiricist theory of knowledge, or an almost equally innocuous materialist psychology. Men were governed, if not by reason, then at least by interest. Interests could be beneficially channelled. This image of man was not based on a biological vision of man, such as was to become persuasive after Darwin. The confluence of several currents – the incorporation of man in a nature red in tooth and claw, and a romantic cult of dark drives and irrationality, and a sense of community – was destined in due course to lead to an altogether different picture. This is a view which, all in all, bears a closer resemblance to the human being we know, and whom psychiatrists know, than does the anodyne accumulator of pleasures and the subtractor of pains, the gourmet-accountant of the Enlightenment.

So later, less benign re-naturalizers argued quite differently. They knew that the rather unusual species of man which had *engendered* modernity was not typical; and they did not necessarily like this sub-species. Sometimes they detested it. They could claim that most men had not taken delight in instrumental rationality and the division of labour. Instead, they had found their fulfilment in violent, uncalculating feeling, or in participation in absorbing communities which did not separate diverse human functions. The cult of violent affect, and of *Gemeinschaft*, were two important constituents of this second version of re-naturalization.

The Second Naturalization of Man, as it might be called, which took place in the nineteenth and twentieth centuries, consisted of seeing man not as a harmless collector of satisfactions, but as a being whose real driving force was found in dark, irrational drives. Moreover, the type of psychology associated with the names of Nietzsche and Freud implicitly or openly devalues the commandments of conscience and compassion. These allegedly higher principles are dethroned, and seen as devious, and perhaps pathological or pathogenic, expressions of the same drives which, in their more brutal form, are at least candid and healthy. Morality, on this kind of view, is but the pursuit of instinctual satisfaction by other means.

The persuasive syllogism ran roughly as follows. Major premiss (dating from Enlightenment): morality must be based on what man genuinely wants, or what he *really* is. Minor premiss (inspired by biology, and/or depth psychology): what man actually wants is rooted in his instinctual drives.

You may choose your own formulation of the conclusion. It is, however, liable to be disturbing, whichever way you put it.

The implications of the Second Naturalization of Man can blend with a number of other trends. The obverse of the Selection of the Fittest, the mechanism allegedly employed by Nature, is the ruthless elimination of the unfit. Ruthless competition, already attributed to the market by *laissez faire* economics, may be attributed to communities rather than individuals. Psychic need and health, economic growth, and the attainment of excellence, may all jointly conspire to undermine and repudiate fraternal, egalitarian, humanitarian ethics.

This vision of the human psyche may also fuse with a more realistic social psychology: an atomized, individualistic, anomic mass society may perhaps have been essential for the breakthrough from productive stagnation. But it is profoundly alien to what men really want from their society. What they really want is to *belong*, to a clearly identified, demarcated, symbolically reinforced community. Moreover, they long to have and know their place within it.

If this is so, universalism and the brotherhood of man go by the board: the obverse of possessing a bounded community is that someone must also be beyond those bounds. The obverse of overcoming anomic status-uncertainty is a return to hierarchy and discipline. All this leads to a re-ritualization of social life and to heavily theatrical politics. The de-sacralized, instrumental, humdrum, ritual-free politics of the new productive order have difficulty in either restraining internal conflict or inspiring resolution in external defence. A revival of ritualistic and emotive politics and of a sense of community, but now expressed in a naturalistic idiom, may then come to have considerable appeal.

The premiss of natural selection is that it operates on entire species. One needs only to treat "races" as a kind of species, and to see the re-integrated, re-sacralized community as a genetic one, to arrive at that blend of racism and ritualized, hierarchical politics and cult of leadership which ruled most of Europe for nearly half a decade during the mid-century, and which aspired to govern it for a millennium. The ingredients which went into it were all taken from stock, from the available themes of Western thought. The repudiation of an atomized, cold and instrumental society it shared with the Left. The repudiation of an unlimited autonomy of the market, and the desire to subordinate the economic to the political, it shared with the moderate centre. The preference for deeply rooted and occasionally ecstatic, uncalculating emotional satisfaction over mere accumulation of humdrum pleasure, it shared with a pervasive romantic tradition.

The whole brew also fits in with some important social factors. It is difficult to run a society consisting of nothing but a desacralized, instrumental political centre and an atomized civil society. Some kind of "corporatism", i.e. settlement of social issues by negotiation between the major new interest groups, is difficult to avoid, though of course it may be informal and unavowed. In a society based on a generalized, school-transmitted "high" (literate) culture, a man's capacity to identify with communities defined by such high cultures becomes the most important factor in his life. "National" sentiment becomes powerful. A society of this kind finds it difficult to tolerate a visible ethnic division of labour. Under the mythology of an old genetic community, there was the insistent reality of a new cultural one.

What passes for a right-wing reaction to post-agrarian society contains a number of ingredients, far from logically coherent with each other, but nevertheless combined in various proportions. These elements also enter into ideological cocktails which are not classified as right-wing:

1 A real desire to uphold pre-modern ideas and principles of organization, inspired by a genuine, literal belief in their validity.

2 A functional, instrumental desire to uphold or revive such ideas, but as a *means* to restoring a sense of community and stability, without literally believing in them. Note: it is often impossible to distinguish, even within the mind and heart of a single man, between (1) and (2), between faith in an old order,

and a functional faith in faith as social cement, rather than as truth. In practice, both these forms of conservatism are rather selective in what they wish to preserve or restore or invent.

3 A belief in competition and ruthlessness, as a condition either of economic wellbeing or of eugenic wellbeing, or of both. (This strand is in logical conflict with the cult of traditional communities, but the logical strain has not prevented many from blending the two elements. Stress on competition between rather than within communities may make it possible to square the two.)

4 A repudiation of the autonomy of the economic sphere and the re-imposition of the polity on it – compatible with (1) and (2) and questionably compatible with the economic element in (3). However, once again, many have found this logical strain quite easy to bear.

5 A cult of community, in effect cultural, but conceived as genetic, and related to the theory of excellence-through-competition-and-discrimination, but applied to collectivities rather than individuals.

6 A cult of communal belonging, associated with an idea that deep, powerful bonds will often consist of love of community and loathing of outsiders.

Acorn or Gate

The mainstream nineteenth-century mind was inspired by the vision of the seemingly irresistible sweep of Western history from Middle Eastern swamp and mud to the power and dynamism of Atlantic civilization, and found further confirmation in its apparent corroboration by Darwinian biology. It may be excused for having been intoxicated by Progress and Evolution. It turned them into key notions of its intra-worldly metaphysics. It may have been a little uneasy about some counter-examples: within Marxism, for instance, there is an awkward and permanently embarrassing chasm between its "dialectical", permanently unstable and progressive characterization of Western society, and its attribution of stagnation to the Orient. Given the pervasive Europocentrism of the thought of the time, the fact that the East will have to be taken in tow did not bother the founding fathers of this movement too much. The asymmetry was more or less ignored. Nowadays, the consignment of non-Europeans to second-class membership of History has become less acceptable.

The one feature which, above all others, characterizes our contemporary revival of these questions is that we are now free of this erstwhile European or Atlantic insularity. This is reflected in the shift from Karl Marx to Max Weber as the single most influential sociologist. There is no reason any longer for embracing the once intoxicating acorn-to-oaktree view of human society. It had guaranteed the eventual coming of a society both rich and free. But in fact there is no series of manifest and inevitable stages, allegedly exemplifying the same principle, both in the mechanics of their succession and in their gradual approximation to excellence. Radical discontinuities and transformations do indeed occur: but they are not inevitable. They are not inscribed into the very essence of the earlier form.

Once upon a time, there were three modish styles of sociological explanation: evolutionism, functionalism and diffusionism. The first is based on the acorn or entelechy model; the second holds that societies are fairly stable, self-maintaining systems; and the third credits change not to endogenous growth but to lateral influence from society to society, by peaceful or other means, by emulation and interaction. Of the three, the first now seems to have least validity, whilst the second and third constitute schemata for the kind of explanation valid in some areas, but lacking it precisely in the one area which concerns us most — that of radical change.

By and large, societies are indeed self-perpetuating. Radical change does occur, but not every day or every century. To this extent, functionalism — attribution of self-perpetuation to societies — is or was a reasonable approximation to the truth. Marxism in effect affirms that functionalism is 98 per cent correct, but that it is the 2 per cent that counts. When a radical innovation does occur – agriculture, literacy, industrialization or science – they manifestly do spread, by a variety of mechanisms. This diffusionism also has its point. So we possess abstract schemata for the kind of explanation which can apply either to stability or to the emulation of a successfully established fundamental innovation. What, however, we cannot take over from our evolution-intoxicated nineteenth-century predecessors is the key idea for explaining fundamental and endogenous change.

The terms of reference now imposed by our data and our problem have led us to quite another pattern. If a name is required, it can be called the Gate-keeper or the Hump model. It is in these terms that the present argument is worked out.

The New Social Contract

The absurdity of the literal occurrence of the social contract is familiar. Bertrand Russell once ridiculed the social contract theory of language: it is hard to imagine an assembly of hitherto speechless elders solemnly agreeing henceforth to call a cow a "cow". The *ex nihilo* establishment of a moral compact is even harder to visualize than a semantic constituent assembly. The logical regress is obvious: without a prior basis of a moral obligation, what could make the contract binding and effective? (*With* a prior foundation of moral obligation, it is redundant.)

Experience and logic converge at this point: the rational establishment of a new social order, even if known to be markedly advantageous to the majority of the participants most of the time, is extremely difficult, and successful instances of it are rare, and only occur in very exceptional circumstances.

The great merit of Durkheim's version of the contract theory is that at least it escapes the more obvious intellectualist absurdities of the old theory. His account avoids the attribution of a precocious, indeed contradictory rationality to the participants in the primal assembly. He ascribes a non-rational origin to the linked emergence of rationality and sociability. In the excitement and hysteria of collective ritual, men are softened and made malleable and receptive. In this condition, the shared, binding and authoritative concepts are imprinted on them. Thereafter they enable men to communicate, and compel them to fulfil their shared obligations and expectations.

It is an old and obvious point that the social contract is eternally re-enacted: the miracle of the persistence of a social order could never be explained by a single event. It requires the perpetual reproduction of whatever it is that binds men together. The present argument insists that mankind has adhered not to one, but to a succession of significantly differing implicit contracts, drawn up in diverse idioms and contexts, and with diverging terms. We have experienced a number of discontinuous identities. We are trying to understand the latest, by seeing how the constraints which operate on it differ from the earlier ones.

The contract implicitly observed by foragers was not the same as that which bound agriculturalists. More complex agrarian societies, obliged to respect a codified and centralized theology, differ from their predecessors who were tied to ritual rather than doctrine. All of them differed from us, their successors, who guard not an exiguous but an affluent storehouse. We have driven a wedge between cognition and legitimation, and we have pushed the division of labour to unprecedented limits. At the same time we refuse, at least in principle, to allow any sphere of it to be the exclusive preserve of any one sub-part of society. Durkheim's scheme is an admirable formula for the maintenance of cohesion in stable societies. It is less persuasive when we come to either the emergence or the perpetuation of a continuously mobile society.

This has a curious consequence: as far as our own social order is concerned, we can investigate the social contract *both* as concrete, dateable, observable historic event, *and* as a permanent, recurring, perpetual mechanism. Past societies generally vindicated themselves in terms of mythical founding events.

THE NEW SOCIAL CONTRACT

These served as justificatory charters for a current, ongoing social order, which its participants were ill-equipped or positively disinclined to investigate. A myth about the past "explained" a current situation. But men could hardly analyse their current situation dispassionately.

By contrast, we can (or at any rate, we fondly hope we can) realistically inquire both into the concrete historical emergence, and into the maintenance and legitimation, of our own social order. Our concern is with the selection of options and the reasons, if any, for our commitment. Compared with our predecessors, we believe our perception of the past to be more veridical and less binding, if indeed binding at all. The past as such is not binding at all. It may, however, highlight the persisting constraints which we must respect.

In recent literature, the rationality of an individual's endorsement of the norms of his society has in effect been discussed in terms of a seemingly technical problem in the theory of games, the so-called Prisoner's Dilemma.[5] Two prisoners are kept in isolation, pending a trial. They are in fact guilty, but the prosecutor only possesses weak evidence which, as far as it goes, would only help him secure a mild sentence (say, two years). If either prisoner confesses, thereby also implicating and convicting the other, he will be rewarded by a free pardon, whilst his non-confessing accomplice will receive twenty years. If both confess, they will each receive ten years. What should either of them do?

Intuitively and morally, we feel that they ought not to confess. (Their crime is irrelevant for us: you can assume it to be some praiseworthy political defiance of an unsavoury regime. Think of it as the political prisoner's dilemma.) By doing so, they will secure what is, from their *combined* viewpoint, the optimal outcome – a relatively mild sentence of two years for each of them.

But note that the rational logic of their individual calculations points in quite a different direction. Neither knows what the other will do (and even if they could communicate, it would make little difference, as neither has any means of enforcing any compact which they might enter on). Prisoner A can and must reason as follows: if B confesses and I do not, I shall get twenty years, instead of ten. If on the other hand he does not confess and I do, I shall get off scot-free, instead of suffering for two years. So, *on either assumption*, it is rational for me to confess. The situation and reasoning of B is exactly similar. Result: they both confess and each gets ten years, though by acting as a moral community they could have escaped with only a two-year sentence!

The reason why this problem has received so much attention is not merely its technical ingenuity and the tension between our morally intuitive reaction and the logic of the situation. The deeper reason is that the conundrum sums up, in the simplest possible terms, the problem of social cooperation, in face of what is frequently the *irrationality* of cooperativeness, when seen from the viewpoint of the single individual. The mechanisms of social control deployed by contemporary authoritarian societies, which characteristically curtail the freedom of association, and above all of loyalty-formation (*solidarity*) of their citizens, follows exactly this logic. How can a society which commends and inculcates both individualism and instrumental rationality, and which in fact could not function without them, nevertheless also hope to maintain solidarity and cooperativeness?

In the real world, the situation is made much worse by the fact that generally there are not two participants, but a very large number of them. If any one of them, or at any rate a small number of them, succumbs to the logic of the situation, the moral resolve of all the others is unavailing, and rebounds to their great disadvantage. It is this logic which inescapably leads, for instance, to panics in fires. The panic is disastrous for all, but restraint by *some* is quite specially disastrous for the restrained, if the others fail to follow their example. Hence no one shows restraint, and all suffer more than they need have done.

More generally, the conundrum merely restates the problem formulated by Thrasymachus at the start of *The Republic*. It arises from the disadvantages, for any one individual, of observing the rules of "justice". Most agrarian societies in effect followed the solution implied by Thrasymachus' position:

political conflict escalated till one power centre monopolized all control. Thereafter, in Ibn Khaldun's words, the surviving unique centre could prevent injustice other than such as it committed itself. This at least made obedience to it rational for all. It became co-extensive with the maintenance of some order at least, as Hobbes insisted.

The agrarian social orders which lived by Thrasymachus' solution nevertheless also piously mouthed some variant of that high-minded language by means of which the Platonic Socrates repudiates Thrasymachus' solution. No doubt men feel happier when able to endorse the order which they have to endure anyway. They prefer to feel *loyal* rather than merely cowed. Our argument has been concerned with the mechanism by which men who had lived under the rule of Thrasymachus, and spoke some variant of Plato's ideology, could break out of the constraints of both.

The normal blockage, the inhibition of any liberating movement within agro-literate society, can be very simply summarized in terms of the prisoner's dilemma schema. It occurs in each of the three main spheres of human activity.

Consider first of all the dilemma in the form in which it arises in the cognitive sphere. Imagine a person contemplating the alternative cognitive strategies, as we have presented them. On the one hand, he can continue to deploy the traditional concepts of his culture, within which moral and natural expectations are conflated. The empirical content of the traditional notions, though probably not a good base for a radical and cumulative exploration of nature, are at least unlikely to be totally in error. By contrast, any single theoretical innovation is most unlikely to be successful. On top of this, the innovation will constitute (at best) a social solecism, or possibly some worse kind of transgression. Under normal conditions, what sane man could opt for the likelihood of cognitive failure and social disaster, as against the near-certainty of social acceptance, combined with at least moderate, customary cognitive success? The conditions which impelled some men at least to take the bizarrely perilous path of a-social cognitive exploration must have been unusual indeed.

In the purely political sphere, the situation is somewhat complex, in so far as mankind has gone through not one, but at least two contracts: the establishment of authority and order, and the establishment of law-bound, accountable authority. In a sense, the first step presents no problem: there is no difficulty at all in seeing how men could be persuaded into such a situation. During the conditions prevalent in the agrarian age, they slide into it only too easily. Dependence on food production ties most of them to the land, and, within any given territory, escalation of conflict and the successive elimination of rivals lead to a single-ruler situation. The political structure of the majority of agrarian societies historically confirms the cogency of this argument. One can only add that the possibility of the arrival of new entrants from outside, and the difficulties of combining delegation with control, and the ambiguity of rules of succession, all help to ensure that conflict frequently revives. The single victor does not remain uncontested for long. It is the sad fate of agrarian humanity to suffer both oppression and anarchy: submission to oppression does not even ensure freedom from disorder.

The overcoming of the second hump, the establishment of limited and accountable government, does not occur through the consent of the parties concerned. It can hardly be conceived as occurring in such a manner, given that this would require the voluntary abandonment of great advantages on the part of the erstwhile possessors of power. It does happen when a society slides into an internal balance of power such as inhibits potential competitors in an internal struggle from, not all conflict perhaps, but at least from escalating the conflict to the limit. The emergence and growth of so to speak fragile wealth, which could not survive confrontation *à outrance* within the society, is clearly an important element in the birth of such a polity. Consent *theories* of government are in the main only formulated after the unplanned, untheoretical emergence of such a condition.

The most interesting sphere for seeing the workings of the compact-makers' dilemma (which is what the prisoner's dilemma should really be called) is the economic. Most men in the agrarian age live in societies divided into coercers and producers, and within which the coercers are markedly at an advantage. Envisage the options facing a producer who can retain, by dissimulation or otherwise, an augmentation of his wealth. In the prevalent condition of scarcity, this confers a certain power on him. Theoretically, the alternative strategies open to him are either to increase his wealth even further by re-investing it, or to turn the potential coercive power of wealth into real coercive power, by purchasing arms and hiring retainers. Given any realistic assessment of the likely strategies of other contestants, whether they be coercers or fellow successful producers, and a world in which coercers habitually trump producers, can there be a shadow of doubt concerning the best strategy? If he has an ounce of sense, our *nouveau riche* producer, whom some accidental concatenation of circumstances has allowed to retain his gains, will promptly turn them into socially more secure forms of power. These might be direct coercive equipment, or the purchase of a status position in a wider coercive organization. He will transform himself into a *nouveau puissant*. This is not merely the most logical option, but it is also the one which men have generally chosen.

What follows is of course that, if the social compact of a productive, industrial society requires men to refrain from coercion and to work and re-invest compulsively, then the contract setting up such a world simply cannot come about. There is no rational path towards "rational", i.e. pacific, rule-abiding, instrumental, un-coercive, cumulative and open-ended productivity. The most important appeal of Max Weber's sociology lies in the fact that he offers a plausible account of how rationality could have come about *ir*rationally. Durkheim explained the rationality of ancient unreason. Weber showed the irrationality of modern reason.

Finally, consider the sphere of religion. This is obviously of some importance, if there is any truth in the argument that a productive society required a rising ceiling of discovery, that this in turn depended on the idea of a unified and orderly Nature, and that such a conception could only be established under the aegis of a monotheist theology, vigorously imposing the idea of an exclusive, hidden, severe and orderly deity. There is an asymmetry between the political and religious experience of agrarian humanity: societies slide into a centralized political system only too easily (even if such systems are fragile and often re-fragment again). By contrast, conceptual, single-apex unification occurs rather less frequently and less easily. Centralization in heaven is less easy than it is on earth. Evidence suggests that it is the occasional absence of political centralization which is exceptional and requires explanation; the reverse is true in the spiritual sphere. Political consolidations frequently take place, but reformations generally fail.

Blaise Pascal is famous as the man who constructed the matrix of available strategies, open to us in this matter of religious faith. He demonstrated, not entirely to his own satisfaction, that commitment to faith constituted the best strategy. On either hypothesis, the existence or the non-existence of the deity, the believer either does better, or at least does no worse, than does the unbeliever. There are various things wrong with Pascal's account of the human predicament: the most relevant defect for us is that he starts from a special situation, in which the options have already been narrowed down to either monotheism or atheism. This simply is not the range of options faced by the great majority of men. Historically, most men seem to have faced Pascal's wager, but with a larger range of options, and they seem to have followed his reasoning, though not perhaps in a way he would have favoured. Notoriously, populations converted to ūnified, centralized, exclusive faiths persist (in perfect accord with Pascal's logic) in insuring themselves in all directions, by also continuing to revere the plural and local, territorial spirits. They often do so to the great indignation of the clerisy committed to the exclusive centralized revelation.

If the conceptual unification of the world was indeed essential for the social compact which underlies our own social order, then once again we must seek some special explanation that will tell us how, for once, this unusual result was secured. We do have some inkling of how it could happen. On the demand side, it requires an atomized and disoriented urban population, seeking generic salvation and doctrine-born orientation, rather than the ritual buttressing of a well-articulated social order (which is no longer present). On the supply side, it presupposes a clerisy oriented towards codified, circumscribed doctrine by its tendency to play up its own monopoly of literacy. Such a clerisy is useful enough to the political authorities eager to enlist its help in administration, and willing to reciprocate by helping it in turn to extirpate heresy. The clerisy may also be capable of avoiding total or permanent subjection to the state (e.g. by possessing a territorial base not under the control of any one state). It does indeed seem possible to discern a historical development of this general kind. Rivalry with shamans leads clerics to stress doctrine, internal rivalry to codify the said doctrine and endow it with a single Apex; extra-territoriality may enable it to escape political control.

So the tacit compact governing our social order, the commitment to certain rules of productive, political and conceptual comportment which had made that order possible, could never have been a real *compact*. It would have gone against the grain, against the rational interests of participants, who were not yet imbued with the spirit of this order. The logic of the situation in which men found themselves precluded them from subscribing freely and rationally to such a contract (or, in most cases, from finding it intelligible). *We had to be tricked into it.* We may see this as the cunning of reason or as a concatenation of accidents.

1945 and Some Recent Clauses in the Contract

1945 and the end of European domination is unquestionably one of the landmarks in world history. The settlement which crystallized out at the end of the war and during the immediate postwar years is still the foundation of our social and international order, even if it was somewhat shaken and modified by the new crisis which began in the early 1970s.

First of all, 1945 meant the elimination, at any rate for some

time, of the extreme right-wing alternative which had (much as
we may dislike recognizing it) conquered continental Europe
and, but for extraneous forces, would have been accepted by it.
The elimination of this option by its military defeat, and by the
laying bare of its atrocities, left the field to the two other main
ideologies. These two theories share a tendency to underrate the
political sphere and coercion.

In the post-1945 world, the two ideologies were left to struggle
for the political souls of humanity. The conditions in which they
did so profoundly affect the nature of the contest. Each vision
had its super-power home base, the homeland of Revolution or
of the non-Revolution respectively. The home base of liberalism
had also sprung from a revolution, albeit an earlier one. After the
acquisition of nuclear weapons by the Soviet Union, the balance
of terror prevented an outright conflict, which otherwise would
almost certainly have taken place. Hence the confrontation had
to be restricted to the ideological plane and to wars-by-proxy.

This greatly accelerated, if it did not actually cause, the
decolonization of the backward world. The conditions of competition for the allegiance of Third World populations makes it
highly unpolitic for developed countries to try to maintain direct
control by force. This was highlighted by two wars in particular,
the Algerian and the Indochinese. Afghanistan may now be
added to the list. So the two competing, nominally anti-political
ideologies struggle with each other by seeking the support of
countries which are often governed by very unscrupulous
regimes, dominating feeble civil societies. The irony is perhaps
more marked in the case of the liberal camp, in which the
Imperial Republic – in Raymond Aron's phrase – and heir of
an Enlightenment Revolution, allies itself with all kinds of
opportunist governments or *ancien régimes*. In the case of the
socialist camp, the contrast is more conspicuous between
nominal ideal and actual practice, rather than between home
base and peripheral allies. The hypertrophy of a centralized
polity is at least as conspicuous at home as in the peripheral
outposts.

After 1945, the preoccupation with why the unique miracle

had *not* occurred elsewhere, and what impediments inhibited its emulation, became something which forced itself to the fore-front of attention. Ironically, the new and less Europocentric vision highlighted the uniqueness of the West. The paradox is easy to resolve. The new vision refrained from imposing the supposed (and misread) pattern of Western European development on other societies, as nineteenth-century thought had done. This made the peculiarity of the new industrial order and its emergence *more* visible. The fact that this order could be incarnated in two quite different socio-political forms under-scored it further. Weber's question became a little distorted[6] perhaps. He had asked: why had it not happened endogenously elsewhere? It now became: why is it not happening, or not happening fast enough, exogenously? It was thus that Max Weber became the most influential sociologist at the very moment when the White Man's Burden was thrust upon America.

Certain other lessons accompanied this rather profound shift of vision. It had already become plain in the seventeenth and eighteenth centuries that a strong state need not pillage its own subjects. A state which taxes a prosperous population in modera-tion does better than one which exploits a population to the limit, and thereby prevents it from prospering. But in the course of their economic expansion, European societies also acquired enormous colonial empires, absorbing the larger part of the non-European world. This contingent association of wealth and empire naturally engendered and encouraged the idea that empire was a condition (rather than a consequence) of industrial wealth. This perpetuated, at the level of national politics, the idea that military power and territorial expansion were paramount goals and/or the conditions of prosperity. The brilliant postwar economic performance of the two prime losers of the war, deprived of all empire (and more), finally put paid to this illusion. Land hunger is a survival from the ethos of the agrarian age.

The sustained and unparalleled economic growth of the immediate post-war decades also underscored both the feasibility of such growth and the manner in which it could allay, or even constitute the solution to, social problems. The multiple fragility of the solution, in face of a built-in tendency of liberal affluent societies to suffer from either inflation or unemployment and eventually both, and from the consequences of either the success or failure of development in the backward countries (their competition or their bad debts alike pose grave threats), only became really conspicuous during the last quarter of the century.

CHAPTER 10

Prospect

The Division of Labour and Back Again

The division of labour has fragmented humanity and, eventually, reunited it. Its most profound aspect, for a long time, was the hiving off of both coercive and ritual specialists. It also eventually engendered a manifold differentiation between diverse kinds of producer within the economic sphere, though the impact of this was initially much less important. A separation of men in terms of their relation to the tools of coercion and cognition became deeply internalized in our souls. It was powerfully enforced and sanctioned by legal, ritual or economic means.

By a miraculous process, the precise secret of which may elude us for ever, this world was eventually displaced by another, with a radically new and qualitatively different division of labour. It abandons the deep-rooted and long-standing tendency towards a profound separation of a military-administrative class and of a ritual-doctrinal class from the rest of society. Modern societies do of course possess a "ruling class", but no formal line is drawn around it. Its personnel rotates, to a greater or lesser degree, and its separation from the rest of the population is gradual. The differentiation, one might say, is deliberately obscured and ideologically denied. It receives no sacramental blessing; these tend to be reserved for the shared humanity of all citizens. Sovereignty is ascribed to "the people", not to the transcendent. Office-holders claim to be delegates of the people, not emissaries of the transcendent. There may be a distinction between the state and civil society, but there is no clear and formalized separation of a state class from the governed population.

Something very similar holds for the old cognitive and

legitimation specialists. Some clerisies do of course remain, but often with the aura of a folkloristic survival. There are intelligentsias, but like their precursors, the Muslim *ulama*, they and their doctrines are by definition open, and they cannot secretively monopolize their wisdom. Modern society is inherently democratic, at any rate to the extent that the notion of a distinct political-military class is absent and felt to be repugnant. Producers have become fully political, rather than politically castrated animals. Similarly, modern society is inherently protestant, in that it cannot seriously bring itself to hold important cognition to be accessible only to a ritually segregated minority.

So much, for the moment, for those two deep ditches, chasms perhaps, which had marked the face of agro-literate society, and which have led its members to feel their society to be made up of radically different species of being. But there has also been a profoundly significant change in the mass of little specializations which make up the economic aspect of the division of labour. The idea underlying the division of labour is that if you do one thing at a time you do it better; and, moreover, that one "thing" is to be defined by one criterion, for only then can you tell whether indeed it is being done better or worse. In due course you can improve your performance by freely selecting means from the infinite reservoir of possibilities, without heeding social constraints and criteria of propriety.

The subdivision of tasks and processes and the clarification of criteria, permitting a genuine instrumental rationality, have both progressed far beyond that which prevailed in the agrarian era. And lo and behold, contrary to what one might have anticipated, this accentuated division of labour has led not to a further extension of human differentiation, but, on the contrary, to its diminution. People do even more diversified things, but what they do is done in the same style. What they do is governed by the same principles, and is conceived in the same idiom. They are free to switch from one activity to another, but the idiom in which the activity is specified remains similar.

The pervasive tendency towards species of a generic protestantism, egalitarianism, democracy and nationalism are but the expression of this push towards a more homogeneous humanity. It is made such by the common subjection to an ethos of instrumental rationality, linked to the productive base of this society. Egalitarianism springs from the inherent mobility, imposed by means–ends rationality, by the free choice of means and their frequent replacement, on the occupational structure; nationalism reflects the fact that this mobility occurs only within a homogeneous, literate, education-transmitted culture, which must needs be homogeneous in any one area, and politically protected by, a centre committed to that culture. The mastery of this culture constitutes the only real passport to genuine citizenship, and consequently constitutes the core of a person's moral identity, defining the limits of the zone within which he can effectively interact and be acceptable. Democracy and protestantism reflect the abolition of fundamental political or cognitive privilege.

Is instrumental rationality, linked to a mobile division of labour, completely pervasive in this society? The answer is that it is not, and cannot be. It is impossible for it to exist at the top – whether one is referring to the logical or to the social summit. By the logical summit I mean the most general issues facing a society: overall decisions cannot be effectively disaggregated into separate, single-aim issues.

Multi-stranded, cosy, humanly rich "irrationality", or, if you wish, transcendence of rationality, thus occurs in this kind of society only in isolated pockets – high above, or in the recesses of private life. Is the non- or counter-rational sphere liable to expand again? Will cold rationality once again retreat into its ghetto? It is conceivable. It is conceivable that efficient institutions now possess an internal *esprit de corps* and sense of loyalty, and that the Japanese "feudal" business ethos, with its paternalism and cult of loyalty, is the model of the future.

The expansion of leisure also means the growth of "expressive" activities, whose importance in life may greatly increase. Brazenly and provocatively anti-rational cults may cease to be peripheral and become dominant. An emotive, ritualistic and anti-rational style of politics may revive again. The paradigmatic

263

contemporary man is perhaps no longer the instrumentally rational producer of modern consumer goods, but on the contrary their consumer. He is habituated to intuitively obvious, simple, and easy controls, which guide him to facile and unreflective deployment of the gadget in question. Some contemporary fringe ideologies have just such a facile, permissive quality. They suggest a user-friendly and undemanding universe, far removed from the severe and orderly vision which had originally engendered our world.

The fate of the three strands of human activity – production, cognition and coercion – are not identical under the newly emerging dispensation. Intimately related though they are, their logic and predicaments remain rather different.

The Future of Production

From one viewpoint, the productive explosion is the most conspicuous aspect of the great transformation. It is taking mankind out of the Malthusian age, in which politics were dominated by the struggle for scarce material resources, and into an age of plenty. But the continuing exponential growth of the productive industrial machine has, like the sorcerer's apprentice, in the end produced far more than it could control. The early industrial system could emerge within the social and political framework of Britain, which in turn could cope with it, with some, but not too much, difficulty. The relatively simple and uncentralized political and social machinery of Britain at the time could contain and manage the new order, though of course it had to expand and transform itself in the process.

The industrial machinery, however, which now exists in developed societies, cannot manage without an incomparably larger and centrally supervised and financed infrastructure. This in turn cannot be taken for granted, like the social order of eighteenth-century Britain, or that of its newly independent North American colonies. The infrastructure now inevitably absorbs an enormous proportion of the total output; its disposal, in the nature of things, is inevitably a political issue. It is contentious, and the disagreement can only be settled politically. This does not mean that, within a politically determined framework, all kinds of relatively minor issues, notably those concerning the detailed arrangements of production, may not be left to "the market" and will not benefit from this. Nor does it mean that the political determination may not be done informally, in an economically liberal idiom and by nominally non-political, informal methods, but the repoliticization of the economy, formal or informal, is upon us. This, at any rate, is the valid element in "socialism", or at least in the abandonment of economic liberalism.

The fact that, in the very nature of things, there *cannot* be a single well-defined overall aim for production, that there is no inherently neutral entity that constitutes "wealth", means that, in the long run, instrumental rationality cannot govern us in this sphere. Men seek life styles, roles, positions. These are many-stranded and culturally defined. They involve the use of material objects as tokens, but they are not made up of such objects. Power helps men to attain them, but power assumes a complex variety of forms.

The illusion of clear criteria had been engendered by conjunction of the old scarcity with a temporary outburst of the "rational" spirit guided by a single-minded pursuit of monetary wealth. In the long run, a multi-stranded evaluation must return, simply for lack of any alternative – hampered though this must be by the absence of a cogent background vision which could guide it. Wealth constitutes only tokens for the attainment of positions, which can also be attained by other means. Affluent society simply chases its own tail.

The Future of Cognition

Cognition does not seem to be in a parallel condition. Its open-ended perpetual growth does not engender any internal contradiction, nor even any collective human *accidie*. It can continue along its instrumentally rational, *zielmaessig* way. Its single aim, the formulation of ever more powerful and more general explanatory, predictive theories, does not, like wealth, contain any inner absurdity. Its implementation is feasible and, judging from the astonishingly consensual – all in all – nature of the scientific community, appears to be relatively easy. The idea of placing an interdict on some kinds of cognitive advance, which poke too disturbingly into matters we might prefer to remain outside our understanding and control, has indeed been mooted. It would seem unlikely that it will be imposed, at any rate for the time being.

The internal coherence or consistency of the ideal of science differentiates it from the ideal of wealth, which is internally contradictory. Above the level of basic physical necessity, what is materially valuable is culturally determined. Hence you cannot in the end assess a culture by its ability to produce wealth, because you would be judging the effectiveness by criteria which are themselves invented by the very process which is to be judged. This is not a logician's conundrum, but a genuine problem. Though wealth was an aim genuine and legitimate and identifiable enough in penury, it ceases to be such once the transition is well and truly behind us. Mankind will eventually notice that this carrot is attached to the cultural harness on the back of the affluent donkey. It is conceivable that some donkeys will fail to act up to this realization. Some societies may, on the other hand, remain committed to a perpetual potlatch.

One question which arises is whether the explanatory and hence manipulative effectiveness, which attaches to natural science, will in due course be extended to the study of man himself. One of the most striking features of our collective situation is the extent to which, so far, this has failed to happen. A number of dictatorial and ideocratic regimes exist which would be only too eager to avail themselves of an opportunity to manipulate the mentality and convictions of men, if suitable techniques were indeed available. They would consider their successful deployment a glorious vindication of their own ideology. Notwithstanding their unquestionable eagerness to use such techniques, there is little evidence of their success.

In liberal, non-ideocratic societies, the combined effects of social disorganization, secularization, lack of certainty, and the fact that, for most men, the environment means other people rather than nature, have meant that psychiatrists and practitioners of related skills have inherited the burden of pastoral care and solace from the old clerisies. Indeed, surviving members of the old clerisies emulate the idiom and style of modern therapists in the exercise of their pastoral duties. Given the demands made on them, and the strategic role they play in contemporary life, and the rewards which would accrue to them if they really were effective, their failure to be successful is all the more conspicuous. It constitutes a dramatic demonstration of the failure, so far, to extend the power of natural science and technology to the human field.

The techniques available to these specialists amount to very little other than the crudest trial and error. The one major and initially plausible doctrine to have emerged in this area at the turn of the nineteenth and twentieth centuries comes in the end to consist of hardly anything other than a skilful evasion of its own falsification. Whether this failure to extend the scientific revolution to the human field will be corrected, or whether it is due to fundamental causes which will protect man from effective comprehension for ever, is not something which is as yet decided. Our neo-romantics take pleasure in affirming the latter view, but their demonstrations of it fall a very long way short of cogency.

If, however, the contrary view were valid, and effective understanding and manipulation of man became feasible, this would indeed, once again, totally rewrite the basic rules of our game. Effective manipulation of human material, whether by genetic or psychological or any other methods, would once again fundamentally transform the terms of reference of human life. The same is true of the re-conceptualization of "wealth", and the re-stabilization of the occupational structure, if indeed these come to pass.

At present, a kind of circularity haunts us: our cultures are not given, but are profoundly transformed by our own activities and policies. That which inspires us with our aims is also visibly modified by us; what then is the authority of our aims? The urgency of this query is diminished by the fact that the effects of our policies on our souls are not immediately visible, and the changes we produce cannot be anticipated or manipulated with any precision. Thus, in short-range terms, the social order and the values emanating from it have at least a kind of relative independence and authority. If human nature became manipulable with effectiveness and precision, the problem would become incomparably more acute. We should need to cope with the same circularity as that which must have faced the deity when it created the world: with no prior world, what on earth (literally) could incline it to create *this* rather than *that*? It lacked either aims or constraints. If man ceases to be a datum, what principles could govern the optional moulding of human nature? We should then lack a human as well as a transcendent premiss, even more conspicuously than we do now.

The Future of Coercion

This is perhaps the most serious, the most problematic of the three areas. The new productive efficiency may be assumed, once it has ushered in plenty, to return production to its erstwhile more modest condition, where its shape is moulded by the other requirements of social life. The visions which for a time gave it so central a place, either by hoping to make politics into its servant (liberalism), or by claiming, contrary to all evidence, that it was ever the motor of all history (Marxism), are visibly mistaken. Cognition, in turn, may perhaps be destined for indefinite expansion, but may (if the present argument is correct) have to accept a permanent divorce from legitimation and culture, from social vindication and from the conceptual ordering of ordinary life. Whether we can live with this divorce, is another question.

But the organization of power, the political ordering of

society, and indeed of the international community, is an inescapable issue. The arguments which claim that this problem is ceasing to be acute are misguided. An enormously complicated socio-economic machine, which has a tremendous and costly and indivisible infrastructure, requiring very major, long-term, irreversible, fateful decisions – that is our lot. So politics, far from being on the way out, encompass more and not less of our lives. A stable and fragmented economy could be politically taken for granted. A holistic one on skids cannot.

Societies with feeble technological powers had little which they could hand over to the state: the traditional state was seldom much good at anything, really, other than killing people and taking away their surplus. It may have, as Clifford Geertz has insisted, constituted a kind of national theatre, though this practice was certainly not a monopoly of the Far East.[1] Modern society, on the other hand, has tremendous power over the environment, over its own members and organization, and the decisions about how those powers are to be employed, for what ends and in what way, have to be taken somewhere, somehow, by someone. The decisions must often be concentrated at some one point – not necessarily the same one for each successive decision. This among other things transforms the very nature of "power". In the past, key decisions seemed to be inscribed into the nature of things, and were in fact determined for us, given the near-impotence of humanity. Our new technology has freed us from impotence. The new knowledge on which the technology is based has also made plain that the nature of things does not dictate any decisions to us. Physically and logically, we may now have a good deal more elbow room than is comfortable. A few more constraints, logical or physical, might even be welcome, just to reduce this vertiginous range of options. But genuine constraints cannot be invented for our convenience. We may, in a sense very different from that intended by Rousseau, be forced to be free.

In another sense, our liberty may be more problematical. What factors now make for liberal or for authoritarian politics? The scarcity which underlay the authoritarianism of agrarian politics is on the way out. This cuts both ways. It means that the beneficiaries of privilege and possessors of powers no longer need to suborn and intimidate the rest, so as to discourage them from reversing a markedly unfavourable material distribution. It also means that men are no longer constrained into accepting a social order and their own position within it by the menace of imminent destitution. One important form of secondary coercion, which worked by menacing with hunger those who defy the rules, becomes harder to apply. The productive process is also complex, requiring intricate cooperation, accurate performance, and, often, independent initiative. It does not easily lend itself to direct coercion and a simple command system, and attempts to impose them lead to diminished efficiency.

The quantity and complexity of relevant technical information is such that efficiency also requires that specialists be selected on merit for special posts, and that the overall social climate be such as not to inhibit unduly either the fairness of the selection or the freedom of expression of the specialists in question. All these factors no doubt in some measure militate against authoritarianism and ideocracy, penalizing such traits with lowered productivity. This consideration will continue to be weighty, though not necessarily decisive. If output ceases to be important, liberty may lose this important support.

The complexity and interdependence, which make it difficult for authorities to be unduly oppressive also, on the other side, make individuals and subgroups heavily dependent on the society and ill-equipped to defy it. Local autarchy is almost inconceivable. The military balance between centre and civil society is of course totally different from that which, in the key country, enabled civil society to defeat the state in the seventeenth and eighteenth centuries. On the other hand, the sheer scale and weight of these weapon systems makes them hard to use, either against small groups hiding within civil society, or against a civil society which is fairly united and capable of maintaining solidarity in its opposition to the centre.

It is difficult to imagine the overall system to be anything other than corporatist in some measure, with decisions arrived at by consultation between the organized expression of the major groupings and interests in society. Societies which are ideologically anti-corporatist may of course refrain from formally avowing that such a system exists, and from endowing it with legal or ritual sanctions.

Corporatist-style haggling between major interest groups may be, and perhaps often will be, complemented by the sovereignty of elections at which individuals vote as individuals, and at which parties soliciting votes can present themselves in any form. Among other things, this effectively symbolizes the fact that the corporate segments of this kind of society are not permanent, nor their membership hereditary. It does contribute an important check to the system.

Developed industrial societies at present come in two main forms, liberal and ideocratic. It is worth asking whether and how either species is liable to become transformed. Marxist ideocracies are of course impelled towards reform by the requirements of efficiency and international competition. Even the modest level of affluence they have attained (not at all modest when compared with their own past) requires to be serviced by a large technical and administrative intelligentsia, which instinctively prefers rational criteria of genuine performance to sheer political patronage, toadyism, verbiage and subservience. But against the liberalizing pressure springing from this, one must put the fact that in a society which is, in effect, a single employment system linked to a single orthodoxy, it is exceedingly hard for any one part of the system to give without imperilling the whole. Right-wing dictatorships with a plural economy can liberalize, and they have done so successfully: the rulers can retain their wealth even when they abandon their power positions, and thus they can be bribed into compromise. In a left-wing authoritarian system, where wealth comes *only* in the form of perks attaching to hierarchical positions, to give up these positions is to give up everything. So far, there is no example of a successfully completed liberalization of a left dictatorship, though admittedly some such liberalizations have been forcibly inhibited.

Will liberal regimes perpetuate themselves? No one knows the consequences of the imminent universal leisure-without-privilege. Leisure classes in the past have had some psychic difficulty in disposing of their free time, as Pascal eloquently noted, notwithstanding the fact that they were free to contemplate, with joy, their own elevation. What will be the state of mind of a universal leisure class, devoid of any elevation to contemplate? We know the patterns engendered by the agrarian need to *work*; what may be the patterns of leisure? So far, the only individualists we have known were also endowed with the work ethic. Is dilettante individualism also conceivable? Production may continue to be instrumentally rational and analytic, but consumption is many-stranded and intuitive, and products are designed to encourage this: what happens when consumption overtakes production and becomes the dominant element in forming the human psyche?

Liberal societies have deprived themselves of powerful legitimations. Referential unificatory truth is a species of instrumental rationality: both the species and the genus corrode belief systems. Social cohesion cannot be based on truth. Truth butters no parsnips and legitimates no social arrangements. There are at least two reasons for this. One is the failure of genuine knowledge to be socially subservient. The second is that publicly accessible truth fails to separate members of a community from non-members.

Will the need to counteract the discontent of a swollen, leisure-endowed but status-less class bring about the revival of a new central faith, centrally enforced? Will this be facilitated by the decline in that instrumental rationality which had brought about the new world, but is no longer required when that world is fully developed? The same solution need not prevail everywhere.

Summary of Argument

The division of labour is not unique to humanity. It occurs within animal and insect societies. What does seem to be unique is the astonishing diversity of forms which it can assume and has assumed in human societies. Among other species, something resembling "cultural" diversity may occur: the identical genetic equipment may allow some variation in conduct and organization of (say) a herd. That diversity may then only be explicable in terms of the history of that grouping and not by the genes of its members. (Ethologists do not seem to be sure whether such diversity is to be explained by environmental pressures or by the history of the herd in question. Only in the latter case can one speak of "culture" in an important sense.) Such "cultural" diversity, however, is very limited. By contrast, among men it is truly enormous. The variety of human societies is staggering.

This diversity is not explicable genetically. The nature and extent of the contribution of genetic make-up to social forms is a contentious and unsettled issue, bedevilled by its political associations and implications. What is obvious, however, is that a *very* large part of the explanation of the form human societies assume must be social-historical and not genetic. The same genetic base permits wide diversity. This is obvious from the fact that populations which can be safely assumed to remain genetically identical, or very nearly so, can and do assume totally different social forms at different times. Very often, social change is simply far too rapid to be explicable by genetic change.

To say all this is not to say that genetic constitution makes no contribution whatever to history. It is conceivable that some genetic constitutions have a greater predisposition to some social forms than others. The issue is difficult, but it can also be ignored, and has indeed been ignored in this argument. The unquestionable and tremendous importance of social factors, of socially transmitted and instilled traits and features, is such as to allow one, and indeed oblige one, to evade the other problem for the time being. One can go a very long way by explaining the social by the social, and this is all we have tried to do.

273

One crucial aspect of the way in which human societies maintain and transmit their distinctive features can be called *culture*. Culture can be defined as the set of concepts in terms of which a given population acts and thinks. A concept is a shared way of grouping experiences and of acting and reacting, and usually has a name. A culture is a system, and not just a collection of concepts: the notions which constitute it are interrelated and interdependent in various complex ways, and it is plausible to suppose that they could not exist at all in isolation. Concepts, like men, are gregarious. It does not follow that any one culture is a fully consistent or coherent system, whatever the criteria of coherence or consistency might be.

It is, however, important not to *equate* culture with the manner in which a social order perpetuates itself. Culture is one way in which it does so, but there are others. Anthropologists distinguish between structure and culture, and the distinction is useful and important. If one supposed that culture alone was responsible for the perpetuation of a social form, one would in effect be saying that *only* concepts constrain men to act in the way they do. This view is false, and constitutes a thoroughly misguided form of Idealism. For instance, a society may change its organization radically because some sub-group within it acquires control of the means of coercion, military or economic, and compels other members to obey it. This can happen without any change in the conceptual system in terms of which the community thinks and acts.

Such conceptual compulsion and perpetuation of order as does exist (and it is pervasive and important), cannot be assumed to be automatic. Concepts need to be instilled. The authority of concepts is not self-evident or self-imposing. The Durkheimian hypothesis that the prime role of ritual is the instilling of important concepts, and that this is what endows a community with its shared ideas and obligations, deserves the greatest respect. In a sense, every concept has and *is* a ritual. Important notions are served by important rituals.

Mankind can be said to have begun when a group of primates acquired a degree of genetic plasticity, so to speak, which made cultural constraint mandatory: when genetics became insufficient for constraining conduct within required limits. Then culture was born and language became indispensable. Potentially unbounded conduct needs to be constrained within some limits, the limits need to be indicated by markers, and language constitutes those markers. In the beginning was the prohibition. Initially, diversity could only be extreme *between* herds, and not inside them. The story of the division of labour is the account of the mechanics by means of which diversity could in the end also develop internally.

Mankind has passed through three fundamental ecological stages: hunting/gathering, agriculture, and industry. The earliest stage provided us with a kind of starting point. For the present argument, however, it is used largely as a kind of contrast or baseline. We are interested mainly in what could *not* have happened then.

Agricultural society is defined by the systematic production and storage of food, and in a lesser measure of other goods. The existence of a stored surplus inevitably commits the society to some enforcement of the division of that surplus, and to its external defence. Hence violence, merely contingent amongst hunters, becomes mandatory amongst agriculturalists. Predators of animals were not necessarily predators to each other. Agrarian societies can and do grow to very large size, and they are Malthusian.

Their scale and the existence of a surplus generally lead them to a complex internal differentiation. The internal conflict for which the presence of a store destines them leads them to great inequality and sharp stratification. This is their most general feature. Generally speaking, they also despise work: they live by work, but prestige goes to those who coerce, or those who manipulate the signals which tell coercers how to gang up. This is indeed the commonest conception of nobility. Agriculture destined much of mankind to hunger and oppression.

There seems to be no general reason why specialists in coercion, and specialists in ritual and legitimation, should not be identical. These two supremely important specializations are indeed sometimes combined. But it is a fact crucial for the history of mankind that they were very often distinct to a greater or lesser degree. The sword may dominate, but the priests help crystallize cohesion among swordsmen. They arbitrate among them, and enable them to gang up successfully. So thugs and priests between them inherit domination of the agrarian world.

The possibility of storing, organizing and transmitting meaning by means of writing is as fundamental as the production and storage of wealth. It makes possible far more effective unification and centralization of polities, of clerisies, and of doctrine. The self-interest of those in privileged positions, plus the inherent logic of perpetuation of a social order, jointly ensure that agrarian society is, all in all, stable. If turbulent, and it often is turbulent, its turbulence leads only to cyclical and not fundamental change.

Agrarian society continues to be, like its predecessor, a concept-implementing rather than an aim-pursuing society. Its notion of truth is that of compliance with a norm, rather than that of echoing an extraneous fact. Truth is for it the fulfilment of an ideal, which in turn is moulded by complex and plural concerns. This is wholly different from truth as satisfaction of the simple, isolated requirement, such as the collating and predicting of facts. The truth of agro-literate society is essentially different from the truth of scientific-industrial society.

There are various reasons why the older notion of truth should have prevailed so long. The nature and importance of coercion is one of them. Coercion in its crude form, the threat of violent conflict and death, lends itself to no fine gradation but invokes a kind of unnegotiable totality and commitment. Loyalty, not reference, is the key value. There is, however, one field in which such instrumental rationality, the subjection of activity to the criteria of effectiveness alone, is possible: specialized production, where an activity can aim at one isolated purpose. In practice, in most agrarian societies, such activity is nevertheless ritually circumscribed, a small island in a sea of producers of subsistence.

How could this world have transformed itself into ours? What are the implications for us of this transformation? How was the switch from concept-implementation to generalized instrumental rationality, from a norm-conception of truth to a referential one, from rule of thugs to rule of producers, from oppressed subsistence farmers to a free market economy – how was all this possible?

The answer is that at most times and in most places, it was not possible, and did not happen. On a single occasion, it did happen, and the technical superiority of the societies within which it occurred then transformed the entire world. All three spheres of human activity – cognition, coercion, production – had to be simultaneously in an unusual and favourable condition for the miracle to take place. In cognition, the shift of stress from ritual to doctrine, the unification of the vision by endowing it with a single apex, led to a vision of a unified, orderly world. The Protestants might well have said – *Ein Gott, Eine Welt, Eine Regel.* The notion of a unified orderly Nature and an egalitarian generic Reason led, by a miracle we cannot fully explain, to an effective exploration and utilization of nature. The subjection of cognitive claims to the verdict of insulated and independent data precludes a justification of the miracle itself by its own cognitive standards. No data can underwrite the sovereignty of data. Those who benefit from it and understand it are for ever precluded from explaining and guaranteeing it. They cannot enjoy the kind of reassurance which their ancestors enjoyed.

In the economy, a rise in productivity tilted the balance in favour of instrumentally efficient specialists and towards a more extensive and eventually an all-embracing market. In the polity, an unusual balance of power, internally and externally, and prevalent in the ideological as well as in coercive institutions, prevented an effective suppression of the new development. The cognitive explosion provided the expanding economy with an ever-receding frontier of opportunity. Perpetual innovation and continually increasing returns, and hence bribery of opponents and temporary non-beneficiaries, was possible. The old qualitative division of labour between the three orders of men, those who fight, pray and work, was finally eroded. It was replaced by a homogeneous population of *functional* specialists, free, able and willing to change their specialisms. They communicated within one and the same literate but secularized idiom, drawn from a script-carried but non-exclusive high culture. Concepts as well as men ceased to live in castes or estates. A single conceptual currency accompanied and sustained an egalitarian humanity. The division of labour is dead, long live the division of labour!

It is the sphere of coercion, of politics, which is now crucial. Contrary to the two main ideologies born of the age of transition, the political order can neither be diminished and consigned to the dog-house, nor will it wither away. A new kind of need for coercion or enforcement of decisions has arisen. The new affluent economy requires an enormous and largely lumpy, indivisible infrastructure. Strategic decisions concerning its deployment and form affect enormous populations for long periods and often do so irreversibly. This infrastructure is not, and cannot be, spontaneously generated, but needs constant attention and servicing, unlike its predecessor at the time of the inception of the new world. The state is now largely the name for the cluster of agencies that perform this role. How it is to be organized and checked, in conditions simultaneously of moral premiss-lessness and of great economic leeway – that is the question.

NOTES

I IN THE BEGINNING

1. J. M. Keynes, *The General Theory of Employment Interest and Money*, London, 1936, 1946.
2. This view is presented in a remarkable recent Soviet book, *Sovremennaia Filosofia Istorii* (Contemporary Philosophy of History) by Eero Loone, Eesti Raamat, Tallin, 1980. In a covert kind of way, trinitarianism is also present (if we subtract a hypothetical future condition) in G. A. Cohen's *Karl Marx's Theory of History*, Oxford, 1978. See p. 178.
3. Karl Polanyi, *The Great Transformation*, New York, 1944, Boston, 1957 (Chapter 4).
4. John Rawls, *A Theory of Justice*, Oxford, 1972. Robert Nozick, *Anarchy, State and Utopia*, Oxford, 1974.
5. Michael Oakeshott, *Rationalism in Politics and Other Essays*, London, 1962.
6. F. A. Hayek, *The Three Sources of Human Values*, The London School of Economics and Political Science, London, 1978, p. 20.
7. Ibid, p. 18.
8. Cf. K. R. Popper, *The Open Society and its Enemies*, London, 1945.
9. Thorstein Veblen, *The Theory of the Leisure Class*, New York, 1899.
10. Ibid, p. 29.
11. Ibid, p. 25.
12. Ibid, p. 32.
13. Marshall Sahlins, *Stone Age Economics*, London, 1974.
14. Ibid, pp. 11, 13, 14, 17. A remarkable attempt to rework a vision of early humanity in Marxist terms is to be found in Yu. V. Bromley, A. I. Pershitz, and Yn. I. Semenov, *Istoria Piervobytnovo Obshohestva* (History of Primitive Society), Moscow, 1983.
15. Sahlins, op. cit., p. 27.
16. James Woodburn, "Hunters and gatherers today and reconstruction of the past", in Ernest Gellner (ed.), *Soviet and Western Anthropology*, London, 1980, or Woodburn, "Egalitarian Societies", *Man* (N.S.), Vol. 17:3, 1982.
17. Karl Marx, *The German Ideology*, London, 1965, pp. 44–5.

2 COMMUNITY TO SOCIETY

1. E. E. Evans-Pritchard, *Nuer Religion*, Oxford, 1956, pp. 128, 141–2.
2. Lucien Levy-Bruhl, *How Natives Think*, translated by L. A. Clare, London, 1926. Lucien Levy-Bruhl, *Primitive*

Mentality, translated by L. A. Clare, London, 1923.

3. E. R. Leach, *Political Systems of Highland Burma: A Study of Kachin Social Structure*, London, 1954.

4. E. R. Leach, "Time and False Noses", in *Rethinking Anthropology*, London, 1961.

5. Ibid.

6. Cf. S. Weir, *Qat in Yemen: Consumption and Social Change*, London, 1985.

7. Emile Durkheim, *The Elementary Forms of Religious Life*, translated by J. W. Swain, London, 1915, 1976.

8. Willard van Orman Quine, *From a Logical Point of View*, Cambridge, Mass., 1953.

3 THE COMING OF THE OTHER

1. For a general discussion, see Jack Goody (ed.), *Literacy in Traditional Societies*, Cambridge, 1968. An interesting examination of this is to be found in Jonathan Parry, "The Brahmanical Tradition and the Technology of the Intellect", in Joanna Overing (ed.), *Reason and Morality*, New York and London, 1985.

2. Cf. M. Bloch, "Literacy and Enlightenment", in a forthcoming work edited by M. Trolle-Larsen and K. Sousboe.

3. Cf. Patricia Crone and Martin Hinds, *God's Caliph: Religious Authority in the First Centuries of Islam*, Cambridge, 1986.

4. S. N. Eisenstadt (ed.), *The Origins of Diversity of Axial Age Civilizations*, New York, forthcoming.

5. K. R. Popper, *The Open Society and its Enemies*, London, 1945.

6. Cf. E. A. Burtt, *The Metaphysical Foundations of Physical Science*, London, 1925.

7. Cf. W. Bryce Gallie, *Philosophy and the Historical Understanding*, London, 1964.

4 THE TENSION

1. Fustel de Coulanges, *The Ancient City*, New York, 1956.

2. See, for instance, S. N. Eisenstadt (ed.), *The Protestant Ethic and Modernization: A Comparative View*, New York and London, 1968. For a critical view of the thesis, see H. R. Trevor-Roper, "Religion, the Reformation and Social Change", in *Historical Studies*, Vol. 4, 1965, republished in *Religion, the Reformation and Social Change*, London, 1984; or H. Luethy, "Once Again: Calvinism and Capitalism", in *Encounter*, Vol. XXII:1, 1964 (reprinted in Eisenstadt (ed.), op. cit.). S. Andreski, *Max Weber's Insights and Errors*, London, 1984. A. Giddens, *Capitalism and Modern Social Theory*, Cambridge, 1971.

3. Denis de Rougemont, *Passion and Society (L'Amour et l'Occident*, 1939), translated by M. Belgion, London, 1940.

4. Alan Macfarlane, *Marriage and Love in England 1300–1840*, Oxford, 1986.

5. Cf. Sevyan Vainshtein (edited with an introduction by Caroline Humphrey), *Nomads of South Siberia: The Pastoral Economies of Tuva* (first published in Moscow, 1972), Cambridge, 1980.

5 CODIFICATION

1. David Hume, *The Natural History of Religion*, edited by

A. W. Colver, Oxford, 1976, p. 60. David Hume, "Of Superstition and Enthusiasm", in *Essays Moral, Political and Literary*, Oxford, 1963, p. 79, also published in R. Wollheim, *Hume on Religion*, London, 1963, p. 250.

2. Cf. Louis Dumont, *Homo Hierarchicus*, London, 1970. Charles Malamoud, "Semantique et rhetorique dans la hierarchie hindoue des 'buts de l'homme'", in *European Journal of Sociology*, Vol. XXIII:2, 1982.

3. For contemporary thinkers who deplore this insulation and seem to aspire to reverse it, see Charles Taylor, *Hegel*, Cambridge, 1975; or Alasdair MacIntyre, *After Virtue: a Study in Moral Theory*, London, 1981.

4. I. C. Jarvie, *Rationality and Relativism: In Search of a Philosophy and History of Anthropology*, London, 1984.

5. Werner Sombart, *The Jews and Modern Capitalism* (1911), translated by M. Epstein, Glencoe, Illinois, 1951.

6. A. V. Chayanov, *The Theory of Peasant Economy*, 1925. D. Thorner, R. E. F. Smith and B. Kerblay (eds), Irwin, 1966. Theodor Shanin, *The Awkward Class, Political Sociology of Peasantry in a Developing Society: Russia 1910–25*, Oxford, 1972.

7. A. E. Wrigley, *People, Cities and Wealth*, Blackwell, Oxford, 1987.

8. Karl Marx, "Preface to a Contribution to the Critique of Political Economy" (1859), in *Karl Marx and Friedrich Engels, Selected Works in One Volume*, London, 1977, p. 182.

9. Cf. Mark Elvin, "Why China Failed to Create an Endogenous Industrial Capitalism: A Critique of Max Weber's Explanation", in *Theory and Society*, Vol. 3:3, 1984.

10. Baron d'Holbach, *The System of Nature*, translated by H. D. Robinson, New York, 1970, p. 338.

6   THE COERCIVE ORDER
AND ITS EROSION

1. A. M. Khazanov, *Nomads and the Outside World* (1983), translated by J. Crookenden, Cambridge, 1984.

2. Cf. Jack Goody, *Technology, Tradition and the State in Africa*, Oxford, 1971. Eric de Dampierre, *Un Ancien Royaume Bandia du Haut-Oubangui*, Paris, 1967.

3. Stanislav Andreski (previously Andrzejewski), *Military Organization and Society*, London, 1954.

4. Cf. Clifford Geertz, *Negara: The Theatre State in Nineteenth-Century Bali*, Princeton, 1980.

5. Louis Dumont, *Homo Hierarchicus*, London, 1970. Stephen M. Greenwold, "Buddhist Brahmans", in *European Journal of Sociology*, Vol. XV:1, 1974. Anne Vergati Stahl, "M. Greenwold et les Newars", in *European Journal of Sociology*, Vol. XVI:2, 1975.

6. Jack Goody, *The Development of the Family and Marriage in Europe*, Cambridge, 1983.

7. Cf. Perry Anderson, *Lineages of the Absolutist State*, London, 1974.

8. Cf. A. Hirschmann, *The Passions and the Interests: Political Arguments for*

Capitalism before its Triumph, Princeton, 1977.

9. Lawrence Stone and Jeanne C. Fawtier Stone, *An Open Elite? England 1540–1880*, Oxford, 1984.

10. E. A. Wrigley, *People, Cities and Wealth*, Blackwell, Oxford, 1987.

11. Alan Macfarlane, *The Origins of English Individualism*, Oxford, 1978.

12. John Hajnal, "Two Kinds of Pre-Industrial Household Formation System", in Richard Wall, Jean Robin and Peter Laslett (eds), *Family Forms in Historic Europe*, Cambridge, 1983. Peter Laslett, "Family and household as work group and kin group: areas of traditional Europe compared", in Richard Wall *et al.*, op. cit. Peter Laslett, "The uniqueness of European modes of production and reproduction" in John Hall, Michael Mann and Jean Baechler (eds), *Europe and the Rise of Capitalism* (Oxford, 1988). Richard M. Smith, "Some issues concerning families and their property in rural England 1250–1800", in R. M. Smith (ed.), *Land Kinship and Life-Cycle*, Cambridge, 1984. Richard M. Smith, "Fertility, economy and household formation in England over three centuries", in *Population and Development Review*, Vol. 7:4, 1981.

13. Alan Macfarlane, op. cit. (1978).

14. Alan Macfarlane, *Marriage and Love in England 1300–1840*, Oxford, 1986.

15. Louis Dumont, op. cit. (1970), and his paper in Michael Carrithers, Steven Collins and Steven Lukes (eds), *The Category of the Person: Anthropology, Philosophy, History*, Cambridge, 1986.

16. Louis Dumont, *Essais sur l'Individualisme*, Paris, 1983.

17. Ibid.

18. Jack Goody, op. cit. (1983).

19. See Chapter 4, note 2.

20. Ibid.

21. John A. Hall, *Powers and Liberties: The Causes and Consequences of the Rise of the West*, Oxford, 1985.

7 PRODUCTION, VALUE AND VALIDITY

1. T. S. Kuhn, *The Structure of Scientific Revolutions*, Chicago, 1962.

2. There is an excellent summary of the anthropological debate by Yu. I. Semenov, "Theoretical Problems of Economic Anthropology", in *Philosophy of the Social Sciences*, Vol. 4, 1974.

3. Karl Polanyi, *The Great Transformation*, New York, 1944, Boston, 1957.

4. M. I. Finley, *The Ancient Economy*, London, 1985 (2nd edition).

5. M. I. Finley, "Slavery and the Historians", in *Social History – Histoire Sociale*, Vol. 12, 1979. Keith Hopkins, *Conquerors and Slaves*, Cambridge, 1978.

6. G. E. R. Lloyd, *Magic, Reason and Experience*, Cambridge, 1979.

7. Mark Elvin, "Why China Failed to Create an Endogenous Industrial Capitalism: A Critique of Max Weber's Explanation", in *Theory and Society*, Vol. 3:3, 1984.

8. Keith Thomas, *Religion and the Decline of Magic*, London, 1971.

9. Frances Yates, *The Rosicrucian Enlightenment*, Cambridge, 1978.
10. Richard Popkin, "The Third Force in 17th-century philosophy: scepticism, science and Biblical prophecy", in *Nouvelles de la Republique des Lettres*, 1983:I.
11. G. E. Lessing, *Nathan the Wise*, Act III, scene 7.
12. Cf. W. W. Bartley III, *The Retreat to Commitment*, London, 1984.

8 THE NEW SCENE

1. J. G. Merquior, *The Veil and the Mask: Essays on Culture and Ideology*, London, 1979.
2. Gerhard Lenski, *Power and Privilege: Theory of Social Stratification*, New York 1966.
3. Louis Dumont, *Homo Hierarchicus*, London, 1970. Louis Dumont, *From Mandeville to Marx: The Genesis and Triumph of Economic Ideology*, Chicago and London, 1977.
4. Stanislav Andreski, *Military Organization and Society*, London, 1968.
5. Ronald Dore, *British Factory – Japanese Factory: The Origins of National Diversity in Industrial Relations*, London, 1973.
6. Keith Hart, *The Political Economy of West African Agriculture*, Cambridge, 1982.
7. Daniel Bell, *The Cultural Contradictions of Capitalism*, London, 1976.

9 SELF-IMAGES

1. Cf. Fred Hirsch, *Social Limits to Growth*, London, 1977.
2. Keith Hopkins, *Conquerors and Slaves*, Cambridge, 1978.
3. See Eero Loone, *Sovremennaia Filosofia Istorii* (Contemporary Philosophy of History), Eesti Raamat, Tallin, 1980.
4. Hannah Arendt, *The Origins of Totalitarianism*, New York, 1951.
5. See, for instance, Amartya Sen, *Choice, Welfare and Measurement*, Oxford, 1982, or W. G. Runciman and A. K. Sen, "Games, Justice and the General Will", in *Mind*, Vol. 74, 1965, or J. W. N. Watkins, "Imperfect rationality", in R. Borger and F. Cioffi (eds), *Explanation in the Behavioural Sciences*, Cambridge, 1970.
6. David Gellner, "Max Weber, capitalism and the religion of India", in *Sociology*, Vol. 16, 1982.

10 PROSPECT

1. Clifford Geertz, *Negara: The Theatre State in Nineteenth-Century Bali*, Princeton, 1980.

INDEX

Marxism as genuine cognition, 215
in modern (industrial) society, 60–1,
62, 63–7, 131, 136, 140, 196,
205–6, 261–2
transformation of, since early times,
39–53, 71, 77–9, 197–8, 204,
221–2, 253, 277
see also concepts; knowledge; multi-
strand and single-strand activities;
reason; science
community, see under society
Comte, Auguste, 12, 19
concepts, ideas, 55, 274
binding nature of, 56–7
independent existence of, in generic
Platonism, 76–7, 87–90
inherent in cultures, 14–15, 55–6, 77,
274
levelled out, in modern world, 110,
123–8, 128
neither static nor given, 11–12
origin and validity of, linked, 12
shared, norms defined by, 58, 74
see also cognition
corporatism, 246, 271
Counter-Reformation, 168
culture(s), 14, 67, 195, 206–10, 273,
274
concept-implementing and
instrumental-rational, distinguished,
128
future prospects, 213–15
"high" and "folk", 71, 107
in modern society, 219–23, 236, 263
as precondition of open society, 28
socially transmitted, 14
as systems of concepts, 14–15, 55–6,
77, 274
Czechoslovakia, "normalized" after
1968, 234–5

Darwinianism, 142, 143
democracy, 193, 194, 262–3
Descartes, René, Cartesian tradition,
117–21, 122, 123, 141–2
discovery, ceiling of, 161–2
division of labour, 21–2, 43–5, 63, 117,
261–3, 273, 275, 277–8
in agrarian societies, 17, 21, 121–2,
129, 151
and autonomy of knowledge, 119,
136

in modern (industrial) societies, 18,
123
romantic criticism of, 208–9
doctrine, birth of, 73–4; see also
scripturalism
Dumont, Louis, 164
Durkheim, Emile, 56–7, 110, 111,
127–8, 207, 249–50, 255

economic affairs, see production
egalitarianism, 211–13, 262–3
empire, colonialism, 259
empiricist philosophy, 56–7, 116, 123–4
England, as locus of industrial
revolution, 169–70
Enlightenment, 113–16, 116–17,
133–40, 243–4
British and French styles of, 115–16
circular reasoning, 193–7, 199–200
"vulgar" and "higher", 133–5, 136–7
Evans-Pritchard, Sir Edward, 82
evil, problem of, 91, 142

feudalism, 151, 158–9
Frazer, Sir James, 19, 78
fringe cults, counter-culture, 215, 263–4
Fustel de Coulanges, N. D., 81, 91

Geertz, Clifford, 269
genetic factors, in human history, 14,
67, 273
geometry, 80, 82
ghetto, as source of instrumental
rationality, 129
Goody, Jack, 166
Greece, classical, 22, 198

Hadza, 33
Hayek, F. A., 26–8, 29, 30, 31, 34, 175
Hegel, G. W. F., 12, 19, 34, 142–3
Hinduism, see India
"historicism", 12
history
deification of, 141–4
patterns of, 11–15
not predetermined, 15
selective, 13
sequential, cumulative, 13–14
trinitarian theories of, 16, 19–20
as unfolding of rationality, 39, 45
Hobbes, Thomas, 177, 253
Holbach, Baron Paul d', 134–5

major issues still multi-stranded,
209–10, 263
written doctrine as first single-purpose
system, 74, 75, 79
Muslim world, see Islam

nationalism, 206, 210, 236, 262–3
natural selection, 27, 245
nature
impersonal, not coherent cosmos, 60
orderly, unified, 68, 86, 113, 117,
122, 131, 132–3, 134–9 passim,
202–4
Pythagorean mathematization of, 80
and reason, 134–7
systematic investigation of, 17–18,
117, 202–4, 277
Nazis, 234
neolithic (agricultural) revolution, 20,
31–4, 38; see also agrarian societies
Newton, Isaac, 199
Nuer, 40–1
nuraghi, 130

Pascal, Blaise, 232, 256
pastoral communities, distinctive
political character of some, 22,
149–50, 151
peasant communities, distinctive political
character of some, 22, 150, 151,
162–4
philosophies, two species of, 118
Plato, Platonism, 75–6, 76–7, 79,
84–90, 118–21, 141–2
Polanyi, Karl, 19, 180
politics, see coercion
Popper, Karl, 28, 78, 85
populism, 207
"post-industrial" society, 17
poverty, relief of, 226
power, see coercion
Pragmatism, 143, 204
pre-agrarian societies, see hunting/
gathering societies; also man,
primitive
prediction, social, 15
price, just, 182, 184–6
price, market, 186
Prisoner's Dilemma, 251–2
production, economic affairs, 20–1,
173–6, 182–9, 191, 276, 277
adjustable, negotiable, 176–80, 205

in agrarian societies, 16, 103, 128–30,
151, 176, 182, 276
and coercion, political power, 181–2
future prospects, 182, 264–5, 268
in modern (industrial) societies, 17–
18, 108–9, 140–1, 145
Protestantism and, 100, 104–6, 167–8
solutions to social problems not
determined by, 19–20
three stages of, 180–2
see also market; trade; wealth
Progress, 140–4, 247–8
property, see wealth
Protestantism, 100, 103–12, 132, 160,
167–8, 262–3
Pythagoreanism, 80

Quine, 78

reason, rationality, 39, 45, 76, 93, 110,
117, 128–9, 221–2, 272, 277
economic rationality, 174–6
as independent basis for investigation,
113
and nature, 134–7
see also cognition; multi-strand and
single-strand activities
Reformation, 111–12, 113–14, 168
relativism, see universalism and
relativism
religion, the sacred, 255–7
no room for, in modern world, 66
religious writings, see scripturalism
two types of religion, 75–6, 84, 91;
see also salvation see also church;
clerisies; monotheism;
Protestantism; Reformation; ritual;
transcendent
Renan, Ernest, 205
Revolution, French, 134
revolutions, 147, 232
ritual, 48, 57, 71–2, 75, 86–7, 110, 274
language as, 51
romantics, fashionable, 173, 208–9,
240–1
Royal Society, 198–9

Sahlins, Marshall, 31–3, 34
salvation, 80–2, 214
no longer from extraneous source,
142
salvation religions, 75, 82, 83–4, 91–
3, 111–12, 214